FV

D1261402

The Great Silent Majority

The Great Silent Majority
Missouri's Resistance to World War I

Christopher C. Gibbs

University of Missouri Press
Columbia, 1988

Library of Congress Cataloging-in-Publication Data

Gibbs, Christopher C.
    The great silent majority.

    Bibliography: p.
    Includes index.
        1. World War, 1914–1918—Public opinion. 2. Public opinion—
Missouri. 3. World War, 1914–1918—Protest movements—
Missouri. I. Title.
D570.85.M8G53   1988   940.3′1   88–4835
ISBN 0–8262–0683–2 (alk. paper)

∞™ This paper meets the minimum requirements of the
American National Standard for Permanence of Paper for
Printed Library Materials, Z39.48, 1984.

I dedicate this book to Harry Cochran Gibbs,
Jean Fisher Gibbs, David Kingsland Gibbs,
Buckner Fisher Gibbs, Scott McKinney Gibbs,
David Brock Gibbs, and Jeanne Buckner Gibbs.

"They nursed their idiosyncrasies and took no advice."

—Thomas Hart Benton

Preface

This book examines the immediate impact of American entry into and participation in World War I. There have been a number of excellent monographs on this topic in the past ten years. Some have focused on organizations like the National Council of Defense or the War Industries Board; others have concentrated on one particular segment of society, such as women or workers; and two recent major studies have presented an overview of the entire nation at war. This book focuses on one state, Missouri, between 1914 and 1919, in an effort to examine as many aspects of the war as possible without losing sight of the human beings involved.

My research revealed that Missourians did not want to go to war in 1917. This was not altogether surprising. Other students of the period, including Herbert Peterson and Gilbert Fite and John C. Crighton, have noted the lack of enthusiasm for the war in the Midwest, the South, and the Northwest, indeed, everywhere outside the metropolitan Northeast. While most students of the period agree, however, that eventually the vast majority of Americans fell into line, even came to support the war, the majority of Missourians continued to oppose American participation in the war all the way to the Armistice. Furthermore, they resisted involvement to the extent of refusing to participate in the major mobilization drives organized to enlist them in the war effort. In so doing they came under heavy fire from war boosters at all levels of society, from President Woodrow Wilson to the chairman of the local council of defense; some risked jail. The order of the day was "Line up and sign up," and Missourians refused, in large numbers, despite great pressure to go along. The roots of their refusal, its manifestations, and some of its more immediate consequences are the subject of this study.

The first chapter examines Missouri before American entry into the war, with special attention to certain important traditions that influenced popular attitudes toward the war already raging in Europe. Chapter 2 looks specifically at opposition to America's entry into the war as expressed by Missourians in letters to political leaders and others, in meetings, and in other ways. The aim here is not primarily to prove conclusively that a majority of Missourians opposed the war, but to outline the grounds for opposition and indicate the ways in which opposition grew out of prewar traditions.

The papers of the Missouri Council of Defense provided me with a rich resource through which to examine the people who implemented war mobilization in Missouri. Chapter 3 looks at the council at the state and local levels, focusing on the motives, methods, and effectiveness of the council in its efforts to foster local enthusiasm for the war. During the war, mobilizers at every level stressed the importance of participation in a variety of wartime activities. The level of participation, they argued, would serve as a measure of war support. These activities included war bond purchases, conscription, the pledge to conserve food, the growing of specific war crops by farmers, and the cooperation of workers with leaders in industry and government to guarantee unhampered manufacture and transportation of war materiel. Chapters 4 through 6 use the mobilizers' own yardstick to demonstrate that a majority of people in the state refused to participate in these activities, thereby demonstrating their opposition to the war through active, and dangerous, resistance. The leading study of Missouri during the war has argued that, however they may have felt in early 1917, most Missourians came eventually to support the war. The actions of Missourians during the war indicate clearly that this was not so. By the mobilizers' own measurements, most Missourians failed to support the war at any time. To be sure, America's involvement in the war lasted a mere nineteen months. It is possible that, had the war lasted longer, as the piles of dead mounted up, Missourians might have come to be driven by that hatred and desire for revenge that drove the French, the British, and the Germans. But that did not happen. The sacrifices of American troopers, Missourians among them, brought Germany's swift defeat—and left a bitter taste in the mouths of many of those troopers, as well as the families and neighbors that welcomed them home when the fighting was done.

This story ends there. Some omissions need to be accounted for. Black Missourians were explicitly excluded from official participation in the war at the state and local level. This does not mean that they were not affected by the war, but it does mean that I was unable to find more than a few scraps of information on the subject, and I did not feel confident in drawing any conclusions therefrom. For an imaginative way of dealing with this very problem, see Theodore Kornweible, Jr., "Apathy and Dissent: Black America's Negative Responses to World War I," *South Atlantic Quarterly* 80 (Summer 1981): 322–38. Also, I have dealt only briefly with the experiences of Missouri servicemen and women in the United States and overseas. Here there was almost too much information available, and I did not want to lose sight of the main story, which was the domestic impact of the war. Consequently, while I deal with conscription at length, once Missourians don uniforms I leave them, perhaps for another book. The Twenties lie beyond the scope of this study. I hope, however, that conclusions about the war can serve as a context for an examination of that period. Historians who have argued the war's popularity have drawn conclusions regarding the Twenties based on that assertion. How might we look at the Red Scare, consumerism, the Klan, creationism, or radical politics in the years before the Great Crash if we begin from the point of the war's lack of popularity? This is especially important if the story of the war's impact on Missouri applies to other states as well. The limited research I did on the eight states bordering Missouri implied that the heart of America was not in the war at all, that Missourians were not alone in their opposition and refusal to participate. Obviously, further research is needed. I hope that this volume can suggest relevant lines of inquiry.

Finally, I have many people to thank for their help in a project that has taken much longer than many of us hoped in the beginning. The staffs of the Library of Congress Manuscripts Division, the State Historical Society of Missouri, the Western Historical Manuscripts Collection, the New York Public Library, and the Missouri Historical Society were all that a researcher hopes for. The Department of History, University of Missouri–Columbia, provided funds and teaching opportunities to help finance the early stages of this project. Among those individuals who offered valuable criticism, clues to overlooked sources, or simply the inspiration and the community of ideas without which scholarship cannot occur are (in no particular order) Tom K. Barton, Robert Larson, Larry Gragg, Robert Griffith, David Roediger, David Danbom, Steven Watts, Thomas Alexander, Susan Flader, Ken Plax, Richard Vietor, Phil and Betty Scarpino, Susan Curtis Mernitz, Steve Donohue, R. A. Kendrick and D. P. Kendrick, and the men of the 46th MHD, Republic of Viet Nam, August 1969–February 1971. I owe a special debt to Nancy Nagel Gibbs, whose faith in this project remained strong when mine flagged. David Thelen and Steve Piott read every word of every draft of this manuscript. They were absolutely reliable. They never failed to offer help, ideas, critiques, sympathy, anything, anytime. This brief mention is a small return for all they gave to me.

C. C. G.
Alexandria, Va.
April 1988

Contents

Chapter 1

Before the War

The story of the impact of World War I is in large part the story of clashing value systems. At one extreme stood modernization and a world dominated by economic interdependence in an international market network, bureaucratic organization, large corporations, and interest-group politics. At another extreme stood traditionalism: a world made up of local communities and local markets, organized along the lines of family and faith, age, sex, ethnicity, within which democratic political action was widely regarded as a reliable solution to local problems.

An examination of the early twentieth century reveals few pure examples of these extremes. They coexisted and intertwined as people employed various combinations of both to meet the challenges of daily life. One result was the complex blending of actions and attitudes that has permitted so many different interpretations of early twentieth-century America. World War I increased polarization. Wars are traumatic experiences for societies as well as for individuals, and a close look at a people at war can reveal much about the society in which they live. What has been blurred before may become clear in the flash of crisis. Specifically, a study of World War I can clarify for us the alternative responses employed by people on the brink of the modern world, can show us which were successful and which were not. And it can suggest the origins of some of the patterns that emerged as the war ended.

When World War I began in Europe, the United States stood poised between two worlds. Although the new century was well along, many people lived lives that had changed little for generations. Animals still provided most of the power for farming, for instance, and few homes outside cities had indoor plumbing or electric light. But a few farmers had begun working their land with tractors. Power companies were weaving a nationwide electrical web. Railroad tracks laced the land, and automobiles and trucks moved increasing numbers of people and things. America had become the world's leading industrial power, with giant factories and huge, bustling cities. Yet in Arizona, hostile Indians raided isolated outposts; in Wyoming, mounted bandits robbed travelers; and along the Rio Grande, Texas Rangers galloped in pursuit of desperadoes. Increasingly, however, the modern world of factories and cities grew, while the traditional world slipped into the past.

Americans experienced a variety of contacts with the changing world, and they had a variety of responses to it. For some agricultural workers it meant moving to the city and starting work in a factory, all within a few weeks. For others the process was slower, and manifestations of the modern world crept into their lives all but unnoticed, and not necessarily unwelcome. While some people were relatively untouched by changes, and others were victimized by them, still others hurried them along. In search of money and power, the builders of financial and industrial empires expanded their operations around the world, welding together vast enterprises, creating an extensive and complex market network linked by growing technology and communication, modern transportation, and high-level financial dealings. The number and size of corporations had been growing for twenty years as entrepreneurs slowly, often reluctantly, abandoned competition in favor of the stable profits they hoped would come from cooperation, growing markets, and a bureaucratic organization that created clear lines of authority while it diffused responsibility.[1]

Responding in part to the growth of the market network and the power of corporations in it, federal and state governments used civil service reform to develop their own bureaucracies to supervise commerce, food and drugs, and the collection of revenues. At the same time, many workers, responding to pressure from increasingly organized employers, sought to wield influence through national labor unions. As the loosely organized, radical Knights of Labor waned, for instance, the more conservative American Federation of Labor grew, and labor leaders demanded a place in the decision-making process rather than fundamental changes in it. Specialized agricultural organizations arose as market-oriented farmers, still a minority, sought to improve the quality and increase the sales of crops and livestock. Middle-class professionals, doctors and lawyers and historians, embarrassed by quacks and charlatans, often hounded by reformers, created specialized organizations to set their houses in order. Businessmen, seeking favorable treatment from increasingly powerful government agencies, and hoping to present a united front against opponents, joined together in trade associations, businessmen's clubs, and chambers of commerce.[2]

By 1915 there was available a range of choices for exerting control over one's life in changing America. For some the goal was to put farming, working, government, the professions, even business itself, on a more "businesslike" basis. People created organizations that tended along interest-

1. For the efforts of businessmen to channel reform to their own ends, see Gabriel Kolko, *The Triumph of Conservatism*, and James Weinstein, *The Corporate Ideal in the Liberal State, 1900–1918*. The standard work on bureaucracy is Max Weber, *The Theory of Social and Economic Organization*, trans. Talcott Parsons (New York: Oxford University Press, 1947).

2. For changing middle-class attitudes, see Robert H. Wiebe, *The Search for Order, 1877–1920*. For changes in agriculture, see Murray Benedict, *The Farm Policies of the United States, 1790–1950*; Grant McConnell, *The Decline of Agrarian Democracy*; and especially David B. Danbom, *The Resisted Revolution: Urban America and the Industrialization of Agriculture, 1900–1930*.

group lines with an economic focus: what you did for a living determined your role in the system. People were defined by their role in the market network. Institutionalized with charters, bylaws, and officers, these groups sought intentionally to copy the model provided by large corporations of stability, bureaucratization, and growing influence.

At the same time, many rejected outright the market network, with its growing interdependence and remote centers of power. They rejected the idea that people could be defined in market terms. Factors such as kinship, skill, age, sex, ethnicity continued to operate as determinants of human relationships. Few farmers joined specialized agricultural groups. Physicians were among the most organized of professionals, yet in 1915 only about half belonged to the American Medical Association. Few workers belonged to unions; they gave their allegiance instead to church, to family, and to such voluntary associations as ethnic solidarity organizations, mutual aid societies, and debating clubs. Woman's place was still mainly in the home, and domestic laborers enjoyed no organization at all. Immigrants clung to their old ways in the new land. In a changing world many Americans drew on traditional values and resources to exert control over their lives.

Nor were old-fashioned capitalist values dead in America. Manufacturers and businessmen clung to the ideal of the free market and unhampered competition. They sought to conduct their businesses with as much success as possible, free of interference from large corporations or government regulators. Skilled workers resisted the factory system, which fragmented the productive process and turned craftsmen into machine tenders, because they sought to become independent entrepreneurs, supervising their own shopful of journeymen and apprentices in the time-honored tradition. Farmers continued to believe in the ideal of the independent yeoman who worked his land and provided for his needs without the grain trust, the railroad, or the meat-packing combine robbing him of his small return. In small towns and cities and on farms, people still believed a man should be able to advance as far as his skill and his luck allowed, that he should achieve status through recognized ability and a sense of responsibility to the community. These people could, and did, cooperate with each other to meet local emergencies or to solve current problems, but they resisted the efforts of bureaucratic organizations in business and government to drag them into the growing system of market interdependence.[3]

3. The lingering of immigrant institutions is discussed in Oscar Handlin, *The Uprooted*, 2d ed.; Frederick C. Luebke, *Bonds of Loyalty: German-Americans and World War One*, pp. 27–56 passim; Theodore Salutous, *The Greeks in the United States*; and Herbert Gans, *The Urban Villagers: Group and Class in the Life of Italian-Americans*. Agricultural opposition to modernization is covered in Danbom, *Resisted Revolution*, pp. 2–22, which cover the years before the war; Wiebe, *Search for Order*; and for the role of immigrants in the work place, see Gerald Rosenblum, *Immigrant Workers: Their Impact on American Labor Radicalism*. On business reluctance to modernize, see Robert D. Cuff, *The War Industries Board*, pp. 10–15. See also two articles by David Montgomery, "Workers' Control of Machine Production in the

This study focuses on Missouri, whose residents called their home the "Center State."[4] Like most people, Missourians believed that their state was at once the best and the most typical in the country. Indeed, Missouri did possess many of the characteristics of a region standing between the nineteenth and the twentieth centuries. People in the Ozarks, for instance, lived aggressively traditional lives: remote, independent, almost adamantly primitive. Yet the state was so important in the market network that it was the only one in the nation with two federal reserve banks, one in St. Louis and one in Kansas City. St. Louis, the fifth-largest city in the country, was a hub of river and rail transportation and was the commercial capital of much of the south-central United States. Kansas City was smaller and its prominence more recent, but it was a growing industrial center and the chief city of the central Great Plains.

Missouri's internal economy had changed rapidly in the ten years preceding the outbreak of the war. Manufacturing produced $600 million in goods in 1914 and agriculture produced $480 million, but it had only been a few years since manufacturing had replaced farming as the chief producer of wealth. Thousands of Missourians lived in cities and worked in factories, but over half the state's 3.5 million people lived on farms or in small towns and villages. Missouri's leading industries revolved around farming, as the state sent boots, meat, flour, and beer all over the nation and the world. Yet farmers still brought surplus goods into town on market days, dealing directly with local consumers while they consumed the bulk of their produce themselves. Thus a traditional society characterized in part by local market economies, unity of production and consumption, and face-to-face dealings existed in the midst of a modern system dominated by corporations dealing in a worldwide market.

In 1917, when America entered the war, Missouri was made up of people with varied backgrounds and experiences, which led to diverse assumptions about the war and its place in their lives. Farming was in a direct way the most important element in the lives of over 1.5 million people in rural areas. Approximately 263,000 farms occupied 79 percent of the land area of the state. The average farmer worked about 130 acres, 71 percent of which was improved. According to agricultural experts, the farmer made the equivalent of a dollar and a quarter a day, but he saw little hard cash from year to year. The average farm was worth about $13,000: $9,000 in land,

Nineteenth Century" and "The 'New Unionism' and the Transformation of Workers' Consciousness in America, 1909–1922."

4. For surveys of Missouri before the war, see John C. Crighton, *Missouri and the World War, 1914–1917: A Study in Public Opinion*, pp. 16–20; Missouri Bureau of Labor Statistics, *State Sociology of Missouri, 1913;* Office of Secretary of State, *1910 Census of Missouri . . . Collated From the Thirteenth Decennial Census Statistics of the United States;* Department of Commerce, Bureau of the Census, *Fourteenth Census of the United States, State Compendium, Missouri* (1924); W. L. Nelson, "A Rural Survey of Morgan County, Missouri"; and David Thelen, *Paths of Resistance: Tradition and Dignity in Industrializing Missouri.*

$3,000 in buildings and stock, and the rest in machinery. Tenants operated about 75,000 farms, and the rest were owner-operated. Native-born whites owned 251,000 of Missouri's farms. There were 8,000 foreign-born farm owners, half of them from Germany, and 3,600 black farmers, half of them tenants. Half of Missouri's farm acreage was in pasture, 25 percent in corn, 10 percent in wheat. In the southeast part of the state, entrepreneurs were converting swampland into vast cotton plantations. Almost every farm raised livestock and poultry. Half raised mules and three-fourths raised horses. Some 82 percent raised hogs, 45 percent had beef cattle, and over 65 percent raised dairy cattle. Fewer than 3 percent of Missouri farms had tractors; only about 15,000 had indoor plumbing, or gas or electric lights.[5]

Half the state's population lived in cities or towns. St. Louis was the largest, with about 700,000 inhabitants; Kansas City was a distant second with about 250,000. St. Louis was the more heterogeneous, with 6 percent black, 18 percent foreign-born, 35 percent native-born of foreign parentage, and 39 percent native-born of native parentage. The population of Kansas City was 61 percent native-born. Only 10 percent were foreign-born, while 9 percent were black.[6]

Missouri's urban dwellers came from a broad range of backgrounds. Although Kansas City was relatively new, some old St. Louis families had resided in the city since the eighteenth century, and prominent families in both cities had migrated from Kentucky and Tennessee when Missouri was still a slave state. Most of St. Louis's German, Irish, and Bohemian communities were established before the Civil War. The newer immigrants to Missouri's cities came from the American South and from eastern and southern Europe, especially Italy, Austria-Hungary, and Russia. By and large these people were farmers or peasants driven off the land by the mechanization of agriculture that had occurred in the late nineteenth century. The older families often had the higher-paying jobs and lived in the good neighborhoods, however, leaving the unskilled, low-paying work and the crowded tenement neighborhoods for the more recent arrivals.[7] But regardless of origin,

5. Agricultural statistics come from the *Monthly Bulletin of the State Board of Agriculture of Missouri*, 1910–1920; *Fourteenth Census: Agriculture*, 6:567–614; and *State Sociology of Missouri*, 1913.

6. William Crossland, *Industrial Conditions Among Negroes in St. Louis*, in the series *Studies in Social Economics*, by the Faculty of the St. Louis School of Social Economics, vol. 1, no. 1, p. 6; *State Sociology of Missouri*, 1913.

7. Ruth Crawford, *The Immigrant in St. Louis*, in the series *Studies in Social Economics*, by the Faculty of the St. Louis School of Social Economics, vol. 1, no. 2; Jay Corzine and Irene Dabrowski, "The Ethnic Factor and Neighborhood Stability: The Czechs in Soulard and South St. Louis"; Gary Mormino, "Over Here: St. Louis Italo-Americans and the First World War"; *State Sociology of Missouri*, 1913. Russel Gerlach, *Settlement Patterns in Missouri: A Study of Population Origins*, is a mine of information, complete with excellent illustrations. David W. Detjen, *The Germans in Missouri, 1900–1918: Prohibition, Neutrality, and Assimilation*, deals primarily with the German-American Alliance in St. Louis, but is a useful study.

old residents as well as immigrants had customs and traditions embedded in generations of experience, and these served as primary resources when meeting the circumstances of life in modern America. They also helped influence opinion on the war.

The impact of the war must be seen in the context of this wide variety of values and backgrounds. The war was characterized by different people in various ways: as a moral crusade, as a protection of American interests, as a demonstration of loyalty to the nation's leaders, as the adventure of a lifetime, or as a chance for America to take her place as a great power among nations. All these have received close attention from students of the period. Three quite different attitudes, however, require examination because they informed the behavior of large numbers of people in Missouri with regard to the war. These attitudes—localism, faith in democracy, and anticorporate sentiment—were deeply rooted in Missouri and underlay the responses to the war of many, perhaps a majority of people in the state. They are the basis for this study.

Many saw the corporation as the most influential manifestation of the market network, and the anticorporate sentiment of the war years was in large part a continuation of antitrust attitudes of the late nineteenth century. But the years since 1900 had seen growth in the size and complexity of corporations, and opponents argued that corporations drove up prices paid by consumers while driving out local producers; they corrupted politics and deprived workers of control of production. At the same time, corporations were seen to enjoy all the advantages of citizenship with none of the responsibilities, profiting from the public domain and an open political system while dodging taxes and evading responsibility for their actions.

Such attitudes had deep roots in Missouri. Radical rule following the Civil War had opened the door to corporations, especially railroads. Food and energy monopolies had grown up by 1900. In the 1870s, Missouri was known as the "mother of outlaws," not only because of the James and Younger Gang, but because of the local popularity of these men among otherwise law-abiding citizens who applauded their attacks on banks and railroads. Later, reformers like the Patrons of Husbandry and the populists strove for legislative restrictions on corporate activities, pointing to corrupt links between politicians and corporations. Communities often refused to float the bonds needed to attract companies, or refused to pay when local politicians pushed them through anyway. Between 1900 and 1908, two Missouri attorney generals, Herbert S. Hadley and Elliot W. Major, achieved prominence for their attacks on monopoly, and their successes against the harvester and the oil trusts won each in turn the governorship of the state. William J. Stone built a solid political base on the one thing that seemed certain to bring Missourians together during the late nineteenth century, their hatred of corporations. This power base propelled Stone from the small town of Nevada to the governor's mansion in Jefferson City, then to the United States Senate.[8]

Anticorporate sentiment had two different sources in Missouri. On the one hand, many people still adhered to market relationships dominated by local conditions and face-to-face dealings. Profit was restricted by local standards rather than individual acquisitiveness or events in distant places. And, if some chafed under these restrictions, many defended their customs against the disruptive influence of the market system, where business was conducted by strangers over long distances and profits were determined by the demands of invisible investors.

Still other Missourians were committed to the free market and open competition. They believed in individual acquisitiveness unhampered either by traditional morality or by powerful outside influences. Increasing interdependence within a national market system meant a loss of independence and upward mobility. Local merchants and manufacturers found themselves unable to compete with big New York firms. Small businessmen resented being dictated to by trusts. But, whether local market traditionalists or independent capitalists, Missourians as consumers, as taxpayers, as citizens, believed that large corporations threatened to deprive them of control over their lives.

A 1900 streetcar strike in St. Louis provides an example.[9] An attempt by streetcar workers to unionize in response to the consolidation of St. Louis transit companies meshed with widespread anticorporate sentiment in a months-long battle over control of mass transit in the state's largest city. St. Louis streetcar companies had angered city residents for years. They tore up streets for construction, evaded taxation, raised fares, and endangered pedestrians by their lack of fenders and the carelessness of drivers. In 1899 a pliant state legislature allowed any municipal street railway company to lease or purchase the property of any other street railway company. Within a year the United Street Railway Company, a New York firm with a charter to do business in Missouri, had purchased all St. Louis companies but one. The workers responded by organizing also. They established Local 131 of the Amalgamated Association of Street Railway Employees of America, a national union. The company responded by discharging union members. The

---

8. For a contemporary (1907) indictment of corporate behavior, see E. A. Ross, *Sin and Society* (New York: Harper & Row, 1973). Jack D. Muraskin, "Missouri Politics During the Progressive Period, 1896–1916" (Ph.D. diss., University of California-Berkeley, 1969), pp. 20–70 passim; Ruth Towne, "The Public Career of William J. Stone" (Ph.D. diss., University of Missouri, 1953); Christopher C. Gibbs, "Elliot W. Major," in Robert Sobel and John Rains, eds., *Biographical Directory of the Governors of the United States, 1789–1978* (Westport: Meckler Books, 1978), p. 860; Steven L. Piott, "Herbert S. Hadley," in ibid., p. 559.

9. Piott, *The Anti-Monopoly Persuasion: Popular Resistance to the Rise of Big Business in the Midwest*, pp. 55–72.

union issued an ultimatum demanding they be rehired. The company refused, and in early May 1900, 3,325 employees struck.

Both sides agreed that the issue was union recognition, but the whole city got caught up in the strike, and the issue broadened. In the first place, the strike affected the transportation of thousands. In the second place, both the company and the workers appealed to the public for understanding and help. The union was the more successful. The company's behavior made matters worse by uncovering a groundswell of anticorporate attitudes. While the union strove to provide transportation, even if it meant that ladies had to ride in wagons, the company hired strikebreakers, enlisted the aid of the city police, and joined with other corporations in the city in advising citizens on the rights of trusts. The streets of St. Louis were soon filled with pedestrians wearing buttons that read, "I will walk until the street car companies settle."[10]

St. Louisans demonstrated their dislike of the companies in more forceful ways. One man, crossing the tracks with his family, feared they would be run down by an oncoming car. He pulled a pistol and was arrested for brandishing a weapon. The judge dismissed the case, saying, "Even if Mr. DeDonato pulled a gun, he had a right to do so. Citizens have rights which corporations must respect . . . ." In the words of another observer, "It seemed to many that a quasi-public corporation should exhibit a semblance of courtesy and efficiency for the franchise privileges granted by this city."[11] During the strike a letter to the *St. Louis Star* said that the company, since it occupied public streets and possessed a franchise to be used for the benefit of the public, owed "a duty not only to those who are entitled to dividends on its stock, but to the people of the city as well." The corporation, these and other people argued, had entered into a relationship with the residents of the city: it could use public streets and exploit the public's need for transportation to make a profit, but it was obliged to provide safe, reliable, economical service as well.

The company brought in armed roughnecks as strikebreakers. These men did not know the city well and had little interest in courtesy or service to customers. The company supplemented scabs and police allies with a private posse of bankers, lawyers, and businessmen armed with rifles. But seven hundred of the city's retail merchants supported the strikers, who were also their neighbors and their customers, against the "great organized power of tyrannical trusts . . . crushing down wages and pauperizing the great masses of people."[12] The company's private army lacked discipline, and soon residents were petitioning the mayor to prevent members of the private army from discharging firearms and threatening the lives of women

10. See ibid., p. 61.
11. Ibid., p. 57.
12. Cited in ibid., p. 64.

and children. People complained that a government "of monopoly, by monopoly, and for monopoly" was unable to control the transit company. Further, the company, owned by outsiders, had imported "alien enemies . . . for the purpose of shooting down citizens of St. Louis."

The citizens fought back. They attacked strikebreakers and the policemen who had been put on the cars to protect them. They piled rocks or built fires on the tracks and stoned the cars when they stopped. Middle-class women saved their garbage to hurl at the cars, and one woman attacked a scab motorman with a dead frog tied to a string. Wires were cut, shots were fired, and crowds of angry women faced down a band of patrolmen sent to disperse them. Finally the police resorted to mounted charges with sabers drawn, but the crowds melted away before them, only to reform and again attack the cars, the drivers, and the policemen.

Eventually the company triumphed. Despite appeals from the people of St. Louis, the state court refused to overturn the consolidation act that had allowed the monopolization of St. Louis transit companies. The city refused to revoke the company's charter. The State Board of Equalization ignored a petition from forty thousand St. Louisans to impose higher taxes on the company. The company promised to rehire its old employees, but it broke its promise immediately and continued its open-shop policy. Frustration brought an end to citizen opposition eventually, but the St. Louis transit strike demonstrates the basic elements of anticorporate sentiment in Missouri in the years before the war, including the idea that corporations bear responsibilities to the society in which they operate, and that these responsibilities are at least as important as those to stockholders; that, in short, people are at least as important as profits. The strike also revealed a sharp sense of alienation between people and corporations, and the belief that the corporations behaved the way they did because they were outsiders in the community.

Anticorporate sentiment grew out of a widely shared localist point of view. By 1915 the market encompassed the world. Newspapers stressed the global economic implications of the war in Europe. But many Missourians had more limited horizons. The most important problems were the daily ones, such as transportation, and people sought to deal with them at the local level, where the problems manifested themselves. Since, as in the transit strike, the ultimate source of the problem often lay far beyond the local level, in distance and in organization, localism tended to cripple effective action. But it was at the local level that people felt they had power, especially when united with their neighbors, who shared those same problems. They did not care about the difficulties of scattered stockholders or New York managers. The forces of a changing world might be at work, but many Missourians continued to believe that they could deal with them at home.

Localism helps explain the attitudes of urban Missourians. To a great extent their lives were bounded by the neighborhood and the workplace.

Recent arrivals to the city, whether from Europe or rural America, gathered in enclaves held together by common language, religion, and customs. They often worked in the same industry or trade, perhaps alongside family members. In addition, the hostility that often greeted them only strengthened the tendency to cling together.

This led to a kind of dual localism among Missouri's immigrant population, as they split their loyalties between their new homes and their old. In the neighborhoods they worked to recreate something of the world they had left behind, all the while maintaining close ties to their home villages. St. Louis blacks, who had only a short river or train trip to the South, commuted regularly between the city and their Cotton Belt homes. Some Europeans became known as "birds of passage," working for a time in America, then returning home, sometimes making several round trips. And each time they returned to Missouri, they did so reinforced with cultural resources from their old homes.[13]

It was this localism that prevented many of Missouri's urban dwellers from quickly developing a broader view of American life and a strong sense of nationalism. After more than sixty years in the city, St. Louis's Bohemian population was still a distinct entity. St. Louis Germans were famous for the close ties among themselves and with the fatherland. The wealthier among them, such as the family of brewer Augustus Busch, maintained summer homes in Germany, and the less well off relied on a steady stream of letters and newspapers from relatives and friends. Other immigrant groups can be tracked as they moved around the city and up the social and economic ladder, and it was not unusual for the same house of worship to serve in turn as a Catholic church, a synagogue, and an African Methodist Episcopal church.[14] Kansas City Italians of all classes lived close together and conducted business through Italian bankers and lawyers; they patronized Italian physicians, druggists, and shopkeepers, and subscribed to locally printed Italian newspapers that kept them informed of events in both Italy and America. In St. Louis the boundaries between neighborhoods were often so sharply drawn that on one side of the street the signs might all be in Italian and on the other in Polish.[15]

Living frequently in the worst parts of the city and working in the most difficult and menial jobs, Missouri's urban immigrants clung to traditional values and customs to protect themselves from the harsh new life they had

13. Kansas City Board of Public Health, *Fourth Annual Report, 15 April 1912–22 April 1913*, pp. 56, 130–38; Crossland, *Negroes in St. Louis*, pp. 6–8.

14. Margaret L. Sullivan, "Hyphenism in St. Louis, 1900–1921" (Ph.D. diss., St. Louis University, 1968), p. 198; Crawford, *Immigrant in St. Louis*; Corzine and Dabrowski, "Ethnic Factor and Neighborhood Stability"; Thelen, *Paths of Resistance*, pp. 134–39. For German ties to the old country, see Detjen, *The Germans in Missouri*, pp. 20–30.

15. Sullivan, "Hyphenism in St. Louis," pp. 30–34; Crawford, *Immigrant in St. Louis*, pp. 15–32; Kansas City Board of Public Health, *Fourth Annual Report*, pp. 69–71.

found in America. At the same time, this insularity sometimes reinforced those values, leading them to celebrate national holidays and national heroes with increased fervor. They created ethnic theater and singing societies to keep their language alive, and founded schools to teach their own children the value of their heritage in an alien land. They organized mutual aid societies, often through the church, to provide people some measure of economic security, and they patronized local shopkeepers, keeping the market system at arm's length as much as possible.[16]

Yet all city dwellers, immigrant and native alike, experienced the consequences of the sudden growth of the state's urban areas in the late nineteenth century. Municipal services especially were stretched to the limit by population growth and by the economic consequences of the depression of the 1890s and the downturns of 1907 and 1914. Inadequate sanitation, unreliable transportation, and costly energy brought hardship to city dwellers regardless of their job or place of birth. And if opposition to alien corporations was not always successful, localism permitted organization transcending class and ethnic barriers to attack common problems.

In Springfield, in the southwest corner of the state, the issue was electric rates.[17] Springfield citizens had a record of local action against outside corporations. In the early years of the century, consumers protected their local meat-packing industry by boycotting the national packing trust. Between 1910 and 1912 the city repeatedly and successfully sued the St. Louis and San Francisco Railroad for unpaid taxes, and the Greene County court followed up with an order increasing the assessment of the property of all railroads in the county by 25 percent. In 1912 the people of Springfield took on the Federal Light and Traction Company of New York, owner of the Springfield Gas and Electric Company.

In August 1912 the Springfield Gas and Electric Company offered the city council a contract that called for a maximum rate of twelve cents per kilowatt hour of electricity. The council demurred. It only cost the company a little over a penny to generate that same kilowatt hour. The council appointed a committee to look into the question and began to drop hints about proposing to voters a plan for the construction of a municipal power plant. The council also demanded to see the company's books and promised to fine any company official who refused to testify before the council. The company continued to insist on a twelve cent rate, and people in Springfield began to get angry, especially after the local press pointed out the low rates paid in nearby Joplin and Carthage, where municipally owned plants competed with private companies. Some citizens even announced that they were willing to go back to coal oil lamps if rates were not lowered.

16. Sullivan, "Hyphenism in St. Louis," pp. 32–36; Crawford, *Immigrant in St. Louis,* pp. 15–33; Rosenblum, *Immigrant Workers,* pp. 120–35; *State Sociology of Missouri, 1913,* pp. 37–38.

17. *Springfield Republican,* 14, 20, and 25 August, 18 September, 13 and 15 December 1912; 5 and 22 January, 9 February, 2 April 1913.

Normally the people of Springfield were willing to leave the daily matters of government to their elected representatives. This time, however, they chose to intervene directly. In December, six hundred people jammed the city council meeting to hear the public service committee give its report. They sat or stood silently, until the committee recommended a six-year contract with the company at a maximum rate of nine cents. The crowd gasped. Not only was the rate still too high, they would be saddled with it for six years. Their distress was so apparent that only one member of the committee rose to defend the proposed contract. Later, after the meeting broke up, the manager of the company, C. C. Chappelle, claimed that popular participation had intimidated the committee. He argued that the sentiment of the citizens was against a fair proposal for the lighting company and claimed that any councilman voting for such an ordinance would be ruined politically. The next day the press announced that the people of Springfield were ready for a municipally owned power plant.

A committee of businessmen from the Commercial Club, the Retail Merchant's Association, the Young Men's Business Club, and the Jobber's and Manufacturer's Association met to explore the issue. The group enjoyed the approval of the company, which agreed to abide by their recommendation. To the company's dismay, however, the businessmen, who had to pay the light bills for their businesses as well as at home, announced in late January 1913 that they wanted an even lower rate than the public service committee had recommended: six cents per kilowatt hour. This proposal was along the same lines as one made earlier by Councilman T. H. Gideon, who was earning the reputation of a local consumer advocate.

Once again the council met, and once again six hundred filled the chamber. This time, however, the observers did not confine themselves to loud breathing. Indeed, they angrily shouted down any who tried to speak for rates higher than those suggested by the businessmen or by Gideon. That very night Gideon began enlisting support from businessmen for a municipal power plant. On 29 January, though, the council passed the businessmen's proposal, subject to a vote of the people. The company had twelve days to respond.

Through January and February the people of Springfield awaited the company's response. The press pointed out on 9 February that the city water contract came up for renewal in July, and "the problem of rates for private consumers again, as in the lighting controversy, will be the one uppermost in mind." The company finally, in late February, rejected the "Merchant's Bill." It further entered a suit charging that the proposed rates were confiscatory and asking the court to rule on the fairness of the Merchant's Bill. In the April 1913 municipal elections the people of Springfield passed the Merchant's Bill by an overwhelming majority. In the years that followed, Councilman Gideon became mayor, and in 1916 the people of Springfield once again confronted the Federal Light and Traction Company in an even more bitter fight over local rights. (See Chapter 7.)

Two controversies raged in St. Joseph, Missouri, in 1912–1913, one over streetcar franchises and the other over natural gas.[18] Citizens complained that before the streetcar company would extend its tracks it always demanded perpetual lease on the land plus city maintenance of the line. When pressed, the company agreed to provide free tickets for city employees plus free electricity for city hall. The mayor agreed to this arrangement. He had to back down, however, when it was revealed that the city planned to provide auto transportation for its employees, and there were suggestions that the mayor planned to distribute the free passes among his friends. The mayor insisted that the new transport plan had "slipped his memory." Angry at the company's treatment of citizens and its dealings with the mayor, Councilman C. D. Radford summarized local complaints. "Why is it," he asked, "that we cannot make the streetrailway company do things?" The company seemed able to dictate to the city what it would or would not do, and the city was helpless. "Surely no corporation is greater than the city in which it operates," Radford insisted, adding that St. Joseph might look to Detroit and emulate its relationship with its transit company. As it was, the company was blackmailing the city, and "It is not right to pay the company to do things."

Responding to heavy public pressure, the city council agreed to require the company to extend its tracks into new sections of the city in return for a new franchise. The council further agreed, over the mayor's objections, to place a tax of .5 percent on the company's gross earnings.

The St. Joseph gas controversy arose from demands for lower gas rates and improved service. The Kansas Natural Gas Company, which sold gas to the St. Joseph Gas Company, and which in turn was owned by American Light and Traction of New York, charged forty cents per one thousand cubic feet of gas. The city public utilities commission called for a rate of thirty-five cents. In fact, the city's contract with the company did not specify any particular rate, and city prosecutor W. B. Norris predicted that the company would actually raise rates by ten cents. Councilman John Brendel protested that he had been beleaguered by "scores of consumers" about gas rates and services. There was barely enough gas to heat homes or cook meals, but rates were as high as ever and going higher. At a city council meeting in November 1912, representatives of St. Joseph consumers complained of high rates and poor service. Brendel called for an investigation of the gas company, but the mayor, a former director of the local gas company, was opposed. As the St. Joseph Gas Company could only buy gas from the Kan-

18. See *St. Joseph News-Press,* 14 and 17 September; 1, 7, and 11 October; 1, 5, 19, 26, and 30 November; 5, 6, 9, and 26 December 1912; 7 and 14 January; 8, 12, and 18 February 1913.

sas Natural Gas Company, he pointed out, and as the Kansas Natural Gas Company was in receivership and rates were consequently being set by a federal judge, the city of St. Joseph could do nothing.

The city continued to receive complaints from consumers. Councilman Brendel voiced the general opinion: "If the people of St. Joseph are to be made to pay higher rates for gas, or even if the present rate is to be continued, we are unquestionably entitled to better gas." The mayor countered that he was not against consumers, but the city was helpless as long as the Kansas Company could persuade the court to raise rates. At a December council meeting the city demanded a new franchise calling for a contract that established a specific amount of heat and candle power, one that gave consumers a discount if gas fell below the specified amount. It further established a specific rate for gas and granted the city the right to demand extension of mains as needed, and to require the company to run taps to the property line instead of the curb, as they usually did. Mr. K. M. Mitchell, a company executive, told the meeting, "We should get together like businessmen and settle this thing. Tell us what you want and I will see if it can be had. We ought to be able to come to an understanding." Brendel responded, "We could come to an understanding if you got everything you want."

A few weeks later the president of American Light and Traction came to town to look over the company's property and to confer with city officials. Evidently no one was satisfied by the meeting, however, because the company rejected the city's proposal as too expensive. Consumers kept complaining; the city sued the company and began to suggest municipal ownership. The federal court raised gas rates by ten cents.

As these examples suggest, aroused citizens sometimes triumphed over large corporations, and sometimes failed. More important to an understanding of attitudes toward the war is the localism from which sprang the anticorporate sentiment of Missouri's urbanites. Furthermore, if the community was the arena, and the corporation was the problem, the proper tool for dealing with the problem as often as not was direct democracy.

The issue of democracy is crucial because it is linked directly to the war. Woodrow Wilson sought to rally support for the war by raising the standard of democracy, but the attitudes of Missourians indicate a divergence of definition. To Missourians, democracy was the right of people to control their own lives, to make for themselves the important decisions that affected their lives—indeed, to decide what were the important decisions. A leading student of the period before the war has noted that reformers who tried to streamline municipal governments frequently saw their provisions voted down if they did not include strong provisions for direct democracy.[19] Urban businessmen sometimes sought to change city governments to prevent the kind of popular influence that had prevailed in Springfield and St.

19. Weinstein, *Corporate Ideal*, p. 109.

Joseph. They sought to remove certain economic issues like taxation and franchise privileges from the realm of politics by giving the power to appointed officials, to commissions, or to interest-group leaders. In this way they hoped to apply business methods to government: as Kansas City businessmen admitted, they were "interested in municipal reform as a means of making their community more attractive to outside firms." And in St. Louis, just before the war broke out in Europe, citizens demonstrated what they meant by reform and democracy when they rejected a proposed new charter in 1911 and then approved a revision in 1914.[20]

According to its supporters, the 1911 charter had all the advantages of modern civil government. It was simple and efficient. It placed city government on a businesslike basis by providing civil service, increased power for government, and a greater concentration of authority. Labor leader Owen Miller, who had helped write it, said it was a good charter, but admitted it lacked strong provisions for initiative and referendum.

Opponents agreed, at least with half of Miller's assessment. They asserted that the new charter would deliver city government into the hands of "monopolists and the wealthy few." The Women's Trade Union League and the Missouri Direct Legislation League claimed that "the interests," armed with a $100,000 slush fund, planned to buy the election. Small businessmen and local unions agreed, and the opposition to the charter because of its limitations on "direct popular government" ran high across the city. On election day the charter was defeated by a two-to-one margin.

The 1914 charter enjoyed a different fate. Its opponents were suspicious because the charter enjoyed popular support. William M. Reedy, St. Louis publisher and journalist, had supported the 1911 charter as the most democratic possible, but he and others believed that the 1914 charter went too far. The new document provided for much less efficient government than the old one had. Power was not as centralized, responsibility not as dispersed. Spokesmen for major corporations and leading politicians agreed that the 1914 charter granted entirely too much power to the citizenry. The unicameral legislature was too susceptible to popular whim. Wealth stood in danger of confiscatory taxation. Entrenched power was threatened with unemployment, or at least the possibility of less graft.[21]

But the new charter had more of what the voters wanted. They preferred a unicameral legislature and more direct popular control of city government. The new charter doubled the number of offices subject to electoral control. It allowed the city to own and operate its own utilities. Most important, it

20. See *St. Louis Republic*, 7 January 1911, p. 7; 11 January, pp. 2, 4; 15 January, p. 1; 18 January, p. 2.

21. *Reedy's Mirror*, 26 January 1911, p. 1; 15 May 1914, p. 1; 19 June, pp. 1–2; *St. Louis Republic*, 10 January 1911, p. 12; 14 January, p. 6; 1 February, p. 1; 1 May 1914, p. 6; 27 May, pp. 10–11; 15 May, p. 6; 25 May, p. 3; 29 May, p. 1; 15 June, p. 6; 25 June, p. 6; 30 June, p. 6; 1 July, p. 1.

provided for stronger, more accessible initiative and referendum. As a result, in spite of a poor showing in the heavily boss-influenced wards along the Mississippi River, the new charter passed, 42,340 to 40,153.

In the years just before the war, Missouri was as much a rural state as an urban one, and people in rural areas were, if anything, even more localist and anticorporate in their outlook than their city cousins. It had been rural Missourians who supported the Granger and Populist movements in the state, and they remained strongly traditional in outlook well into the twentieth century. In 1917 Homer Croy, a young writer who would soon enjoy a national reputation, returned from a trip around the world to his native northwestern Missouri farm country. Croy was excited, filled with the wonders he had seen, with a storyteller's urgent desire to relate it all. But he discovered something about his home that had escaped his notice while he was growing up there. His friends and neighbors did not seem to care about the great events of the wide world. Their perceptions, interests, and energies were limited to a great extent by the affairs of the farm and the village, by the county, occasionally by the state. Croy found much to admire in this, for it gave people a strong sense of community and an abiding love of the land. At the same time, it ill prepared them, he believed, for the storm about to break over them.[22]

Travelers in the Ozarks, at the other end of the state from Croy's rolling northern plains, noticed similar attitudes of enduring localism. The region was dominated by log cabins and rocky fields; farms were "off on brushy byways," and houses and lands "were marked by a good deal of careless neglect." The people had a "well-enough" attitude that, according to some visitors, was not the result of shiftlessness. Rather, people "were not ambitious to have a fine house or make a show and out do the neighbors. They had been used to frugal living and with it were content." As another observer pointed out, the "hillman" has made an art of relaxation, "but he does not loaf all the time. He works hard . . . when the occasion demands it."[23] And this attitude, which often left an individual living in rather shabby circumstances, extended to his relations with his neighbors in the marketplace. The market itself was local, and behavior was influenced by factors other than what the traffic would bear. People grew little surplus of any-

22. Homer Croy, *Country Cured* (New York: Harper & Bros., 1943), pp. 80, 134, 167–68; for the views of a large-scale, highly successful farmer in "Swamp East" Missouri, see Thad Snow, *From Missouri* (Boston: Houghton Mifflin, 1954), pp. 78–81, 122–27; see also Thelen, *Paths of Resistance*, pp. 13–17. Loren Reid, *Hurry Home Wednesday: Growing Up in a Small Missouri Town, 1905–1921* (Columbia: University of Missouri Press, 1978), deals with the son of a small-town postmaster and newspaper editor in the northwestern part of the state.

23. Charles P. Cushing, "Floating Through the Ozarks," *Outing*, August 1911, pp. 537–46; Cushing's "The Ozarks," *The Mentor*, July 1927, pp. 23–31, discusses changes in the area during the intervening years. Otto E. Rayburn, *Forty Years in the Ozarks: An Autobiography*, pp. 12–13, 31–37.

thing, and what they did grow tended to stay in the area. Every Saturday "someone from every family has to go to the village to carry the small truck" to sell, and to buy necessities. Cash was normally used for such items as bacon, beans, and tobacco, and barter accounted for much of the rest. "Things ain't bringing as much as they did one while," said a farm wife. "We only get fifteen cents for butter, or ten cents if we sell to a neighbor."[24] Obviously local market values allowed people to worry about making a profit, but did not allow them to profit off their neighbors.

A close look at one county in central Missouri, Morgan County, provides many details of rural life before the war and serves as an example of the importance of localism in the lives of rural Missourians.[25] Morgan County is on the northern edge of the Ozarks. Its southern part is wooded and hilly. In the center lies Versailles, the largest town and the county seat, with a population of just under 2,000 in 1915. North of Versailles the land is rolling prairie. In 1915 there were about 13,000 people in Morgan County, most of whom lived on the county's 2,000 farms. The average farm was 138 acres, of which 75 percent was improved; the rest was woodland or unimproved pasture.

Most farms in the county, and the most modern ones, lay in the prairie region, with less well-developed holdings in the rough country to the south. The vast majority of farms, 1,721, were between 20 and 260 acres, with only 34 over 500 acres. About three-fourths of all farms were owner-operated, and the majority carried mortgages. Most houses, especially in the prairie districts, were wood frame. Over 320 were log, and 106 were log and frame combined, but most of these were in the south. Only 36 farms had indoor plumbing. A handful of farmers owned tractors. Both mechanization and silo construction were considered signs of progress, but only 152 farms had silos, of which 105 had been built since 1912.

The local community played a much larger role in the lives of Morgan County residents than did the national market. For example, while over half of all farms had orchards, only a few were over five acres, and there were no commercial orchards at all. The farm family consumed the bulk of the produce, much of which was preserved. What little the family could not use was sold or given away to neighbors. Trading for variety was popular: apples for peaches, for example, or pears for apples.

In another area, Morgan County dairy cattle produced 1,123,000 gallons of milk and about 284,000 pounds of butter a year. Some 9,599 gallons and 83,000 pounds were marketed locally; farm families consumed the rest. Over 173,000 chickens and other poultry were raised, but only 75,000 were marketed. Farm wives and children earned extra cash by selling 560,000 of the 763,000 eggs laid annually, but they sold them locally, mostly to towns-

24. Clifton Johnson, "Life in the Ozarks," *Outing,* January 1906, pp. 435–42.
25. W. L. Nelson, "A Rural Survey of Morgan County."

folk. The average farmer raised 10 to 20 hogs and roughly the same number of cattle. The average farm family slaughtered and ate about 4 hogs and probably 1 or 2 steers each year. Some of the animals were slaughtered and sold locally, and a few were shipped out to packing houses. Most of the grain grown in the county, corn and oats, was used as feed. Wheat was the only "cash" crop, insofar as there was one in Morgan County. The average farmer devoted ten to twenty acres to wheat. Much of this was milled right in the county and the flour was consumed there also. Farmers took their grain to the mills and either waited for it to be processed or exchanged it on the spot for an equivalent amount of flour. When they had satisfied their family's needs for the coming year, they sold the remainder for cash.

Morgan County farmers relied on local action to solve local problems. There were several "beef clubs" that supplied meat to county residents as needed, but did not market any outside the county. And farmers still joined together for threshing and harvesting, to help neighbors build a silo, or for barn raisings and wood choppings. Such organizations were ad hoc, generating no bureaucracy, with no ties to larger official groups, and they dissolved when the work was done. Yet, while the concerns of Morgan County residents were local, they were not isolated from the outside world. Virtually every family took a newspaper, sometimes three, including one of the farm journals like *Missouri Farmer* or *Missouri Ruralist*. These papers provided popular fiction, jokes, games, household and farming hints, plus national and international news. Further, Morgan County did not lack for transportation. The Rock Island and the Missouri Pacific railroads traversed the county, and the navigable Osage River ran along its southern border.

Thus, with the modern market network growing around them, with water and rail links available, localism continued to dominate the lives of Morgan County residents, not by force of circumstances, but apparently by choice. People in the area had ties to the market network if they wanted to use them. No doubt many did, forging links with remote power centers and perhaps attaining wealth and power in the process. The outlet existed for anyone who wanted to have a commercial orchard, or grow large wheat crops, or run big herds of cattle. But few did.

Missouri, however, was not exclusively a haven of local market economies and direct democracy, nor did all its problems come from alien corporations. The state had its share of men and women anxious to extend the market network, even into the Ozark backwoods. Businessmen from major cities traveled on chartered trains throughout the Midwest seeking to drum up new sources of raw material and new customers. Some looked as far away as Latin America, and they rejoiced when European competitors fell to fighting one another in 1914, for they hoped to move into neglected trade regions.[26]

26. *St. Louis Republic*, 24 July 1914, p. 4; Muraskin, "Missouri Politics During the Progressive Period," p. 68.

But Missouri businessmen sought more than new markets. They also wanted people to like them. They complained of being regarded as "outlaws and outcasts" and sought to prove their patriotism and willingness to serve the public interest. At the 1914 Missouri Banker's Convention in St. Louis, speakers claimed that businessmen must "show people that we are not the embodiment of cold blooded selfishness and thinking only of our profits." As a partial solution, Kansas City meat-packer J. C. Swift urged the assembled financiers to start at the grass roots by winning Missouri's rural population to their point of view. Swift suggested that they work closely with the State Agricultural College at Columbia to wean farmers away from their traditional values, and to teach them about sound business methods and the beneficence of businessmen. Indeed, the State Federation of Commercial Clubs (forerunner of the chambers of commerce) had organized in Hannibal only a few years earlier, seeking to build better agriculture and better relations between farmers and businessmen.[27]

The drive to modernize farming in Missouri had in fact been underway for years. Agricultural reformers in the state knew that the issue was one of values rather than merely technique. Every January prosperous farmers, businessmen, and state agricultural experts gathered in Columbia for "Farmer's Week" to hear the gospel of progress preached. At the 1915 meeting speakers sharply attacked the "well-enough" attitude of so many farmers; their absence from Farmer's Week was proof of this. The farmer who just wanted to get by, and this included most of them, needed to be raised to a higher moral plane, up to "more wholesome living" through "heartier ambition."[28]

Secretary of Agriculture David F. Houston, formerly of Washington University in St. Louis, told farmers that the world was their market. To reach this market they must increase production with the aid of science and technology. Houston advocated improved relations between state and federal agencies and urged farmers to realize that "there is no man in this country who needs to be a businessman more than a farmer." Further, farmers who were "doing business in a market economy for profit" must "offer a standardized product which will . . . be readily acceptable."

The next speaker, Philander P. Lewis, president of the State Board of Agriculture, businessman, and gentleman farmer, continued the theme. He referred to farming as a business or industry seventeen times in his brief speech, telling farmers that it was "good policy to [follow] the example of the great corporations of the country" by centralizing and modernizing operations. Lewis spoke in nearly religious terms of "subduing the earth" and of the "feeding of the multitudes." He said that if he could, he would cross a

27. *St. Louis Republic,* 8 July 1914, p. 6; 19 May 1914, p. 1.
28. State Board of Agriculture, *Forty-Seventh Annual Report* (1918), includes a complete report of the 1915 meeting, including texts of all speeches. Thelen, *Paths of Resistance,* pp. 35–43, discusses the origins of the drive to modernize farming in Missouri.

"honey bee with a lightning bug and have him working twenty-four hours a day." But since he could not, he urged rural Missourians to imitate his mythical hybrid, to grow better crops and breed better livestock, which would result "in the making of better men and women," through the application of the corporate model to Missouri farming.

For decades agricultural experts had been urging this theme on Missouri farmers, trying to get them to abandon primitive methods and the constraints of a local market economy. And for decades they had little impact. The men in Columbia in 1915 were speaking mainly to each other, to the already converted. Partly this was due to the strength of tradition; partly it was because they had as their allies the men most farmers regarded as either suspect or outright dangerous. These included "book farmers" like Houston, gentleman farmers like Lewis, and the owners of the food trust, like Swift. It also included businessmen who stood to profit from the farmer's industry, such as implement manufacturers and dealers, bankers who owned farm mortgages, and the handful of big farmers who sought to grow through modernization. These forces had joined together in commercial clubs and other organizations to promote state fairs, where competition among farmers would, they hoped, lead to greater output and higher profits. They supported model farms to serve as examples of the right ways to do things. Perhaps most important, they hoped to build the Missouri College of Agriculture in Columbia into the center of modern profitable farming in the state.[29]

Cooperating with businessmen and successful farmers, the College of Agriculture and the State Board of Agriculture experimented with new farming methods, which they then tried to pass along to farmers. Following passage of the Hatch Act in 1887, which offered federal funds for agricultural experimentation, the state created the Agricultural Experimentation Station, attached it and its funds to the college, and made the dean of the college the director of the station. The college grew, adding new departments and going from two graduates a year in the 1880s to over fifty in 1917 alone. They too talked mostly to each other, however, as the average farmer paid little attention to what went on in Columbia. So the experts tried to attract farmers to town by offering "short courses" at the college during the winter when farmers had some free time. But, if they had the time, they lacked the inclination, and the short courses suffered low enrollment. So in the 1890s the experts were forced to take the word directly to the people with "farmer's institutes" right in the local community, sponsored by local businessmen

29. For the tone and message of the agricultural experts, see the Missouri State Board of Agriculture's monthly bulletins and annual reports. See also Frederick B. Mumford Papers, Western Historical Manuscripts Collection (WHMC), State Historical Society of Missouri, Columbia, Missouri. Thad Snow's *From Missouri* presents the views of a farmer closely allied with the agricultural modernizers. See also Robert Tontz, "Membership in General Farmer's Organizations, 1874–1960," *Agricultural History* 38 (1964): 155, and *Armour's Farmer's Almanac, 1919* (Chicago: Armour Fertilizer Works, 1919).

and bankers, and designed to "discuss means and methods of making farming more profitable."

Shortly before the war broke out the college broadened the scope of these institutes in their effort to turn farms into food factories. In 1910 they created the Extension Division. For years the effort to convert farmers had met with only limited success. The experts needed a permanent local representative to bring home the new era of agriculture to remote districts and resistant individuals. In 1912 the college established a program of county farm advisors who would be paid, half by the United States Department of Agriculture and the College of Agriculture, and half by the county. The college found local support from businessmen who were willing to put up the money (since few farmers were), and in 1914 the Smith-Lever Act provided further federal funding for the county farm advisors, or county agents, as they came to be called. By the war, 15 of Missouri's 114 counties had agents. The agents and the businessmen who sponsored them, collectively called the county farm bureau, met in Slater, Missouri, in 1915 to create the Missouri Farm Bureau Federation.[30] Thus by the war a whole structure existed to make farming more businesslike. The structure consisted of local businessmen, county agents, the College of Agriculture, the state agriculture board, and the federal government. All of these individuals and institutions were determined to alter the character of life in Missouri. They were presided over by Frederick B. Mumford.

Nobody represented the forces of modernization in Missouri better than Frederick B. Mumford. As dean of the College of Agriculture from 1909 to 1938, as federal food administrator for Missouri during the war, and as chairman of the Missouri Council of Defense, he occupied a central place in Missouri during World War I.[31]

Mumford was born in 1868 in Michigan and attended Michigan Agricultural College. He became a professor at the Missouri College of Agriculture in 1895. In 1900 and 1901 he did graduate work in Leipzig and Zurich. He wrote several important books on animal husbandry. According to one story, Mumford began his career as an apostle of modern farming methods while still a student. During a vacation he overcame his father's skepticism toward "book farmers" by performing on his father's orchards a grafting technique he had learned in school. As soon as the orchard was flourishing, Mumford began to preach the new methods to his father's neighbors.[32]

30. For a history of the college, see Frederick B. Mumford, "History of the Missouri College of Agriculture," *Agriculture Experiment Station Bulletin*, no. 483 (Columbia, Mo.: Agriculture Experiment Station, 1944), pp. 125, 127–28; Vera B. Shuttler, *A History of the Missouri Farm Bureau Federation* (Springfield, Mo.: Missouri Farm Bureau Federation, 1948); also McConnell, *Decline of Agrarian Democracy*, and Danbom, *Resisted Revolution*, for the responses of many farmers.

31. For biographies of Mumford, see *Missouri Alumnus*, June 1936, p. 11; and *Missouri Historical Review* 41 (April 1947).

32. Mumford Papers, WHMC, folders 36–38, contain Mumford's pronouncements on farming.

Mumford combined the training of a scientist with the spirit of a zealot. While his eyes were always on the goal of improved conditions for farmers in general, his approach (although this cannot have been his intention) tended to dehumanize farmers as individuals, making them into units of production within an efficiently operating food-manufacturing process. For Homer Croy's neighbors in Nodaway County, for people in the Ozarks and in Morgan County, farming was a way of life, not a way to get rich. For Mumford a farm was "a combination of factors involved in the production of food." He condemned "artistic additions" to farm buildings as "economically worthless," despite whatever pleasure they might bring to the people living in them. Nor did the farmer's wife escape: "The management of a household is too important to be placed in the hands of ignorant, untrained and inefficient women." Only through modern science could women provide save, healthy homes for their families. Farmers, Mumford insisted, were "the most important industrial body in the state," and as such they must rely on proper use of technology and sound business practices to get the most out of what they had.

Mumford saw himself primarily as a teacher who could lift the farmer from his slough of ignorance and indolence. Modern industry, he pointed out in 1915, used science and technology to increase profit, and so should the farmer. Yet the individual farmer usually could not afford to pay for the technology, so the State Board of Agriculture, the College of Agriculture, and the Experiment Station would provide it for him. Theoretical science, however, had no place in Mumford's plans for the future. To Mumford, that education which did not foster greater efficiency, which did not enable students to "perform the practical duties of citizenship [i.e., working for the betterment of society] is a menace to the state." He did not care about how much his students knew, but rather about how much they could do, how much they could achieve "in agriculture as a vocation."

Mumford's philosophy would have tremendous impact in the months to come. In the months before the war, Missouri was a state in transition: half rural, half urban; half agricultural, half industrial. Her people possessed a complex set of values including the most traditional and the most modern. Missouri culture included faith in the most radical forms of direct democracy and the belief in the need to centralize, bureaucratize, and modernize; it included attitudes so bounded by local affairs that people seemed unaware of the rest of the world, and attitudes and interests that encompassed whole nations; it included those who thought the modern corporation could provide the model for making a new and better America, and those who thought the corporation was the enemy of everything good in the country. It also included a large number of people who were content just going about their daily affairs and wanted very much to be left alone to continue those pursuits.

Mumford and his allies had for years been at odds with the localism, preference for local democracy, and anticorporate sentiments of so many of their neighbors. For years they had enjoyed little success in overcoming these values; but the war provided them with a new opportunity for progress. Depending on their priorities, they could capture new markets and get rich, try out their ideas for modernization in a crisis, prove to people that they were patriotic Americans, or all three. They looked forward to augmenting their own power, to overcoming local traditions, to circumventing local political peculiarities. But first they would have to address the opposition of Missourians to American entry into World War I.

Chapter 2

Silent Majority

The war reached America in the spring of 1917.[1] Events piled up suddenly in a matter of weeks. In January 1917 Germany decided that the only way to break England's stranglehold on her overseas supply lines was to resume unrestricted submarine warfare and hope for victory before America could intervene effectively. On 31 January Germany informed the United States of her decision to create a zone closing off all Europe and to sink any ship, neutral or belligerent, that entered the zone. Secretary of State Robert Lansing urged President Wilson to hold Germany to the *Sussex* Pledge of 1916 and break off relations. Anything less, Lansing argued, would severely damage American prestige. According to Lansing, we would not be able to "hold up our heads as a great nation" if we did not break off relations, even though such an action would lead to war. Edward M. House, the president's close adviser, agreed.

This was not the first time the war had threatened America. In May 1915 German submarines had sunk the British liner *Lusitania*, killing 1200, including 128 Americans. They had sailed despite a German warning not to, and no doubt ignorant of the fact that the *Lusitania* carried munitions, thereby making her a legitimate target. Wilson's demands for an apology from Germany achieved quick results, but were too strongly worded for his antiwar secretary of state, William Jennings Bryan. Bryan resigned to become a spokesman for the opponents of war. He was replaced by the avowedly pro-British Robert Lansing. In any case, Germany's quick apology and Wilson's willingness to accept it restored a measure of calm.

The calm was disrupted a year later. In February 1916 Sen. Thomas P. Gore

1. For events leading to war, see Arthur S. Link, *Woodrow Wilson and the Progressive Era, 1910–1917*, chs. 6–10, esp. pp. 164–67, 211–24, 269–74, 276–82. Also, Robert H. Ferrell, *Woodrow Wilson and World War I, 1917–1921*, pp. 6–16; Ernest R. May, *The World War and American Isolation*, esp. p. 422 for Wilson on popular reluctance to avenge German submarine depredations; Ruth Towne, "The Public Career of William J. Stone"; Jerrald K. Pfabe, "Missouri Congressmen and Neutrality, 1914–1917"; John C. Crighton, *Missouri and the World War*, pp. 165–75; Thomas W. Ryley, *A Little Group of Willful Men*, deals with the armed ship bill controversy; Seward Livermore, *Woodrow Wilson and the War Congress, 1916–1918*; and for the impact of submarine warfare on the American economy and popular reactions to that, see Steven Donohue, "No Small Potatoes: Consumer Consciousness in the American Food Crisis, 1914–1917."

of Oklahoma and Rep. Jeff McLemore of Tennessee sought to prevent another *Lusitania* crisis through a measure warning Americans to keep off the ships of belligerents. Wilson arrayed his supporters against the resolution, and Congress tabled it. Within a few days the Germans sank the *Sussex*, an unarmed passenger ship. Lansing and House urged the president to sever relations with Germany. Instead Wilson, anxious to avoid war, demanded from Germany, and got, a pledge not to sink merchant ships without warning. Germany's announcement of a return to unrestricted submarine warfare in 1917 thus forced Wilson into the arms of House and Lansing.

By 2 February 1917 Wilson decided to break relations with Germany. He still hoped to avoid war, for he believed, and had told House on two occasions, that the American people would not go to war no matter how many of their fellow citizens were lost at sea. On 2 February Wilson spoke with the Democratic chairman of the Senate Foreign Relations Committee, William J. Stone of Missouri. Stone counseled delay, for he too believed that the majority wanted to avoid war. On 3 February, however, Wilson told Congress that the United States had broken off relations with Germany. He insisted that the dignity of the nation was at stake and that, furthermore, he was prepared to ask Congress for authority to "use any means that may be necessary" to protect Americans "in the prosecution of their peaceful and legitimate errands" on the high seas.

War clouds darkened on 26 February when Wilson recommended a policy of "armed neutrality" and asked Congress for permission to arm American merchantmen and to provide U.S. Navy crews to man the guns. Wilson was under considerable pressure. Two American vessels had recently been sunk, and shippers were refusing to put out to sea. Goods piled up at the docks. Railroad cars headed for the docks stood loaded on sidings. The transportation system of the country was grinding to a halt, and domestic shipments of necessities had become sidetracked. Consumers suffered as food shortages developed in cities and prices rose sharply. Food riots had broken out in some eastern cities during the winter. German submarines were threatening to cause widespread civil disorder in the United States and to bring commerce to a standstill.

The House of Representatives voted 403 to 13 to grant Wilson the power to arm merchantmen. In the foreign affairs committee, Dorsey Shackleford of Missouri unsuccessfully opposed the bill because it gave the president the right to wage a war undeclared by Congress. In floor debate Shackleford attacked the war party and the prowar press for setting up such a rattling of sabers that the president and Congress could not decide the issue fairly. He insisted that he was not a pacifist, as some had claimed, but that he was for war if "our interests guided by justice" demanded it. As for the people, how could they make any decision since they could not get accurate information from the newspapers? The press had "been misleading from the time the war commenced until now. They have taken only one side," blowing small incidents out of proportion in order to push America into a war in which we had no interest.

Other Missouri representatives disagreed. Thomas Rubey of Lebanon supported the bill because Americans had to trust their president and stand behind him lest the world think we were divided. Courtney Hamlin refused to permit America to be driven from the seas, but felt that the president was better prepared to handle the crisis than Congress. William Borland told his colleagues that America had the right to defend her interests and the right to trade anywhere in the world, no matter what was going on there. The arming of merchant ships, he insisted, would not bring America into the war. The arming of ships sending war supplies to one belligerent, and then shooting at another belligerent trying to stop those ships, could not possibly involve us in a war with either side. It was just business.

The bill suffered a different fate in the Senate. The foreign relations committee actually strengthened the measure somewhat, over Stone's objections. Stone insisted that he would therefore not manage the bill on the floor and turned it over to Nebraska senator Gilbert M. Hitchcock. The bill then joined many others on the crowded calendar, but only after Wisconsin senator Robert La Follette managed to delay its introduction until the day before adjournment.

Senator Stone, La Follette, and others prevented passage of the armed-ship bill by filibustering it to death. Stone spoke for five hours, his longest speech of the session. He asserted that to allow the president to bring America into the war without a formal congressional declaration represented a dangerous precedent. He denounced the agitation for war that came from munitions makers, bankers with loans to the Allies, and the big city press. "What vital interest," he asked, "has the great mass of our people in this bloody tragedy that they should plunge into it?"

The filibuster succeeded, and the armed-ship bill went out with the Sixty-fourth Congress; but Wilson's supporters got up a statement to the effect that the majority of senators had wanted to pass the bill and had only been prevented from doing so by a handful of their colleagues.

Supporters of war in Missouri and across the nation attacked the filibusterers. Wilson told his secretary of agriculture, David F. Houston, that the bill's defeat was due to the "slipperiness of Stone" and the "vanity of La Follette." He further denounced them as a "little group of willful men, representing no opinion but their own." Editorial cartoons showed the filibusterers receiving medals from the Kaiser. The *Atlanta Journal*, the *Duluth News-Tribune*, and the *New Republic* all supported Wilson. The *New York Times* identified them with Benedict Arnold. Newspapers in Providence, Hartford, Philadelphia, Montgomery, Memphis, and Houston railed against the senators, and the word *treason* appeared frequently. James Cox, governor of Ohio, called the filibusterers traitors; New York City mayor John Mitchell also attacked them. Albert Bushnell Hart called for reforms of Senate rules to prevent such outrages in the future. Theodore Roosevelt seconded that call. At a pro-Wilson rally at Carnegie Hall, one speaker offered Stone thirty pieces of silver for betraying the president. Legislatures in Texas, Colorado, Arkansas, and Delaware issued variously worded rebukes. La Follette was shunned on the Senate floor, and the others were similarly punished for their actions. Finally, Wilson armed the ships on executive authority.

On the evening of 2 April 1917 President Wilson addressed a joint session of Congress. Germany, he said, was at war with mankind, with all nations. Submarines, which violated the rules of warfare, plus German belligerence, made even armed neutrality impossible. The German threat to human life and to the "most sacred rights of our nation" made submission impossible. Now, he said, Americans must summon up their strength and fight. We would not fight against the German people, Wilson promised, but against their despotic government; not for conquest or domination or indemnities, but for the rights of man. Wilson asked Congress to declare war against Germany, and to the winning of that war he pledged for all Americans "our lives and our fortunes, everything that we are and everything that we have." Congress then applauded and departed to consider the matter. By Easter Sunday, America was at war.

The press played an important role during the war crisis. In 1917 newspapers entertained, publishing fiction, pictures, stories of famous people, and sporting news. They also provided useful information on farming, homemaking, and business. They kept people informed on matters affecting their lives, including the actions of the government. At the same time, newspapers reported on the attitudes of the people so that leaders and representatives could keep track of public opinion. Beyond reporting accurately the opinions of their readers and the actions of their leaders, however, newspapers were not expected to be "objective," or simply to report "the facts." The press played an advocative role in American politics, speaking both to people and to politicians; and every interest group, party, or faction that hoped to influence anything had at least one newspaper to publicize its position and boast of its mass following.

The majority of Missouri's urban press supported American participation in World War I.[2] Nonintervention, doing nothing, was not news; intervention meant action, a call to arms, dashing correspondents and rousing editorials. The partisan press followed its standard bearers to war. Theodore Roosevelt and Henry Cabot Lodge derided Wilson's neutrality and applauded intervention, and so did Missouri's Republican press. Democratic newspapers followed Wilson's twistings and turnings and came out for war when he did. But in many instances the management of urban dailies did

---

2. See Crighton, *Missouri and the World War*, which is in large part a study of the editorial positions of dozens of Missouri newspapers.

not have to be dragged along by the force of party loyalty. These were businessmen as well as journalists, and they kept a close eye on sale and advertising revenue. They shared with national leaders in politics and commerce a cosmopolitan view of the world, of interdependence and the generally beneficial influence of the world market network. It was obvious to them that if America did not help the Allies, America would be the worse for it. These men were not warmongers, nor did they plot personal profit from the war. They saw themselves as practical men of affairs who knew that America's interests lay with Britain and France, and that if our interests were severely threatened, then war was the unavoidable solution. Their job would then be to rouse the people to unified support of the government, to whip public opinion to wholehearted belligerency. And when war came, this is what most of them sought to do. As a result, however, people with opposing viewpoints were denied a public forum; and students of the period who rely solely on the editorials of urban dailies are left with the clear impression that the war was widely supported.

In fact, the press was in a difficult position. First, it tended to support the war so vigorously that it proclaimed majority support as well. This is what appeared on the editorial pages and in the banner heads and lead news stories. But a careful reading of Missouri's press uncovers a second level of news that points to another story. Sometimes it was an editorial complaining about slackers, or a small item on a back page by some conscientious reporter noting lack of support for the war, or, indeed, outright opposition.[3] Clearly the press felt obliged to report on opposition to the war, but it never did so in any significant way; nor did it impartially discuss the issues raised by such opposition. It noted, in a minor way, while the major theme remained unchanged.

Small town and rural papers usually followed the urban dailies, but not always. Many local editors were also local politicians dependent upon the party for printing contracts and for office, and their partisanship was often vigorous. Also, some local editors adhered to old-time patriotism, to the spirit of '61 or '98, which could produce as bellicose an editorial as any in the country. But such editors were also much more accessible to their readers than those in big cities. Owners were more likely to be editors as well, and they sometimes shared the localist attitudes of their neighbors. Consequently, some small-town papers in Missouri opposed entry into the war if that seemed to be the predominant local attitude. Others, apparently torn between partisan loyalty and local sentiment, simply ignored the issue whenever possible, and it was not uncommon for rural weeklies to give even the declaration of war no more than a small paragraph.[4]

3. See *Springfield Republican*, 18 February, 12 July, 17 August 1917; *Hopkins Journal*, 20 March 1917; *St. Louis Post-Dispatch*, 15 December 1917, p. 4; 21 December 1917, p. 10.
4. Missouri papers that virtually ignored the war crisis included the *Putnam Journal*,

Local politicians, who also played an important part during the war crisis, were no less confused. Such men controlled party machinery and consequently the electoral process. At the same time, they claimed to represent the opinions of their followers. And yet, pronouncements by politicians regarding popular support for the war can be as misleading as those of the newspapers.

Missouri was staunchly Democratic, and the state party backed Wilson solidly. After all, their success was tied to the organization that dispensed dollars and jobs, but only to the deserving. This influenced Missouri's representatives in Washington as well. Senator Stone, who had a strong popular base of support, apparently felt secure in straying from the fold and opposing Wilson. Missourian Champ Clark, Speaker of the House throughout the war, also opposed Wilson on various issues, notably conscription. Missouri governor Frederick D. Gardner, with his eye on Stone's Senate seat, and junior senator James A. Reed were more cautious. Rep. Walter Hensley of Farmington struggled valiantly against entry into the war, but the opposition of the state machine was evidently too much for him, and he dropped out of national politics, refused to run in 1918, and went home when his term ended.

Philosophy, in addition to party, undoubtedly swayed many of the state's politicians. The president, whoever he was, was the nation's leader and deserved support. After all, he had the information and the expert advisers, so his course of action was no doubt wisest. At the same time, some politicians felt safe in ignoring popular opinion on so crucial an issue as entry into the war. Popular majorities existed to elect representatives, not to make policy. Specific groups might call for legislation affecting them, but in general the people were not judged competent to make the big decisions. The Constitution, according to this approach, had placed certain powers in the hands of the government, and the people must follow.[5]

In early 1917, for example, when they were being "showered" with letters and postcards from constituents, 90 percent of which favored a referendum on the war, Missouri congressmen were unmoved. Hensley had introduced a referendum resolution, but his antiwar colleagues, including Shackleford, had refused to comment on it. The prowar congressmen from Missouri had insisted that an open discussion of the issue, followed by a popular vote, would show Americans to hold diverse opinions on the war, and the rest of the world would think us divided and weak. A referendum was not expedi-

---

Atlanta Express, Princeton Post, and *Ridgeway Journal;* for one that does a sharp about-face in order to keep up with Wilson, see the *Linneus Bulletin,* February 1917. Loren Reid, son of a small-town editor who became postmaster with Wilson's election, makes virtually no reference to the war at all in his *Hurry Home Wednesday: Growing Up in a Small Missouri Town, 1905–1921,* though he was twelve at the time.

5. *Missouri Farmer,* 15 February 1917, p. 2; 15 November 1917, p. 11; *Slater Rustler,* 13 March 1917.

"YOU GREAT BIG SISSY, YOU"

Kansas aint no coward, but Kansas don't like shooting men, and good men too, at that."

"Capper's Weekly, published by the Governor of Kansas reaches thousands of farmers. At the top of the editorial page are these words: Capper's Weekly stands for........a permanent peace alliance for the total abolition of war.'"

2,500,000 farmers belonging to the Grange and the Farmer's Union are on record against increasing the armament of the United States.

ent, they insisted. Even though America was not under attack, nor had it been threatened with attack, there was no time for direct democracy now. Congress, they maintained, speaks for the people and has the constitutional responsibility of deciding the matter of war or peace and, in any case, was much better informed than the people and better prepared by experience to decide the issue.[6]

This suggests a conflict of attitudes regarding representative government. Throughout most of the nineteenth century the men who ran for political office had offered themselves as servants of the people. They were perhaps better fit to hold office because, in a general sense, they were wiser, better bred, wealthier; but they seldom claimed greater expertise, and, while they may not have entirely enjoyed the close supervision of the constituents, they submitted to it, and to the high turnover in office that was a feature of the politics of that time.

In the late nineteenth and early twentieth centuries, however, the people who held office increasingly insisted that the business of government had grown so complex that it could no longer be left even to the wealthy or the vaguely "wise." It required special knowledge and special skills that could only come with long experience. As a result, beginning about the same time as the bureaucratization of the civil service, tenure in elective office began to increase. The rise of a managerial elite in business and of a professional elite in medicine, law, and education went hand in hand with the professionalization of politics. Some in Congress might adhere as closely as possible to the wishes of their constituents, and others might cling to traditional notions of deference, but the rising group of professional representatives and senators felt secure in ignoring such traditions.[7]

The result was a shifting in the practice of representative government. Thus caught in the crosscurrents of change from traditional to modern, the political process responded slowly during the war crisis. Direct democracy threatened the usurpation by the people of the constitutional responsibilities of Congress and so was unthinkable to many congressmen. Yet even within the halls of Congress itself, debate on the war was characterized as treason, and normal political contention was regarded as debilitating. In spite of assertions to the contrary, there was no immediate threat from Germany; indeed, the only crisis the government claimed was one of credibility: America's reputation as a great nation was at stake. Yet democracy received no hearing, and republicanism collapsed. Paralyzed by the crisis, under pressure from people and president, congressmen abandoned politics, at least rhetorically and for the moment, responding with loud calls for

6. Missourians' comments on the war referendum in *Congressional Record*, 64th Cong., 2d sess., 54:4649, 4668–69, 4679.

7. Nelson W. Polsby, "The Institutionalization of the U.S. House of Representatives"; Richard J. Jenson, Steven L. Piott, and Christopher C. Gibbs, eds., *Grassroots Politics: Parties, Issues, and Voters, 1854–1983*, pp. 29–34, 81, 104.

unquestioning loyalty and unity whenever Wilson raised the specter of submarine warfare, failing in their responsibilities even as they proclaimed them, surrendering themselves to the executive branch of government.

In addition to the state's leading press and politicians, many of Missouri's leading businessmen supported the war. For some this was simply good business. Prices rose with demand and scarcity developed as the war took many producers out of the market, making them strictly consumers. The European powers needed food, for example, and were now less able to provide their own. The gap could be filled by American farmers. Lead was another crucial element in the war machines, and Missouri was America's leading lead producer. The war brought a boost in prices. *The American Zinc and Lead Journal*, published in Joplin, frankly rejoiced when Wilson's early peace efforts failed, welcomed American entry into the war, and apparently hoped the war would go on forever.[8]

Other businessmen saw the war as their chance to demonstrate their patriotism and at the same time rationalize the nation's economy. Missouri businessmen were tired of being called names. If they offered their services to the war government, they might boost their reputations and at the same time forestall dangerous reforms, control the process of mobilization, and make some money while they were at it. As a result, public-spirited men like St. Louisan Robert Brookings went to Washington at Wilson's request to join other businessmen on the new federal agencies that sprang up to oversee the war. Brookings and others worked long and hard out of a sense of duty. The owners of Missouri's lead mines were more self-interested. They served in wartime agencies and, wrapping themselves tightly in the flag, pegged the official price of lead at more than 100 percent its prewar price.[9]

As businessmen geared up for mobilization, they also sought to increase their control over the economy through effective organization. Across Missouri they joined into local chambers of commerce, bankers' groups, coal dealers' groups, and others. Economic cooperation hardly represented a startling innovation, but for years it had suffered from popular antitrust sentiment. Now, however, businessmen could claim the national emergency and federal sanction as excuses, and by the end of the war some had virtually raised cooperation to the highest levels of patriotism while condemning individualism as shirking or worse.[10]

8. *American Zinc and Lead Journal* 4 (February 1917): 1; *St. Louis Republic*, 26 June 1914, p. 3; 1 August 1914, p. 1; 8 August 1914, p. 4.

9. For a further discussion of the lead issue, see Chapter 6; for modernization during the war, see Ellis W. Hawley, *The Great War and the Search for a Modern Order: A History of the American People and Their Institutions, 1917–1933*, chs. 2, 3, and 7; Richard L. Watson, Jr., *The Development of National Power: The United States, 1900–1919*, 219–330 passim; Robert D. Cuff, *The War Industries Board*.

10. *Slater News*, 4 January, 22 February 1917; Harold C. Syrett, "The Business Press and American Neutrality"; *St. Louis Post-Dispatch*, 8 August 1918, p. 9 (advertisement by meatpackers).

All these forces joined Wilson in the call to battle. The press ran the flag up the masthead; businessmen organized patriotic demonstrations among employees; politicians urged the state legislature to bring Missouri into line with federal statutes against dissent. Such activities, including suppression of dissent, began even before the declaration of war. During the submarine crisis an editor in Savannah, Missouri, warned local opponents of Wilson's armed-ship bill to "either talk up the country or get out of it."[11] A Springfield editor warned that too much democracy would prove divisive during the crisis. By the end of March, Missourians read that dozens of undercover agents were in their state checking for possible disloyalty. Furthermore, all federal employees, including local postmen, as well as the local police, were reported to be cooperating with these agents.[12] Although it is almost impossible to demonstrate the truth of these stories, they certainly helped to set the tone with which the nation entered the war to save democracy.

With the declaration of war, local officials called "spontaneous" patriotic demonstrations. In accordance with instructions, shops and plants closed and classes were canceled. Students and workers dutifully paraded through the streets. Flags and pictures of Wilson appeared in windows.[13] Soon the newspapers were filled with stories of the fate that awaited those who did not back the war 100 percent. By the summer, policemen in Kansas City, St. Louis, and Springfield raided saloons and pool halls and stopped people on the street demanding proof of loyalty, such as a draft card or a receipt for a war bond. Anyone not possessing such proof was arrested. Judges imposed heavy fines and jail sentences for disloyal talk. The *St. Louis Post-Dispatch* encouraged violence against people "suspected of lukewarmness toward the war," calling such actions "a wholesome symbol" of patriotism. Governor Gardner threatened vigilante action, insisting that Missourians did not care if Congress passed laws regulating disloyalty, that such people in Missouri would "be dealt with unmercifully."[14] And, indeed, a few people did take matters into their own hands. One man, recently fired from his job, turned in his former employer for disloyalty; and in St. Louis a woman and her mother reported the woman's husband for disloyalty.[15]

Suppression of dissent became the order of the day, but the impulse did not come from the grassroots, but from above, from the government, from the press, from business leaders who encouraged and instigated such action. Supporters of war not only assumed such behavior to be necessary

11. *Savannah Reporter*, 23 February 1917.
12. *Milan Republican*, 15 April 1917; *Springfield Republican*, 1 March, 8 September, 10 August 1917; 23 September 1918.
13. *Springfield Republican*, 2 March, 7 April 1917.
14. *Warrensburg Star-Journal*, 3 April 1917; *St. Louis Post-Dispatch*, 6 October 1917, p. 1; 1 November 1917, p. 28; 6 April 1918, p. 1; *Springfield Republican*, 10 August 1917.
15. *Springfield Republican*, 18 August 1917; *St. Louis Post-Dispatch*, 6 April 1918, p. 1; 23 April 1918, p. 1.

and proper, but were reluctant to deal seriously with the possibility that the war lacked wide support and that, consequently, their actions were indefensible. They feared that was the case, and they railed angrily at that fear. Out of their anger and anxiety grew extravagant claims of patriotism. The same anxiety—that they might be in the minority—led them to try to silence not only dissent, but even debate on the war and on their behavior during the war. Thus, in their fear, the state's leaders and opinionmakers altered the definition of democracy. No longer could democracy be characterized by conflict, by argument, debate, and finally majority rule. The prowar position could not bear debate, by the admission of its advocates, so in place of a mere majority they required total support, 100 percent compliance, or total silence. "Keep your mouth shut," ordered government officials, and the press seconded the command. A prowar women's organization in St. Louis issued ten new commandments for the war period. The first instructed, "Thou Shalt Not 'Chatter'"; the second, "Thou Shalt Not Listen to 'Chatter.'" The *Post-Dispatch* thought these improvements on the originals so worthwhile that it recommended they be applied to everyone. In Kansas City a Canadian war veteran who was touring the country to boost American enlistments was arrested by local police because his stories of the horrors of trench warfare were too accurate. The truth, local authorities feared, would give aid and comfort to our enemies.[16]

Under the circumstances, Missourians for the most part kept quiet. Careful searching disclosed no organized antiwar demonstrations, and observers noted that even at official prowar functions people were unusually quiet. It seemed, after all, the safest course. Threats can frighten some people, real oppression can frighten many more, and fear can lead to a kind of lethargy. No one would speak for them, and people were not allowed to speak for themselves. But, cautioned one Missourian, "Congress should be warned by the awful silence of the masses."[17]

Warned of what? How can popular attitudes on the war be determined? Most of the news media and the majority of elected officials clamored for war; virtually everyone else kept quiet. Why not take the attitudes of the former to be representative, especially when a negative, opposition to the war, is so difficult to prove? Besides, it is possible that the press and the

16. *Warrensburg Star-Journal*, 13 April 1917; *St. Louis Post-Dispatch*, 28 November 1917, p. 4; 23 December 1917, p. 1; *Springfield Republican*, 4 February 1917.

17. H. M. Horn to Robert M. La Follette (RML), 25 March 1917. See La Follette Family Papers, Series B, Manuscripts Division, Library of Congress. Among the thousands of antiwar letters to Senator La Follette, filed alphabetically by year, are over two hundred from Missourians. These letters illuminate the issues surrounding America's entry into the war as they were perceived at the grassroots level. For comments on "lethargy and fear," see Laura Fuhr to RML, 19 November 1917, and Louis Erb to RML, 10 November 1917; Rev. J. T. Hartman to RML, 6 March 1917, for the comment on the silence of the masses; J. H. Allison to RML, 17 March 1917; for somber "prowar" rallies in St. Louis and Johnson County, see *Missouri Farmer*, 20 May 1917, p. 3; 5 June 1917, p. 3.

politicians really did represent the people. Certainly most historians have so concluded. In fact, however, there are clear early indications that Missourians, at least, hoped to avoid the war in Europe. These feelings surfaced during the fight in Congress over the Gore-McLemore Resolution, for the struggle in Washington reverberated in Missouri.[18]

Stone took the lead for Missourians. In a conference with the president he pointed out that the administration's stand could mean war for America, and that no amount of talk about principle would disguise that fact. The Missouri delegation, all but two of them Democrats, met, and the majority favored some form of warning to Americans to stay off the ships of belligerents. Perl Decker of Joplin expressed his fear that America stood on the brink of war and that strong measures were necessary to avoid that calamity. Republican Jacob Meeker of St. Louis believed that Wilson was trying to maneuver them into voting for war at some later date. Stone claimed that those who risked their lives traveling on endangered ships committed "moral treason against the Republic" by threatening to embroil it in war.

Several leading newspapers criticized the state's representatives. Both the staunchly Democratic *St. Louis Republic* and the Republican *St. Louis Globe-Democrat* attacked the delegation for its opposition to the president. The *St. Joseph News-Press* claimed that these "insurgents" did not represent public opinion in Missouri. Both the Democratic State Committee and the Democratic Press Association adopted resolutions upholding their party's national leader. At least two Missouri representatives, however, claimed that they had support from their constituents. William Igoe of St. Louis said, "I know the people of my district do not want to go to war." Leonidas Dyer, another St. Louisan, agreed, claiming to have received over two thousand telegrams, all but five in support of the warning resolution. Wilson had his way, however, and the resolution failed.

There was more disagreement the following year. The *Globe-Democrat* insisted that the resumption of unrestricted submarine warfare and the consequent break in diplomatic relations surely meant war. The *St. Joseph News-Press* positively welcomed it, claiming that America had been pushed around enough and it was time she stood up for her rights. Senators Stone and Reed supported Wilson's decision to break off relations, more out of party loyalty than out of conviction, for Stone at least still hoped to avoid war. And on 5 February, the Missouri legislature passed a resolution expressing confidence in the president, adding that "Missouri and its people stand united and ready to uphold his hands and follow his leadership . . . regardless of the cost or sacrifice."[19]

Others disagreed. The *Kansas City Journal* claimed, "There are probably

---

18. Crighton, *Missouri and the World War*, pp. 102–4, covers the controversy; also Pfabe, "Missouri Congressmen," pp. 75–76, 100–112; *St. Louis Republic*, 24 February 1916.

19. Crighton, *Missouri and the World War*, pp. 165–66.

few soberminded Americans who believe that the new situation means even the severance of diplomatic relations with Germany or that it justifies such action." The *Warrensburg Star-Journal* warned Americans to stay out of the "zone" and let the European powers fight it out. The leading German newspaper in St. Louis, *Westliche Post,* tried to defend Germany's actions, blaming England and France for the crisis. The socialist press vigorously opposed any tendency toward war. *St. Louis Labor* insisted that "the Big Biz interests" were behind the whole thing, trying to make more money from the crisis, while the people opposed the war. The *Sedalia Railway Federationist* claimed that the United States had no business in the European war. In Congress, Representative Hensley, a friend of antiwar spokesman William Jennings Bryan, introduced his ill-fated resolution calling for a popular referendum on the question of entry into the war. It was quickly crushed.[20]

The crisis provoked other comments on the possibility of war, ranging from macabre humor to pathos. "After the war," said the *Slater News* in January, "the history of the war in thirty-seven volumes, dollar down, two dollars a month until the next great upheaval." War-induced inflation angered many, and one poet commented on it in "On Account of the War," which included the following passage:

> The baker reduces the weight of his bread,
> The butcher sends steaks that could muster as lead,

---

20. *Kansas City Journal,* 2 February 1917, p. 6; 4 February 1917, p. 8; *Warrensburg Star-Journal,* 6 February 1917; *Westliche Post,* 1 February 1917; 2 February 1917, quoted in Crighton, *Missouri and the World War,* p. 166; *St. Louis Labor,* 10 February 1917; Crighton, *Missouri and the World War,* p. 168, quotes Hensley as defending the referendum resolution not on the grounds of pacifism, but of direct democracy. Hearings were held on a war referendum in late February. See U.S. Congress, House of Representatives, Committee of Foreign Affairs, *Hearings on H.R. 492, Referendum of Declaration of War,* 64th Cong., 2d sess., which includes the following exchange between Rep. Clarence Miller of Minnesota and a witness (pp. 9–10). The witness is asking the questions:

Q: If you trust people to elect you to Congress, could you not trust people to vote on a proposition of this kind?
A: If you can put before the people an issue, with the facts on one side and on the other, and let them come to a decision on it, I think their will ought to control. But in this kind of a vote, the same facts are not before any two minds.
Q: If we declare war on Germany, with Congress not knowing just how they feel, why should not the issue be placed up to the people? If the issue is concrete enough for Congress to declare war, why should it not be concrete enough to put it up to the people?
A: We are glad to get your viewpoint on this matter.

Another witness, Guy Marchand, of the Initiative and Referendum League (which included St. Louisan James E. How), also questioned the committee: "The principle is . . . the rule of the people. What have you to fear? If your proposition of war is sound, you should not be afraid to submit it to your constituents and let them vote upon it. Are you afraid of the American people?" (p. 16).

The tailor's wool suits are of shoddy instead,
"On account of the war."

And the *Bethany Democrat* noted that "with Kaiser Bill, John Bull, and Uncle Sam saying in concert 'This is my ocean,' like the Kilkenny cat fight, it is just possible that there will be little left of either but the fur when the fuss is over." Even the atrocity stories used by the belligerents in their efforts to enlist American sympathy began to wear thin. "One great difficulty in the latest atrocity reports," commented one observer, "is that the fighters are unable to report anything new." The *Savannah Reporter* pointed out that to have the great Christian nations of the earth declare war on each other during Passion Week was something to think about, though it did not mention that the United States was the only nation declaring war at that time. And, finally, the *Missouri Farmer* published a grim reminder of the meaning of war a mere five days before the declaration:

Laughing, crowing baby boy, what knows he of tears,
Partings bitterer than death, anguished hopes and fears,
Cooing, babbling joyously, little does he guess,
Soon the darkling war clouds may make him fatherless.[21]

If there was a great outcry in Missouri against those men in Washington who opposed Wilson on the armed-ship issue, it all tended to come from the same sorts of sources. In Kansas City, Joplin, St. Joseph, and St. Louis, papers attacked Stone, Decker, and Shackleford, claiming that they had betrayed the sentiments of their state. They called for Stone's removal from the chair of the foreign relations committee. The Missouri legislature reprimanded them for their actions. The Democratic Club of St. Louis's fashionable West End condemned Stone, as did the St. Louis chapter of the Sons of Confederate War Veterans.[22]

A handful of newspapers in the state supported Stone and the others, perhaps because they discovered that their readers did. Both the *Hannibal Morning Journal* and the *Houston Herald* granted the senator the right to voice his opinion. Newspapers in the towns of Columbia and Paris agreed. The *Nevada Post*, in Stone's hometown, went so far as to endorse the senator's stand against the sort of one-man rule that Wilson seemed to seek. The *Warrensburg Star-Journal* claimed that Stone "represents three-fourths of the people of Johnson County." J. M. Ward, editor of the *Bonne Terre Register*, insisted that not 1 percent of the people in his area supported Wilson. The editor of the *Kirksville Daily Express* found, to his surprise, that his readers

21. *Slater News*, 4 January, 15 February 1917; *Weekly Saline Citizen*, 3 February 1917; *Bethany Democrat*, 8 February 1917; *Missouri Farmer*, 15 February, 1 April 1917.
22. Crighton, *Missouri and the World War*, pp. 172–74.

also supported Stone. After running an editorial attacking the senator, the editor conducted a local poll. The people of Kirksville backed Stone by a two-to-one margin. Despite this, however, the editor continued to criticize the senator and to boost the war.[23]

While some newspapers supported Stone, the majority probably opposed him. Why should we believe one group rather than the other? The prowar press and politicians claimed that all real patriots, all real Americans, backed Wilson. Yet there is evidence that most people in Missouri opposed the war. Usually they did so in ways that gained them little publicity. Nor could they alter significantly the nation's course, and history tends to ignore the road not taken, sometimes to the extent of pretending it never existed. One by one the traditional channels of communication closed to them, and few Missourians were accustomed to the new politics of interest-group organizing and lobbying. There were a few antiwar meetings, but the press provided scant coverage, and federal agents attended to identify the vocally disloyal. Opponents of war believed themselves to be in the patriotic majority; the press and their elected representatives told them that they were a treasonous minority and threatened to treat them as such. But there were a few antiwar spokesmen in government and the press, and people could, and did, write to them, thanking and encouraging them. Consequently, there were rumblings of opposition to the war, and astute observers noted them.

Jess Tollerton, an old-time politician from Springfield and a friend and close adviser to former governor Herbert S. Hadley, wrote Hadley in the summer of 1917. The people, Tollerton admitted, were not being allowed to express themselves, but he assured his old friend that 75 percent of the population opposed the war.[24] Congressman C. W. Hamlin supported the war but found that he had run afoul of his constituents' wishes. Hamlin received so many antiwar letters that he finally made public his answer to one and let that stand as answer to all. Hamlin admitted that the war was unpopular, but insisted that he had to follow the nation's leader in time of crisis. "The same mail that brought me your letter," he wrote, "brought me several [others like it]. The truth is that each mail brings me similar letters." But Hamlin, like the Kirksville editor, continued his support of Wilson despite popular opinion.[25]

In July 1917 the *St. Joseph Gazette* reported a poll on the war in Atchison County. The voting was by secret ballot to prevent any overt pressure, and it

23. *Hannibal Morning Journal*, 11 March 1917; *Houston Herald*, 8 March 1917; *Warrensburg Star-Journal*, 9 March 1917; *Kirksville Daily Express*, 17 March 1917; Towne, "Public Career of William J. Stone," p. 222; Crighton, *Missouri and the World War*, pp. 175–80; J. M. Ward to RML, 5 March 1917.

24. "Jess" to Hadley, n.d. [Summer 1917], Hadley Papers, WHMC, folder 657.

25. *Slater Rustler*, 13 April 1917.

ran twenty to one against the war.[26] People in Macon County petitioned Robert La Follette to keep working for peace and assured him of their support even after war had been declared.[27] In late 1917 prowar advocates circulated a petition calling for severe punishment of the disloyal element in one Missouri county. The effort collapsed when fewer than 10 percent signed up.[28] In January 1918 a woman in St. Clair County lamented her neighbors' lack of patriotism in tones that echoed across the state: "Why is it that so many people feel indifference, and even disgust, at the government's [war] plans? Many talk even now as if we ought to have kept out of this war. They feel like opposing all our country does."[29]

People noticed that most of their neighbors opposed the war. Some were content with claiming a simple majority, but others claimed more: 70 percent in some cases, as high as 90 percent in others. A man in Cass County wrote to La Follette, "There is just one old man [here] for this THING [and] his wife inherited a small bunch of STEEL STOCK years ago." The *Missouri Ruralist* noted antiwar meetings in scattered locations around the state as late as July 1917, and in June the *Missouri Farmer* paid an oblique compliment to William Jennings Bryan's opposition to war by asserting that the people, had they been given a chance, would have voted against war by sixteen to one. From St. Louis and Kansas City came reports that only one in ten citizens wanted war, and the same held true in rural areas. A. M. Spencer of Milford wrote La Follette, "In the last two dayes I have talked to 40 of my nabors and only one wanted war." In the words of L. W. Hilker of St. Louis, "the great silent majority" opposed the war.[30]

Some tried to remain calm in the crisis, pointing out that those who did support war usually wanted someone else to fight it for them. "I am not going to get excited over this European war," wrote a columnist in the *Missouri Farmer*. "In the first place, this International Law stuff is too deep for me anyway. In the second place, I am not going over to Europe to fight—and their hands are too full to come over here after me." A former army officer in Kansas City wrote President Wilson, "Among my social and business associates I find those most inclined to war are the men that are past military age." An editor in Harrison County made the same point, and in Greene County an observer noted that the first man to take off his hat for "The Star-Spangled Banner" was not necessarily the first man to enlist when war

26. Reported in *Springfield Republican*, 12 July 1917. For the results of straw votes and polls reported by congressmen ranging as high as 200 to 2 against war, see *Congressional Record*, 64th Cong., 2d sess., *Appendix*, 515, 389; 65th Cong., 1st sess., 239, 224, 238, 326, 338.

27. Arch Hilton to RML, 18 April 1917.

28. Theo Lunde to RML, 23 November 1917.

29. *Missouri Ruralist*, 5 January 1918, p. 6.

30. F. Smith to RML, 1 May 1917; *Missouri Farmer*, 15 June 1917, p. 2; *Missouri Ruralist*, 5 July 1917, p. 3; L. W. Hilker to RML, 1 April 1917; A. M. Spencer to RML, 4 April 1917.

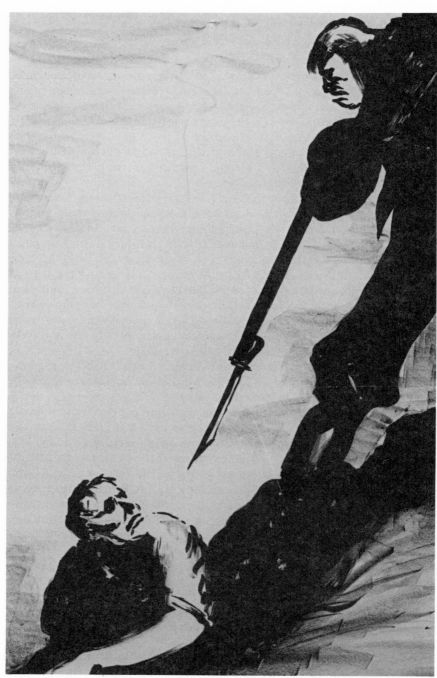

Poster published by the American Union Against Militarism, Washington, D.C. The cartoon was identified as being originally drawn by Robert Minor for the *St. Louis Post-Dispatch*. Courtesy Special Collections, Ellis Library, University of Missouri–Columbia.

came. The rabidly prowar editor of the *Hopkins Journal* sputtered, "We never before imagined there are half as many traitors in this country as there now seem to be."[31]

The grounds upon which Missourians opposed the war are just as important as the fact that they opposed it. The prowar element accused them of pacifism, of pro-Germanism, of being radicals and Bolsheviks, of being unpatriotic. Missourians were, in the main, none of these. Their opposition to the war grew out of long-standing economic and political traditions, and their criticisms of the war, like their views of the world before 1917, were based on localism, faith in democracy, and anticorporate sentiment.

It is clear that Missourians were not pacifists in any deeply rooted ideological sense. They did oppose entry into what they regarded as Europe's war, but there was little objection to American incursions into Mexico in 1914 and 1917, when the Missouri National Guard was called to patrol the Mexican border. Nor had there been a great outcry against the war with Spain a generation earlier. Even the protracted and bloody Philippine War seems to have excited little notice. These were more or less legitimate military actions for the government to undertake; they were why America had people in uniform. The nation's interests lay traditionally south and west in any case, not east, toward the "old country."[32] At the same time, the bare facts of the war in Europe—the interminable months of fighting over the same few yards of shattered ground, the mounting casualties—were by themselves enough to give people pause. Sending a few professionals to deal with swarthy natives was one thing, but sending the flower of American manhood to wade in the mud of the Western Front in the face of the machine guns of the crack Prussian army was something else again.

It is also unlikely that Missourians' attitudes on the war were determined solely by their ethnic origin. Missouri ranked tenth in the nation in the number of German-Americans. Of Missouri's 688,108 residents of foreign stock in 1920, 298,177, almost half, were German, and the next largest group, Irish-Americans, were a distant second with about 82,000.[33] German-Americans had been the leading ethnic minority in St. Louis for fifty years or more, and they dominated both banks of the Missouri River as far west as Gasconade and Montgomery counties. These were the people who had kept Missouri in the Union in 1861, and they represented a strong Republican element in a state dominated by Democrats.

The German-language press in the state tried to justify Germany's behavior during the first years of the war. People with German names wrote letters

31. *Missouri Farmer*, 1 March 1917, p. 9; J. M. Shook to Wilson, 1 March 1917, copy to RML; *New Hampton Herald*, 11 January 1917; *Springfield Republican*, 4 March 1917, 3 March 1918; *Hopkins Journal*, 20 March 1917.

32. *Wayne County Journal*, 12 March 1917.

33. Department of Commerce, Bureau of the Census, *Fourteenth Census of the United States, 1920: Population*, 2:895–96, 903–4. See also Gerlach, *Settlement Patterns in Missouri*.

to national leaders protesting the war, and occasionally St. Louis Germans got arrested for shouting pro-German slogans in saloons or on the street. But those on the lookout for such activity noticed that "good Anglo-Saxon" names appeared in court for disloyalty as often as "Teutonic" names. Many who wrote to Stone, La Follette, and Wilson sought to counter assertions that only German-Americans opposed the war by pointing out their long native ancestry, or their patriotism as demonstrated by veteran status. Many of Missouri's German-Americans were circumspect in their opposition to the war in any case, and antiwar meetings tended to be dominated by "native" Americans.[34]

Ethnicity played a role in the attitudes of other Missourians of foreign stock. The Italian-American community in St. Louis, for example, most of whose residents were born in Italy, demonstrated strong allegiance to their native land. They kept a close eye on the battles along the Italian front and engaged in editorial combat with the German press in St. Louis over which was the better nation. But only a handful of St. Louis Italian-Americans returned to fight in the Italian army. While the war reinvigorated their love for their homeland, they demonstrated that love with a burst of ethnic solidarity here in America. St. Louis Italians joined mutual benefit societies and attended Italian-language theater in greater numbers than ever before, but they showed no desire to rush to the battlefield.[35]

Ethnicity influenced other Missourians as well. When the war broke out in Europe, and at various times thereafter, the consulates of the belligerent powers appealed to their nationals living in America to join the colors of their homeland. But most immigrants from the Austro-Hungarian Empire were so glad to have gotten out that they were not about to return voluntarily to the oppression and militarism from which they had fled. And Mr. Dooley undoubtedly spoke for many Irish-Americans when he said, "We are fightin' for freedom of speech—if you will only keep your mouth shut . . . . The bands are playin' that beautiful chewn beloved be the demicrazy: 'Gawd Shave the King' "; he noted that a congressman wanted to lend "that champeen of democracy, King George," ten billion dollars, "and he doesn't care if he ever pays it back so long as we do." Finally, German-Americans reacted in much the same way as the Italians: they waged their battles in St. Louis beer halls and the press, but only a few joined the German army.[36]

34. *St. Louis Post-Dispatch*, 12 May 1918, p. 1. Detjen, *The Germans in Missouri*, pp. 138–46, deals with divisions within the German-American community over the issue of the war; the issue of close cultural ties with the Old Fatherland was, he asserts, of concern only to an elite minority. For the rest, he finds little support, whatever the reasons, but points out that most German-Americans in Missouri found silence to be their best defense against attacks from the media and local officials as well as from the "quasi-governmental" state council of defense (p. 141).

35. Gary R. Mormino, "Over Here: St. Louis Italo-Americans and the First World War."

36. *St. Louis Republic*, 29 July 1914, pp. 1–2; 30 July 1914, p. 4; *St. Louis Post-Dispatch*, 11 January 1915, p. 13; Finley Peter Dunne, "Mr. Dooley on the Freedom of the Seize" (n.p., n.d., pamphlet in New York Public Library).

Missouri's ethnic population was in a difficult spot, caught between old-country ties and the bonds of their new communities in this country. By and large they did not want to fight for the fatherland, but they showed a similar reluctance to support the American war effort. After all, what was the point of fleeing conscription in Austro-Hungary or Russia only to encounter it in America? While the fact is that few of Missouri's German-Americans joined the German army, they cannot have been anxious to join the American army to fight their relatives. Nor can the Irish have been eager to rush to the aid of Britain. But people in Missouri not only opposed entry into the war, they resisted participation in it, and the widespread opposition to bond drives, food pledge campaigns, and conscription outlined in later chapters cannot be explained by ethnicity alone.

Nor does radical politics alone explain opposition to the war. Socialists played a leading role in the Missouri labor movement, and Missouri's socialist press, including *St. Louis Labor* and the *National Ripsaw,* commanded wide audiences. Nevertheless, Missouri was never a stronghold of socialism, despite concentrations in St. Louis and a few other localities for a time. Few Missourians voted socialist in 1912, and most people seem to have relied on Wilson to keep them out of war in 1916. Socialists were probably the largest organized group opposing the war, but there were not enough of them in Missouri to account for the extensive opposition noticed by Jess Tollerton and others.[37]

Widespread opposition to the war grew out of the political and economic implications of the crisis for all citizens, not just ethnics or radicals. People believed that a majority opposed the war, but that special interests were drawing the country into it anyway. Congress and the president, they insisted, ignored the popular will. The press misreported public sentiment in order not to offend wealthy allies and advertisers. Wall Street bankers, arms dealers, food speculators, all the old enemies, wanted war because they would get richer while the common people paid in money and blood. This was the theme that dominated Missouri's opposition to the war in 1917 and 1918.

Missourians had already felt the war's impact. Wilson's preparedness efforts raised taxes and prices. The war caused dislocations in the international market network, and entrepreneurs sought to profit from these dislocations—"on account of the war." Missourians complained bitterly of "HCL," the high cost of living, and American intervention only promised to make matters worse. The people knew what was going on, according to the *Warrensburg Star-Journal:* the politicians and the financiers were trampling on "the welfare of the consuming element of our people," and democracy was under attack.[38] For years Missourians had sought to defend their roles as

37. See *St. Louis Labor* and *National Ripsaw* for January through March 1917. Only 2 percent of Missourians voted Socialist in 1912, and 1 percent in 1916; *Official Manual of the State of Missouri for the Years 1913-1914,* p. 753; ibid., 1916, p. 427.

38. *Missouri Ruralist,* 5 April 1917, p. 5; *Missouri Farmer,* 15 March 1917, p. 6; *Warrensburg*

taxpayers, as consumers, as citizens in a changing America. For years they had watched large corporations amass great economic power beyond the control of the average citizen. For years they had struggled to maintain local democratic control over their lives against the encroachments of growing central power. And now, in the spring of 1917, the war threatened to sweep them all away, strengthening their enemies, forcing the people into a European conflagration against their will, destroying their communities and their lives.

From a political perspective, many Missourians believed that, despite all his talk about democracy, President Wilson sought greater power for himself. The president and his supporters argued that unusual circumstances demanded unusual solutions. Congress, as indicated during the armed-ship bill struggle, seemed inclined to give Wilson what he wanted. In that instance Wilson had sought to wage war in lieu of a formal declaration. But if that attempt had been scotched by a handful of insurgent senators, the threat of actual war was worse, even though it might be arrived at in the proper way. War would enlarge the power of the federal government and thus would further restrict the voice of the people in deciding the fate of their nation.[39]

To some Missourians this represented a threatened "Europeanization" of American politics. Americans had traditionally believed themselves to be a new world in contrast to decadent Europe, and they had long feared the corruption of American virtue by the spread of European economic and political systems. They believed that the president listened more closely to a few advisers than he did to the people who elected him. Thus he imitated a European potentate and not the leader of a democracy. Some Missourians accused Wilson of harboring "Caesarean" ambitions, of seeking imperial powers. Others, in the unkindest cut of all, compared him to Germany's Kaiser.[40]

Many others saw Wilson as a hypocrite. The man had, after all, been elected on a peace slogan. He had spoken out forcefully on the rights of neutrals and the glories of democracy. Yet he obviously favored the Allies, ignored the wishes of the people, and sought to bring America into the war against her will. Such a man could not be trusted: Richard D. Kathrens wrote to Stone, "What is the difference between a President and a Kaiser when it comes to herding men into military camps against their will . . . . If we make our President drunk with the power of an autocrat, how shall we be sure that he will not go to excesses in his delirium and use his powers to

---

Star-Journal, 17 February 1917.

39. For expressions of these opinions, see P. M. Litton to RML, 6 March 1917; G. R. Ruby to RML, 5 March 1917; J. V. Beltz to RML, 5 March 1917; C. C. Williams to RML, 7 March 1917; John E. Wilson to RML, 28 February 1917.

40. Hans Ballin to RML, 30 March 1917; F. Smith to RML, 1 May 1917; N. Holman to RML, 5 March 1917.

crush and oppress . . . ?"[41] But pointing out the president's failings could only bring trouble, as a man in St. Louis discovered when he was arrested for muttering, "Wilson kept us out of war. Like hell he did."[42]

The issue of the presidency aroused considerable controversy. Supporters of Wilson claimed that those who opposed war were not standing behind America's leader in time of crisis. By their terms, whatever the president declared to be a crisis was thereby beyond debate, indeed, was removed altogether from the realm of free choice. If America was to be a great nation, this argument ran, she had to appear united so that her enemies, as well as her friends, would not think her weak. The appearance of disunity, which was an inevitable result of the democratic process, threatened America's safety. Thus Americans, not Germans, were the real enemy, for only Americans could make America appear divided and weak and thereby invite attack by Germany.

Missourians did not, however, follow the newborn cult of the imperial presidency; nor did they ascribe to what might be called a public relations interpretation of democracy and foreign policy. They preferred to regard whoever filled the office of president as an elected official, and they retained to themselves the right to decide ultimately the correctness of national policy. To promise to support the president simply because he was the president would be to abdicate their responsibility as citizens.

This raised the issue of patriotism. Supporters of a strong stance against Germany sought, rhetorically at least, to deprive their opponents of citizenship by proclaiming them traitors, calling them unpatriotic, un-American, for refusing to follow President Wilson to war. To such people the president transcended the status of a human executive and became a symbol, like the flag, that commanded constant respect and unswerving loyalty. But to M. D. Collins, "This 'claptrap' of standing by the President is not fooling the people; the President is not standing by the people." And that, after all, was his job.[43]

At the same time, the press had failed. W. F. Hupe, of Montgomery County, warned Wilson, "This sentiment for war is not from the people as the news Papers [sic] would have us believe. Since the newspapers do not represent them the people have no way to express themselves."[44] Under these circumstances, national leaders could not judge accurately what was going on in America. The war-mad press "truckled" to the jingo element, and some angry Missourians suggested that editors be sent first into the front lines to see the results of their efforts.[45]

41. R. D. Kathrens to Stone, 21 April 1917, copy to RML.
42. *St. Louis Post-Dispatch*, 21 December 1917, p. 10.
43. Rev. M. D. Collins to Stone, 28 February 1917, copy to RML; J. P. McCann to RML, 4 March 1917, uses the word *imperial*.
44. W. F. Hupe to Wilson, 31 March 1917, copy to RML.
45. Elsie Fischer to RML, 9 February 1917; Rev. J. T. Hartman to RML, 6 March 1917.

Behind it all lay "the interests": the bankers with loans to Britain and France, the middlemen, the profiteers, the munitions makers and food speculators. A farmer in Blue Lick complained to La Follette, "Our glorious country [is being] led by schemers into every conceivable way into war that a few men may gather to themselves so much of the goods of this world that they cannot resist the temptation to go to great extremes to rob society of more and more." Missourians agreed that Wilson listened more to "the siren song of the speculators" than to the voice of the people. One citizen wrote Senator Stone, "How can a people have confidence in those Congressmen and Senators who are known to have Wall Street investments?"[46] And in addition to the president and Congress, the press as well had been "subsidized," "polluted," "poisoned," "prostituted," and "Morganized" by those who sought to profit from the war.[47]

The findings of the Nye Committee of the 1930s, the whole "merchants of death" theory of those years, was thus only an echo of popular sentiment in Missouri in 1917–1918. People who believed that railroads and banks impoverished the masses, corrupted politics, and deserved what they got from the likes of Jesse James had no trouble believing that the same interests had grown powerful enough to force an unwilling nation into a horrible war for no other reason than profit. Missourians had seen with their own eyes the lengths to which greed could drive corporate executives when the issue was merely union recognition or a utility franchise. By 1917, however, the stakes spanned oceans. The bitterness and frustration was poured into letters to La Follette, Stone, and Wilson as Missourians heaped abuse on the corporations, calling them jackals, mercenaries, pirates, plutocrats consumed with the lust for gold. Patriotism, lamented one man, had become "a dollar piece."[48]

Missourians offered a variety of solutions to the problem. Some wanted to send not only jingo editors to the front, but also munitions makers and other wealthy men, including DuPont, Rockefeller, and Schwab. If men must be conscripted to fight, insisted James T. Roberts, then conscript "all corporations entirely . . . and all individuals [making] in excess of one hundred dollars a month." Some called for a law to prevent sending draftees out of the country. Others wanted to impeach Wilson. One man pointed out that the cost of killing a person in war could be calculated. That amount of

---

46. J. M. Allison to RML, 17 March 1917; J. L. Switzer to RML, 1 March 1917; Rev. M. D. Collins to Stone, 28 February 1917, copy to RML.

47. C. E. Patterson to RML, 31 March 1917; R. D. Kathrens to Stone, 21 April 1917, copy to RML; Richard Ivie to RML, 16 April 1917; Roy J. Hocksmith to RML, 23 April 1917.

48. Jacob Koch to RML, 7 March 1917; P. M. Litton to RML, 6 March 1917; Elsie Fischer to RML, 9 March 1917; Mrs. G. L. Hanking to RML, 12 November 1917; George W. Meyer to RML, 9 February 1917; Phil Dietzen to RML, 8 March 1917, made the dollar piece comment; J. R. Stull to RML, 6 March 1917.

money should then be put at interest and drawn upon to give every deserter from the armed forces one thousand dollars.[49]

But the most popular solution arose from traditional faith in democracy. "Look to the common people," said J. L. Switzer, "for sufficient integrity to guide the ship of state."[50] Specifically, many sought a popular referendum on war.[51] They believed that America stood in no danger of an immediate invasion by Germany, and they were not interested in the extremities to which German submarines had brought England. There was plenty of time for a vote, they believed, and it would settle the debate because people would surely abide by a majority decision more readily than one imposed upon them from above. Besides, Wilson was proclaiming to the world that we were the bastion of democracy. How could we fight for democracy abroad if we did not allow it at home? Missourians also hoped that they could still rely on traditional political mechanisms to stem the tide of corporate power and federal centralization that the war would only exacerbate.

The call for a referendum rested upon the soundest of bases. Since all power came from the consent of the governed, why not prove the system through a popular vote? If those in favor of war had as much support as they claimed, they should be more than willing to offer a referendum and find out. W. F. Hupe made his argument directly to President Wilson: "If left to a vote, I believe that four-fifths or nine-tenths of [the people] would vote against war with or in Europe . . . . Of course, in cases of invasion or imminent danger of invasion we are all ready to fight. Leave it to a vote and see." Hupe added that a referendum would relieve the president of the responsibility of making war, placing it instead "where it belongs—with the people."[52]

There was no referendum. The press, the businessmen, the politicians, the president's advisers all agreed: America had to go to the aid of the Allies, and quickly. A delay for a referendum might mean that America would intervene too late or not at all. Personal profit or advancement might have motivated a few of these men, but they were not "merchants of death," at least not intentionally. They simply believed that their interests and those of the nation were identical, and so they sent their sons to war with clear consciences. Missourians often tended to see the supporters of war as mon-

---

49. J. Lincoln Bishop to RML, 7 March 1917; M. C. Saul to RML, 31 March 1917; J. M. Shook to RML, 1 March 1917; John M. Gomes to RML, 19 November 1917; Charles L. Dalbridge to RML, 13 March 1917; F. S. Elder to RML, 4 April 1917.

50. J. L. Switzer to RML, 7 November 1917.

51. For examples of those calling for a referendum, see J. Havlin to RML, 1 March 1917; A. J. Sladek to RML, 12 March 1917; and F. Smith to RML, 1 May 1917. While not all favored such a course (Shook, for instance, did not), all agreed that the majority wanted a referendum on the war and that the vote would be overwhelmingly against going to war.

52. Hupe to Wilson, 31 March 1917, copy to RML.

sters; at least this is the tone of many of the letters to La Follette, Stone, and Wilson. But that was not the case. It was, rather, a matter of a major difference of opinion regarding America's place in the modern world. It happened that this difference of opinion, which had existed for some time, suddenly had mortal consequences. Finally, with the war an established fact, Missourians stopped writing letters to the antiwar spokesmen in Washington. Protest had become pointless—but not resistance.

Opposition to the war in general, and to specific programs designed to prosecute the war, continued until the Armistice. Champ Clark, representative from Bowling Green and Speaker of the House, led the abortive fight against conscription, claiming that it would bring militarism upon the United States and thus make us just like our enemy. James Reed in the Senate kept up a constant harassing fire on Herbert Hoover's Food Administration and other war agencies. And his actions brought down upon his head attacks by his colleagues as violent as any launched against the "willful men."[53]

Missourians back home hoped wistfully that the war might not touch them. They spoke of its being over in a few months, before American boys could get into danger, despite the fact that the war had already dragged on for three years with no end in sight. Others insisted that America's role would be exclusively naval and logistical, convoying needed supplies to the Allies and stopping the submarine menace, and that there was no need for Americans to endure the inhumanity of trench warfare. Some Missourians tried to make the best of a bad situation. Now, they insisted, the federal government would conscript wealth along with men, would impose confiscatory taxation on war profiteers, and would force the financiers to pay for their war. Now perhaps the government would fulfill the dreams of reformers as far back as the populists by nationalizing transportation, communications, and natural resources in the name of the war emergency.[54]

In general, however, Missourians grew progressively quieter. Prowar hysteria and suppression of dissent mounted as the government mobilized, and an uneasy stillness settled over the state. The declaration of war and the process of mobilization would teach Missourians a new definition of democracy: within a pluralist framework, experts and spokesmen would make the decisions and run the country; citizens would play a sort of plebiscitarian role, approving decisions already made, providing not just majority support, but total, unquestioned support. Under these circumstances the leadership could claim that any dissent that might appear was the work of a

53. The draft controversy occurred during the two months after the declaration of war. See *Springfield Republican*, 1 July 1917, for an example of Reed's attacks on Hoover; also *St. Louis Post-Dispatch*, 30 June 1918, p. 14.

54. *Missouri Farmer*, 1 June 1917; 1 April, 21 November 1918; *Missouri Ruralist*, 20 January, 5 March, 5 May 1917; *Kansas City Journal*, 10 March 1918, p. 3; *Slater News*, 4 January 1917; *Savannah Democrat*, 19 January, 17 February, 23 February, 9 March, 30 March 1917.

small minority of Americans, or perhaps they were not Americans at all, but dangerous aliens who could be oppressed safely in the name of the united people. Politics, in the sense of open debate and clear alternatives at the polls, would be suspended, since it implied dissent. The government spoke of making the world safe for democracy with one mouth, and with the other it ordered citizens to line up and sign up: keep their mouths shut; support the country or get out.

Missourians continued to resist. Some sought to work through the new system. Others fell back on traditional forms. Still others turned determinedly to their own affairs, withdrawing, minding their own business in ways that some historians have taken for tacit support, but that war boosters knew to be tacit opposition. These forms of opposition will be discussed below, but first the process of mobilization must be discussed, especially as it developed at the local level. If the federal government had attempted to mobilize the nation from Washington, for example, then resistance might have taken other forms. In practice, however, the government reached out and established links with local war supporters, giving them jobs to do, and in exchange providing them with a valuable source of power. In Missouri, the chief agent of mobilization was the Missouri Council of Defense.

Chapter 3

Council of Defense

A question might be asked at this point: if there really was such opposition to the war in Missouri, and if Missouri was not exceedingly different from most other states in the Union, then how was the government able to conduct its war? Randolph Bourne, in an essay written in 1917, had the beginning of an answer.

> It makes not the least difference whether you or I want our activity to count in aid of the war. . . . As long as the effective managers, the "big men" in the staple industries remained loyal, nobody need care what the millions of little human cogs who had to earn their living felt or thought. This is why the technical organization for this American war goes on so much more rapidly than any corresponding popular sentiment for its aims and purposes. Our war is teaching us that patriotism is really a superfluous quality in war.[1]

As perceptive as Bourne's comments were, and as accurate as was his assessment of popular sentiment, he missed an important point regarding the war boosters. The "big men" were loyal, to their own pocketbooks if to nothing else. But the people who were fervently for the war were not content with that; they *did* care what the millions of human cogs thought. They wanted those millions to love the war too, and to devote their lives and fortunes to the winning of that war. As a result, while effective mobilization went on at the national level, the war boosters sought 100 percent patriotism. They wanted to reach into every city, village, and farmhouse across the land to enlist every single American in the great crusade. In most states, Missouri included, the local agency responsible for this was the council of defense.

The Missouri Council of Defense was an organization of men and women whose mission was to coordinate war activities in the state. Established in April 1917 at the request of the secretary of war and patterned after the Council of National Defense in Washington, the Missouri Council of Defense was created by bankers, businessmen, and state officials. Reaching down to the county, township, and eventually community levels by November 1918 and

1. Randolph S. Bourne, "A War Diary," p. 38. This essay deals at length with the widespread apathy and "unconcerted hostility" toward the war on the part of most Americans, and why it was irrelevant.

composed mainly of elites at each level, the Missouri Council of Defense attempted to bring modern organization to the state in the name of the war emergency. It was only partly successful.

The American people entered the war unprepared and unwilling. The federal government had to organize the nation materially and psychologically for the war effort. At the same time, the government sought to avoid the direct application of federal power upon a public of uncertain loyalty. Federal officials instead granted broad powers to local officials, who were charged with whipping up local support for the war, with keeping an eye on slackers, and with implementing specific programs designed to provide the government with the resources necessary for waging war. There could be no shirking by anyone, male or female, adult or child, for the duration of the struggle against Germany. In practice this marked a major change in the relationship between the American people and their government. For most people, most of the time, the government had been remote. During the war, however, it not only grew in size and power, but it also tried, through its local surrogates, to influence every citizen, to link together all of society's institutions in one vast national system with headquarters in Washington. Thus it was no longer remote; it was ubiquitous—at least in theory. In practice, though, the same forces that limited the war's popularity at the local level worked to limit the government's spreading power.

The parent organization of the Missouri Council of Defense was the Council of National Defense, created on 29 August 1916 during the preparedness stir and fully organized in early March 1917, when war looked inevitable to national leaders. The national council's goal was "the coordination of industries and resources for the national security and welfare" and the "creation of relations which will render possible in time of need the immediate concentration and utilization of the resources of the nation."[2]

On 6 April, the national council set up a Section on Cooperation with the States to coordinate the activities of the handful of existing state war agencies and to help set up new ones in the rest of the country. On 9 April, the secretary of war, as chairman of the national council, requested the governors of all states to create state councils, and by June every state had complied. Further, the Section on Cooperation asked the states to establish county (and eventually township and community) councils, so that the "Federal Government may reach every individual" and help "him find his place in the work of the war." The Section on Cooperation would work with the state councils to transmit data between state and federal bodies and

2. On the founding of the Council of National Defense, see *First Annual Report of the Council of National Defense* (Washington, 1917), p. 6; Franklin K. Lane to Walter H. Page, 16 March 1918; Lane to John Lyon, 15 March 1918, in *The Letters of Franklin K. Lane, Personal and Political*, ed. Anne W. Lane and Louise H. Wall, pp. 11–28; William J. Breen, *Uncle Sam at Home: Civilian Mobilization, Wartime Federalism, and the Council of Defense, 1917–1919*, pp. 17–36.

among the states, and would also keep tabs on "the general temper of public opinion." These agencies were to awaken the people "to the war issues, the war needs, and the possibilities of assistance in the prosecution of the war by all citizens," paying special attention to "apathetic and apparently disloyal persons."[3]

The way Missouri's state council was created set a precedent that was followed in creating the lower levels of the council and illustrates who was in charge of mobilization in Missouri. In response to the secretary of war's request, Gov. Frederick D. Gardner called for Missourians "from all walks of life" to meet in Jefferson City for a war conference. The governor employed the mechanism of the State Board of Agriculture to implement his call, no doubt partly because it was one of the few agencies with branches and influential members in all parts of the state. Whatever the reason, this move guaranteed that certain walks of life were better represented than others. Of the three hundred who answered the call, some twenty-six were farmers, while eighty-two were businessmen, including railroad presidents, publishers, lumbermen, druggists, plus representatives of dozens of local commercial clubs and chambers of commerce. There were also sixty-three bankers, thirty-seven state agricultural experts, thirty-six state and local officials, and a scattering of journalists and professionals. Workers, blacks, and women were hardly represented at all.[4]

Philander P. Lewis called the conference to order on the morning of 23 April. Governor Gardner gave a speech calling for unity and repeating Wilson's promise that we were fighting the German government, which had trampled upon our rights, not the German people. Gardner went on to praise the virtues of the state, emphasizing farming, mining, and lumbering, but ignoring manufacturing altogether. The only people he spoke of were the farm family: "the farmer, the golden sheaf of wheat in one hand, and the Stars and Stripes in the other"; beside him stood his son, holding an ear of corn wrapped in the flag; and in the doorway of the farmhouse were the mother and daughter, "ready, if the country calls, to see the father and the son go to defend the nation's honor." The farms would feed the soldiers, Gardner asserted, though with the farmer and his son at war, he did not say how. At the same time, Missouri's mines would produce shot and shell, while "the thousand ships which the President wants will be built from the timbers of Missouri's forests." All of those would be carried by the Missouri River to the sea. This, said Gardner, "is the mobilized State . . . one people, one sentiment, and one flag; ready to cooperate; ready to sacrifice; ready to

3. *First Annual Report of the Council of National Defense*, pp. 42–45; *Second Annual Report of the Council of National Defense* (Washington, 1918), pp. 11–28; Breen, *Uncle Sam at Home*, pp. 18, 166.
4. Missouri State Board of Agriculture, *Monthly Bulletin* 15 (August 1917): 58–61, names and identifies virtually everyone at the meeting.

suffer."[5] Thus Gardner at once demonstrated an almost charmingly archaic notion of the nature of modern warfare (wooden ships?) and a chilling version of the modern militarized state. His overblown remarks might simply be ascribed to the rococo oratorical style of that time, except for the fact that he and his colleagues began attempting to implement such a plan.

Two committees, one on permanent organization and one on resolutions, then withdrew to determine the precise nature of the sacrifice. While the committees deliberated, the conference enjoyed more speeches. In the afternoon, Frederick B. Mumford, chairman of the resolutions committee, delivered his report, which was unanimously adopted. The report, not surprisingly, stressed agriculture from the first sentence. It dealt with low world food reserves and with family garden plots. It called for universal service, cooperation, and the elimination of waste. It praised the farmer's patriotism and urged all commercial and banking interests to aid him in producing more. And producing more was something Mumford could talk about, which he did at length and in familiar terms: grow more crops; grow more staple crops for cash; build silos; improve stock through careful breeding. Finally Mumford recommended that the governor appoint a Missouri Council of Defense, since the legislature was not in session to do it.

After pledging loyalty to state and federal leaders, the conference adjourned on the morning of 24 April. That afternoon Gardner created the Missouri Council of Defense. Its duties were (1) to mobilize and conserve all the resources of the state; (2) to cooperate with the War and Navy departments, the secretary of agriculture, the Federal Trade Commission, and the Council of National Defense; (3) to assist in the prevention of profiteering; (4) to take the lead in all movements for assisting the farmer; and (5) to be the supreme authority for war in the state. Gardner then named twenty-nine wealthy and influential men to serve on the council.[6]

The council quickly became like a private club where membership depended on a network of personal relationships, thereby obviating the possibility of a modern, efficient bureaucracy. Since only the legislature could provide state funds, the council was forced to seek money from private citizens, and it relied on a handful of wealthy individuals who immediately became members. In setting up the lower levels of the council, the founders naturally sought people they knew, people like themselves, with the time and the inclination to serve, people they believed they could rely on. Thus personal relationships rather than any objective criteria determined membership. In setting up the lower levels of the council, the founders hoped to create a responsive statewide agency in which each level replicated the lead-

5. Missouri Council of Defense, *Final Report of the Missouri Council of Defense* (n.p., n.d.), pp. 4–5.
6. Ibid., pp. 8–9.

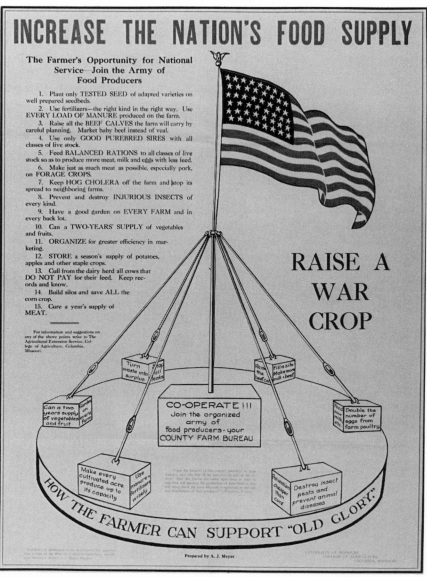

Small type at the bottom of this poster identified it as being distributed "in furtherance of the Smith-Lever Act, approved May 8, 1914, by the Missouri College of Agriculture, Agricultural Extension Service, A. J. Meyer, Director. University of Missouri, College of Agriculture, Columbia, Missouri." Courtesy Western Historical Manuscripts Collection, Columbia, Missouri.

ership, one in which dissent on major issues would not arise and in which all would operate as one. But despite talks on efficiency and modern methods by Mumford, Lewis, and others, tradition weighed more heavily than modernization in the founding of the council, and its effectiveness was limited from the start.

The leaders at all levels did, to some extent, share certain assumptions that helped guide their actions and facilitated coordination. Most supported, for whatever reasons, the government's position on the war as outlined by President Wilson. This meant that the war, however tragic, had been forced upon the United States by German militarists, and that Americans should arise as one and commit their full strength to making the world safe for democracy. In addition, the leadership seems to have shared a distrust of the majority, whom they believed opposed the war. This distrust, stated publicly and privately, is a predominant theme throughout all the council's papers. Apparently some council members began the war with this attitude, while others acquired it in their work; but regardless of how the belief was acquired, eventually most of the people who worked for mobilization in Missouri came to feel distinctly in the minority. This feeling was combined with efforts to arouse loyalty and enthusiasm from everyone, to determine who was loyal and who was not, and to punish the disloyal. The council employed pressure tactics and justified their actions by proclaiming the war emergency. Further, they established themselves, with federal sanction, as the arbiters of patriotism in the state. In so doing they drew a line between themselves, the federally designated official minority on one hand, and their neighbors, the apathetic, possibly disloyal majority on the other. This division often tended along familiar traditionalist-modernist lines, with the government on the side of the modernizers, but not necessarily. It did, however, lend considerable weight to the modernizers' position, so that mere numbers would not determine the outcome of the confrontation. It also meant that the issue of mobilization went beyond politics and economics, since the government and its local agents were trying to persuade the majority to participate in a war they probably opposed.

The council that Gardner and Mumford created was made up of leaders from across the state. Of the forty-six who eventually served, nine were bankers; thirteen presided over businesses, including meatpacker C. W. Armour, Benjamin F. Bush of the Missouri-Pacific Railroad, George Brown of Brown Shoe, and R. A. Long of Long-Bell Lumber. The mayors of St. Louis, Kansas City, St. Joseph, Jefferson City, and Joplin served, as did representatives of the State Federation of Labor, the Grange, and the Farmer's Union.

The performances of these men varied. Only about half attended meetings, held once a month at various localities in Missouri. Governor Gardner served as honorary president, but most of the real work was done by council secretary William F. Saunders, formerly of the St. Louis Chamber of Commerce, and by council chairman Mumford. In between regular meetings, Mumford from his office at the College of Agriculture and Saunders in the council offices in Jefferson City kept up a steady correspondence with each other, with council members, and with local chairmen, sending out directives and answering letters from Washington and from local war workers. In day-to-day matters, then, Mumford and Saunders were the state council.

The process of organizing the lower echelons of the council occupied the attention of the council leadership throughout most of the summer of 1917. To make their work more effective, the council established committees to oversee such things as labor, finance, education, mineral resources, and publicity. Generally a council member plus several other individuals with experience in that particular field made up each committee. For example, the council member on the Mineral Resources Board, Hugh McIndoe, was mayor of Joplin, a lead and zinc mining center. State Geologist H. S. Buihler served as chairman, and the director of the School of Mines also lent his time. In this way the council planned to establish control over all aspects of the war effort by using existing agencies and personnel and coordinating their activities rather than by creating new agencies and thus causing needless duplication of effort.

The council wanted to organize the entire population to ensure that each citizen did his or her part. They appointed county councils of defense in each of Missouri's 114 counties, instructing them to appoint in turn township councils, subject to state approval. Mumford directed this project. He received suggestions for potential members from others on the council, in addition to relying on his own extensive network of acquaintances. He then wrote these individuals, asking them to serve as county chairmen and to pick six good men to help, or to recommend someone else for the job. Also, each county had a women's committee whose chairman, often the wife of a council member, later was given a seat on the county council. Mumford and Saunders thought that allowing women such a high level of participation was perhaps a radical step that some might condemn, but they agreed that the emergency demanded such action. They did not go so far where race was concerned, however, and refused to allow blacks to serve on the council at any level, even in an auxiliary role, thus denying Missouri blacks official participation in the war effort. In any event, of those white males who served on county councils, certain types predominated. Of 155 men identified serving on 35 councils, 96 were businessmen or officeholders and 59 were farmers. Further investigation revealed that the farmers tended to be wealthy, successful men whose position resulted from the businesses they owned in town rather than the farms they owned as a sideline.[7]

7. For the workings of the Missouri council and the attitudes of its members, see the extensive and well-organized Papers of the Missouri Council of Defense (Papers), Western Historical Manuscripts Collection, Collection No. 2797, State Historical Society of Mis-

The process of organization not only guaranteed the domination of the Missouri Council of Defense by a fairly restricted group of individuals, but it also meant that its operations were removed from any expression of the popular will. The council had no legislative authority, having been created when the legislature was out of session. The national council urged states in which this situation arose to seek legislative approval as soon as possible, but Missouri never did. Nor did the council ever operate with state funds, relying instead on the one hundred thousand dollars that was donated by wealthy members. They planned to ask the legislature for reimbursement after the war, but at no time during the council's operations did elected officials exercise any control over the purse strings. Furthermore, when the question of seeking legislative approval arose, the council vetoed it. Saunders and Mumford agreed that "legislation giving authority generally has the effect of limiting authority." Imbued with a strong sense of mission and believing themselves to be the official agency for prosecuting the war in Missouri, the council wanted no limits on its powers.[8] Therefore the Missouri Council of Defense became, by design, separate from the people of the state. It had control, through its members, of the executive branch of government, of major city governments, and of the leading educational, financial, and manufacturing institutions of Missouri. And it answered only to Washington. Consequently, in its attitudes and its methods, the Missouri council made mobilization for war a program imposed from above by a powerful elite upon a balky population that was given no legitimate channels through which to express its opinions.

Many council members, in fact, harbored deep distrust of their neighbors, who were, they suspected, opposed to both the war and the government's mobilization efforts. Instructions from Washington directed the council to counter this opposition with campaigns boosting enthusiasm, to bombard people with propaganda, pressuring them to climb on the bandwagon and keeping a watchful eye on them at the same time. Missouri's leadership needed no such instructions. Mumford and others agreed that one of the main functions of the county councils was to spy on citizens and "report back . . . the attitude of the people . . . and the extent to which they are cooperating with the government in winning the war, or are hindering the conduct of the war by indifference or opposition."[9] The Henry County

souri, Columbia, Missouri. See minutes of meetings, folders 496–500, for initial organization. William F. Saunders to Frederick B. Mumford, 27 February 1918, folder 95; Saunders to Mumford, 26 July 1917, folder 107; also folders 71–73. This official exclusion of blacks makes it extremely difficult to trace the war's impact on Missouri's black population. See folder 1088 for an example of a farmer who was mainly a merchant.

8. Mumford to Saunders, 17 June 1918; Mumford to Frank McAllister, 17 June 1918; Saunders to Mumford, 4 January 1918; Mumford to Saunders, 5 January 1918; all in *Papers*, folders 91, 104.

9. *Missouri on Guard* 1 (November 1917): 8; questionnaire in *Papers*, folder 586; Breen, *Uncle Sam at Home*, pp. 82–85. *Missouri on Guard* was the house organ of the council.

Council instituted a three-card warning system for dealing with the disloyal. A "secret committee on disloyalty" sniffed out suspected individuals and then sent each a white card warning against dangerous "attitudes and utterances." The white card advised "CAUTION" and a complete change of behavior. If the committee observed no change it sent a blue card of "WARNING," which was followed by a red "PROTEST" card threatening physical harm to the individual if he or she did not support the war and the government completely. This system won the approval of the federal government. Other Missouri counties adopted similar plans. In Texas County the spies were called "agricultural reporters." Qualifications for the job included proven loyalty over agricultural expertise, and the first duty was to spy. If the "reporter" had time, he was to record agricultural data. The chairman of the Cape Girardeau County Council boasted of forcing everyone in his county to think alike on the war, or at least appear to do so. "At the beginning of the war," he wrote in 1918, "the expressions of pro-German sympathies were very frequent and somewhat defiant." But the county council had put a stop to that, and "by the end of the war there were left no people in this county who openly expressed any pro-German sympathies."[10] Given that the term *pro-German* included antiwar sentiment as well as questions regarding specific programs, the chairman may well have been right.

In addition to spying, the problem of the production and consumption of food dominated much of the council's activities. During the war America had to feed not only herself and her armies, but her allies as well. Concern with food began at the April War Conference, partly because of the importance of farming and food processing in Missouri, partly because of the dominant role played by Mumford and other agricultural reformers in creating the council.

At its first meeting the new council agreed unanimously that its most important task would be the increase of food supplies, first through increased production, then through conservation. Programs to increase the food supply, which will be dealt with in a separate chapter, met the needs of war supporters in that it gave them a concrete program with visible goals. It also allowed agricultural reformers to try out new programs and businessmen to forge an alliance with farmers in the cause of patriotism. Finally, it gave Mumford and others a way to separate patriots from slackers, since "it gives," in Mumford's words, "every American citizen a chance to show whether he's for, or against, or on the fence."[11]

The government needed billions of dollars to pay for the war, and they decided to let the American people pay for it through bonds. The sale of war

10. *Final Report of the Missouri Council of Defense*, p. 5; Minutes of Meeting of 28 April 1917, *Papers*, folders 496–500; Mumford to "Bankers of Missouri," n.d., folder 70; Breen, *Uncle Sam at Home*, pp. 84, 101.

11. *Missouri Ruralist*, 20 July 1917, 5 May 1918; *Slater Rustler*, 11 April 1918; Mumford to "Bankers of Missouri," n.d., *Papers*, folder 70.

bonds, which will also be treated separately, was not strictly a council responsibility. Bankers had been influential in establishing the council, however, and they played important roles in running it at state and local levels. Thus the council provided a great deal of support in the actual selling programs. Many councilmen and councilwomen were anxious to help, and the sale of bonds provided others with yet another measure of patriotism, another way of enrolling the entire population of the state while singling out slackers for special attention.[12]

In addition to these specific efforts, the council tried to generate broad enthusiasm for the war. In a conscious attempt to counter the popular belief that the war was being fought for the political and economic advantage of "the interests," the council publicized a "holy war" aimed at "saving humanity and preserving civilization." The council hoped their neighbors would look on "every service as an act of privilege and a labor of love," and that emotional fervor would thereby replace apathy or stubborn resistance.[13]

As in the case of food and bonds, the council took the word directly to the people, calling for mass demonstrations across the state on Patriotic Day, 28 July 1917. Speakers with special instructions from the council explained why the United States was at war, what the war meant for the average Missourian, and "how the winning of the war means the establishment forever of the principles of democracy and the liberating of the people of the world."[14] In fact, the council soon took charge of all patriotic speakers in the state, usurping the authority of the Committee on Public Information and its Four-Minute Men. It set up the Patriotic Speakers Bureau, which sent speakers on particular topics on tours, even enlisting preachers in the cause, sending them packets of information stressing God's approval of the war "whenever we wanted sermons preached upon some certain Sunday on a special subject."[15]

In its efforts to spread the word of war and mobilization, the council entered every place where people might gather. They did not want anyone to escape their message. Council members complained that the flag was not displayed often enough and asked that the "National aire" be played before the start of the show in moving-picture houses. The Historical Service Committee, led by Missouri University history professor Jonas Viles, held a patriotic essay contest among the state's teachers, each of whom was asked

12. *Missouri on Guard* 1 (January 1918): 4; Breen, *Uncle Sam at Home*, pp. 24–29, on the council's role in bond sales nationally.

13. *Missouri on Guard* 2 (July 1918): 1.

14. Saunders to Arthur H. Fleming, 7 June 1918, *Papers*, folder 29; "LHG" to Council of Defense, 14 June 1918, folder 15.

15. *Missouri on Guard* 1 (November 1917): 1; Saunders to George Porter, 13 August 1917, *Papers*, folder 135; Mumford to Saunders, 22 October 1917, folder 83; "LHG" to Saunders, 14 June 1918, folder 15; Breen, *Uncle Sam at Home*, p. 34.

to write an essay explaining America's role in the war in language students could understand. The council had a special exhibit at the state fair in August. It conducted a patriotic film service, offering such one-reelers as "Hoover's [Food] Army," and "Labor's Part in Democracy's War" to communities for showing in theaters and at meetings. Libraries, colleges, and other state institutions were asked to spread "educational propaganda."[16] The Women's Committee organized "Liberty Choruses" to perform at all meetings on the theory that "a singing nation cannot be defeated."[17]

As late as January 1918, however, the council could still detect widespread lack of popular sentiment for the war, so it called a statewide rally to "reinfuse" Missouri with patriotism. The rally, they hoped, would "reinvigorate and thoroughly energize people." They sent twelve thousand invitations to county and township members, patriotic speakers, and labor representatives to gather in Columbia to prepare for the event. Speakers from Washington, from England and France, as well as local leaders, were on the program to discuss various aspects of the war. Those who attended were expected then to return home and hold local war rallies, relaying the knowledge and enthusiasm absorbed at the Columbia meeting. Unfortunately, only about four thousand attended, most of them already in town for Farmer's Week, which coincided fortuitously. And there seem to have been no local mass rallies afterward. The council did, however, succeed in making patriotism the theme of the state fair that August, and it provided speakers for some forty county fairs.[18]

The council considered alternative programs to attract total support for the government's war policy, including secret lists of the disloyal, plus extralegal bands of armed men to "maintain order." This followed almost naturally from the council's original intention of keeping an eye on everyone. In fact, the council seemed to have a fixation on lists of names telling who was who in the state, recounting loyalty, abilities, and other characteristics. By the Armistice, the council had called for the enrolling of all women, all men between eighteen and forty-five, all people over ten, and all children between birth and sixteen. Obviously some overlapping was liable to occur, but there is no evidence that such plans were carried out. Chairman Mumford wanted a special list of the disloyal, which he thought "would be a splendid adjunct to our other activities calculated to check up [on] disloyalty." He noted that the Kansas Council of Defense (headquartered at the state college of agriculture in Manhattan) was "planning to card index the attitude toward war activities of every person . . . of eighteen years of age or over, and to begin systematically working on men who are indifferent or

16. *Missouri on Guard* 1 (November 1917): 1.

17. Saunders to Mumford, 18 December 1917, *Papers,* folder 90; *Missouri on Guard* 1 (January 1918): 2.

18. *Missouri on Guard* 2 (June 1918): 1, 3; Saunders to Mumford, 3 June 1918, *Papers,* folder 103.

unpatriotic." Mumford believed Missouri should follow suit, but warned Saunders not "to give too much publicity to the fact that a list of names of persons who [are being investigated] is being preserved for the purpose of taking some action against such persons." Saunders replied that the idea of a card index "has always been very alluring to me," but added that it was prohibitively expensive. Evidently this was as far as the matter went, but it indicates that in some cases the behavior of the council leadership was moderated only by lack of money and experience.[19]

The Home Guards program met with greater success. With the Missouri National Guard called into federal service, the state was left without a military force. This worried state and local leaders. They had been unconcerned when Missouri Guardsmen served on the border against Pancho Villa, but now they feared violent demonstrations against the war. Indeed, labor unrest with antiwar overtones in July 1917 in St. Francois County proved to many that there was something to fear. Widespread labor unrest during the winter, which almost brought war production in the state to a halt, confirmed their suspicions.[20] (See Chapter 6 below.)

Some local councils tried to address the problem on their own. In Kansas City, businessmen fearful of labor violence practiced drilling and military formations under the council's approving eye. The Cass County Council created a band of "marshals" to "go after the pro-German element" it believed was fomenting dissent locally. However, the Cass County marshals served only to stir up local residents, and the county chairman tried to calm his neighbors with a circular that was in itself unnerving: "No tru [sic] American Citizen need have the least bit of fear." The marshals would not "take part in the dealing with the unlawful, The Traitor, or any kind of Criminal." Rather, they would, somehow, "help enforce the law . . . and see that no guilty person be he of whatever nationality creed political faith or what not, be left to go free." The chairman was sure the people would "stand united and inseparable for the President." Just to make sure, his marshals, with their frighteningly vague duties, were waiting.[21]

Other local leaders called for state action, however. After the riot in St.

<hr>

19. Mumford to Saunders, 19 November 1917, *Papers*, folder 87; Mumford to Saunders, 20 April 1918; Saunders to Mumford, 22 April 1918, folder 99. See Frank W. Blackmer, ed., *History of the Kansas State Council of Defense* (Topeka: State of Kansas, 1920); Blackmer boasted that the Kansas card index would be preserved after the end of the war and used to punish not only slackers, but also their descendants: "Their pathway to public honors will be closed. Business opportunities will not be open; society will be cold and hostile . . . they will be without a country . . . . If you can't talk for America, keep your fool mouth shut" (p. 2).

20. For the Lead Belt riot, see Christopher C. Gibbs, "The Lead Belt Riot and World War I." For fear of revolt nationwide, and use of Guards to silence opposition, see Breen, *Uncle Sam at Home*, pp. 82–85.

21. *Missouri on Guard* 1 (July 1917): 1; for Cass County, see J. F. Kircher to Mumford, n.d., *Papers*, folder 501.

Francois County, the county chairman wrote for instructions on how to form a Home Guard. R. A. Anthony, of neighboring Madison County, wrote the council in August 1917 urging the formation of a local council expressly "so that we may complete the organization of a Company of Home Guards." Anthony feared that the riot might be repeated in his area and warned the council, ". . . just how soon trouble may break out we do not know." Chairman George Bailey of Adair County believed that men not otherwise employed might suddenly break into antiwar violence, and he expressed a need to "compel the idle man to work" to avoid such an eventuality. The only difficulty, Bailey pointed out, was that antiwar sentiment was so widespread that "it is mighty hard to get local officers to do their duties along this line." In order to guard against potential outbursts, therefore, Bailey insisted that "an organization for home protection could and should be established." And P. Taylor Bryan, a St. Louis attorney, expressed the feelings of many supporters of war when calling for Home Guards. "People *will* form mobs and there *will* be riots, and nothing but force will maintain peace."[22]

The council did its best to meet the demands of local leaders for protection against antiwar demonstrations. There was some question of the legality of such protection, but the leadership decided not to let that hamper them. Saunders wrote a Moberly man, "We regret the unfortunate conditions which prevent the legal organization of Home Guards," a reference to the lack of a clear law regarding the establishment of additional militia forces. He added, "We urge also that this dilemma be not given undue publicity," because they were going to form the Guards anyway and did not want to give opponents further grounds for complaint. Saunders insisted, "There is a very distinct service to be performed by the Home Guards and . . . prudence as well as patriotism calls for such an organization in every community." Obviously Saunders felt that antiwar sentiment was widespread indeed, and Mumford agreed, so they went ahead and authorized formation of the units, noting that "the Home Guards organizations in our judgment have no legal basis, but it has been our policy to encourage such organizations."[23]

Missouri finally got its Home Guards. Their mission was to prevent "the sinister possibilities of riot, rebellion, sabotage." Over seven thousand men served in five regiments of infantry, plus five separate battalions and twenty-two separate companies scattered around the state. Most weapons and equipment were furnished locally, in the time-honored tradition of such organizations, but the federal government did provide twelve hundred obsolete rifles. Generally these units did little more than drill and march in parades. The Kansas City unit, however, proved so effective in keeping the

22. Anthony to Saunders, 30 August 1917, *Papers,* folder 381; Bailey to Saunders, 20 November 1917, folder 383; Bryan to Saunders, 18 July 1917, folder 378.

23. See R. Glenn to Krug, 31 December 1917, and Glenn to Fritz, 31 December 1917, in *Papers,* folder 383.

peace during a general strike in that city that it was commissioned the Seventh Missouri National Guard Regiment and, probably much to their surprise, taken into federal service.[24] But even if most of them did little more than demonstrate, the Home Guards showed their neighbors the strength of the council's resolve in dealing with the possibility of public expressions of antiwar sentiment.

The council preferred to keep many of its activities secret, in fact. Believing that the loyalty of the mass of Missourians was not what it should be, feeling surrounded by potentially dangerous traitors, they felt better hiding the truth about things like the card index program and the legality of the Guards. Thus when an editorial appeared in *Reedy's Mirror* discussing American military weaknesses, with an eye to improvement, Saunders wrote disapprovingly to a friend, "You can't feed babes on strong meat." Such discussions "may be good enough for highly intelligent men, but do break down the morale of the unintelligent patriot," to say nothing of encouraging the slacker. "I am not at all sure that the people ought to know all these things," Saunders concluded.[25]

Mumford likewise felt that the truth was often dangerous to their cause, and he opposed publication of statistics on the number of farmers drafted because "there is much complaint among farmers generally" over conscription. More information would only confirm their fears and further upset them, so it should be withheld.[26] At the same time, other members of the council suggested that even lies and secrecy were not enough. The secretary of the Nodaway County Council wrote that patriotic speakers "reached the hearts of those who are leaders in the civic life of the county" but apparently missed the hearts of the majority. And the chairman in Montgomery lamented, "I can't get anyone to do anything" in support of the war.[27] So in April 1918 the council launched an attack on suspected slackers. Announcing that "WAR COMES HOME TO MISSOURIANS," as "Thousands of Her Sons" left for France, the council called for the smashing of Hun propaganda. This was a reference to stories of Germany's impending economic and military collapse due to labor unrest and mutiny in the armed forces. Such stories posed a danger to the war effort because they could lead to "premature peace." Such an outcome might prevent the complete destruction of Germany, which would frustrate American war aims. It also concerned those safe in their council offices that Missourians might thereby miss the chance to achieve lasting glory on the battlefield.[28]

---

24. *Final Report of the Missouri Council of Defense*, pp. 55–56; *Missouri on Guard* 1 (May 1918): 1.

25. See *Papers*, folder 182, for a discussion of the controversy arising over the Reedy editorial.

26. Ibid., folder 85.

27. Ibid., folder 185; questionnaire, folder 586.

28. *Missouri on Guard* 1 (April 1918): 1.

As the ships sailed, therefore, the council's tone approached the hysterical. While before it had cajoled and urged and propagandized and plotted in secret, now it threatened openly, publicizing its fear that there were traitors everywhere. Echoing national leaders, the state council equated partisan politics with pro-Germanism. It declared that "politics are Ousted" and forbade its members from running for office. It fired the dutiful secretary Saunders merely for endorsing a candidate in the 1918 U.S. Senate race. Some members began to accuse political opponents of treason. "This is no time for weak-kneed pacifism, carping laments or pro-German leaning," proclaimed the council. While the soldiers were doing democracy's work in the trenches, those who remained at home had a difficult and dangerous fight on their hands too. They had to "punish the slacker and traitor" at home in Missouri. If there was any of this "cancerous condition," local leaders were instructed to "rout it out." The council proposed a state disloyalty law based on a Texas statute that provided up to twenty-five years imprisonment for disloyalty (defined as criticism of the war effort or speech calculated to provoke a breach of peace). The council proclaimed "English the Language of Missouri" and tried to stamp out anything written or spoken in German.

While the legislature seems to have taken its time in getting around to the council's disloyalty law, the attack on Missouri's German population enjoyed somewhat greater success. The campaign against the German language was in fact only part of a broad front designed to stamp out all traces of German culture in Missouri. The council established an honor roll of "schools, churches, business or social institutions who are willing to assert their Americanism by relinquishing the alien tongue." While fighting militarism abroad, the council urged, America must not allow "the enemy tongue to betray [America] to her back." Uel Lamkin, state school superintendent, opposed the teaching of German, or indeed of any foreign language, in Missouri elementary schools and urged the elimination of German from high schools as well. Local councils also took action, and the active Cass County leaders outlawed the use of German on the telephone.

The council backed two other drives against the state's German-Americans. It called for a strengthening of the naturalization and voting laws so that no one who could not speak English could take out naturalization papers, and no one not completely naturalized would be allowed to vote. In addition, it tried to make a statewide survey of "enemy owned property," that is, property owned by Missourians of German birth, which would then be confiscated. The attorney general, a council member, announced that enemy aliens could not vote in Missouri, but the property survey failed altogether. Councilmen at the local level lacked the time and the inclination to do the work. Most of the state's German-born were long-time residents; no one knew if they were naturalized, and few seemed to care. Certainly in counties dominated by German-Americans, such as Gasconade or Montgomery, no action at all was taken. In fact, there is evidence that the council's campaign against all things German met with almost no success, regardless of the ethnic background of local residents. People who spoke German continued to speak it, even on the phone in Cass County. Churches that had conducted services in German before the war continued to do so, and Eden Seminary, near St. Louis, continued to teach in German throughout the war years and into the 1930s. Only where it could operate by executive fiat did the council enjoy much success. Thanks to Uel Lamkin, classes in German began disappearing from curricula in the state's schools. But where widespread popular participation was required, anti-Germanism failed.

In the autumn of 1918 the council held its last great drive to get the slackers. Council members operated as part of the federal draft registration process. Missouri Adjutant General and council member J. H. McCord, who also operated as executive officer for the Selective Service Law in Missouri, instructed county councils to aid law enforcement officers in publicizing the penalties for failure to register, and to "arrange for a general round up . . . of all who failed to register." In this the council promised to assist in the registration of all patriotic citizens as well as "all those other than patriots." Governor Gardner announced that the big day, 12 September 1918, would be historic because it would prove to the world that America would not sheathe the sword "until the very vitals of Hunism have been pierced." Only the abrupt end of the war barely two months later brought an end to this latest council drive.[29]

Missouri women played a vital role in this and other aspects of the council's work, expanding woman's traditional role in society and encroaching on fields usually dominated by men. They were led by Mrs. B. F. Bush, wife of the president of the Missouri-Pacific Railroad, and by Mrs. Walter McNab Miller, a prominent suffragist. Their organization paralleled the men's, and women in council work tended to be educated and well off, with the time to devote to "community service." In many cases their participation on the council was merely an extension of their customary charitable activities. Meanwhile, the daily grind of council work was carried out by the secretaries of the businessmen who served as county chairmen, since the secretary's time usually got "volunteered" along with her boss's.

To a considerable extent the Women's Committee did ordinary "women's work" expanded for the war effort. Councilwomen knitted woolens for the boys overseas. If troop trains passed through town, the women met them and distributed travel kits containing tobacco, candy, and other items useful to young men leaving home. The Military Camp Mother Movement sought to organize women living near army bases to provide a homelike environment where soldiers could relax in their off-duty hours, thereby offering an alternative to the saloons and brothels that inevitably sprang up near the

29. For the rising pitch of hysteria, see *Missouri on Guard* for April, May, and June 1918.

camps. Women in St. Louis provided a place where soldiers from Jefferson Barracks could read, watch or participate in skits and shows, or just talk. The Women's Committee in St. Joseph sought to aid in food conservation and to make home kitchens more efficient by teaching canning techniques to lower-class women. In rural areas women's committees tried to attract home demonstration agents from the College of Agriculture to show local women how they might run their homes better, how to avoid wasting food, and how to deal with wartime inflation. In Callaway County, councilwomen provided school lunches for poor students.[30]

The leaders of the women's war effort in Missouri did not want their work confined to such traditional roles, however, no matter how important they were. On Patriotic Day they tried to register all women in the state for war work. "A little knitting and a little of keeping the home fires burning," they promised, "will not satisfy our women."[31] Women who registered were asked to put down what they felt they could best do to aid the war effort. As the war continued, women participated in the Hoover Food Pledge, securing two hundred thousand signatures. The Women's Committee on Patriotic Education produced a pageant called "The Progress of Liberty," which toured small towns. The Second Liberty Loan Drive raised an additional sixteen million dollars thanks to Missouri's women. As part of the effort to save food, women campaigned for "sane holidays," asking people to avoid overeating during Thanksgiving and Christmas. And because the war created a demand for nurses, women's committees tried to recruit girls for nursing school.

The leaders demanded still more, calling on women to serve the state and forget their own needs. "The whole [food] campaign," wrote Mrs. Miller, "is going to be a wonderful educator of women . . . . Many have never realized that any personal duty rested upon them in this crisis, and many there have been who were indifferent to duty's call. The army of thrift has been a great leveler." Mrs. Bush agreed, adding, "The nation must see that all the time and ability that the women are ready to put at the service of their country should be directed so as to accomplish one great work . . . ." And that was Victory. Women, under these circumstances, would have to replace men. Women's committees began holding classes in stenography, typing, and bookkeeping to enable them to work as clerks. Women also adopted the antislacker stance of the men on the council: "If you are not conserving wheat and meat, you are a slacker. Worse than the man who evades military service."[32]

---

30. See *Missouri on Guard,* which, beginning in December of 1917, reported regularly on women's activities.

31. Mrs. Miller to Mrs. Ira C. Wood, 24 July 1917, *Papers,* folder 408.

32. Ibid.; also, Mrs. Miller to Mrs. Hugh Ward, 26 July 1917, folder 408: ". . . we cannot afford to have any division of Women's work and Men's work . . . ." See also *Missouri on Guard* 2 (March 1918): 5.

Women on the council participated in the drive to register everyone in the state, calling for a "Save the Babies" campaign to lower infant mortality and thereby provide more soldiers for the future. The Women's Committee asked five thousand men and women in Missouri to contribute one dollar each to the effort. They planned a card index of every child in the state from birth to age sixteen, showing especially "the degree of divergence from normality." Although normality was not defined, the committee planned to correct any such divergence with clinics and home nursing programs. Thus Missouri women, led by the wives of council leaders, and by reformers like Mrs. Miller, were simply participating in an extension of progressivism. But the war gave it new meaning. Coinciding with the start of the Save the Babies campaign, Governor Gardner announced that the war was certain to last for years, and that youths today would have to be trained to fight the Hun when they grew up, a prophecy that not only indicates the depth of faith in the "war to end war," but one that came horribly true in 1941. In any case, whereas before the war, work with children had originated with amateur or professional social workers for the betterment of society, this new effort was clearly designed to meet the needs of a new, militarized state.[33]

The council gave heavy publicity to this and all its campaigns, especially through *Missouri on Guard*, its monthly newspaper. The image presented was one of thousands of patriotic men and women all working in unison for a common end. This, the council believed, would persuade the average citizen to fall into line because obviously everyone else was doing so. Any slacker should thus believe that he was alone and should consequently keep quiet. At the same time, such an effort was necessary to the self-image of the council members. They were attracted by the picture of everyone marching together toward a common goal and wanted to play a leading role in this process. But, as has been suggested, this image is distorted. In the name of the modern state, the Missouri council really tried to coerce the entire population into unanimous support of the war, really tried to suppress dissent and wipe out any divergence from their idea of normality. In practice the council's authority was often inversely proportional to the distance, administrative as well as geographic, from the Columbia–Jefferson City axis. As a result, while many county councils did display a high degree of efficiency and enthusiasm, just as many deviated wildly from council orders. The council's dream of total participation failed to materialize at the community level.

Several factors account for this. The federal and state administrations were Democratic, and this affected council organization despite protestations to the contrary. Thus in strongly Republican regions people often found themselves organized by their political opponents. Also, communications were not perfect in Missouri in 1917. Not every council could be

33. *Missouri on Guard* 2 (May 1918): 2.

reached by telephone; telegrams were expensive, and letters took several days and were easy to ignore. In addition, many people in rural areas and small towns had little experience in organization on this large scale. In spite of enthusiasm and hard work, the crisis of war overwhelmed some council members, and their efforts were ineffectual. The motives of some who joined the councils also help explain organizational breakdown. Some joined to advance favored projects, such as agricultural reform or women's suffrage, and tended to let other matters slide. Some seem to have joined for personal gain: a local banker trying to sell his bank's allotment of war bonds could find a position on the county council useful in boosting sales. A man in Moniteau County tried to use his membership to keep his draft-age son out of the military.[34] Some men and women may have been forced into council work by pressure from state leaders whose favor they sought, or by peers, or simply by their own desires to live up to their responsibilities as local leaders. A personal telegram of congratulations from Herbert Hoover could have great importance to a rising young businessman in Sullivan County.[35] None of these factors, however, would make a person an effective war worker, or even loyal to the government. They simply swelled the membership roles.

Some county councils clearly abused their authority. The state council felt it had to caution the Pettis County Council that its instructions to citizens were "pretty strong" and might cause offense.[36] The council in Henry County was really just one man, the chairman, who became a sort of petty dictator. He insisted on doing everything himself and refused even to call meetings. Local members complained to the state council, which suggested a reorganization, but this plan failed and the local chairman continued his activities. The Buchanan County Council was so rabidly anti-German that it refused to permit a representative of the Committee on Public Information to speak in St. Joseph. The proposed speaker was of German ancestry, and his talk presented what the county council called a balanced view of the war, including a few minor criticisms of American policy. The Buchanan County Council felt that a few were too many, however, and that the man was obviously pro-German. Assurances to the contrary from Washington and from Jefferson City did not persuade them to change their minds.[37]

Some county councils failed to operate effectively because German-Americans dominated the area. In Cole County, residents of German descent refused to sign the Hoover Food Pledge. Gasconade County proved a special trial to the state council. The local school board refused to open the

34. Saunders to Mumford, 31 December 1917, *Papers*, folder 90.
35. See the letter from Hoover to Lenny Baldridge, Milan, Mo., "Washington looks to you . . . ," published in *Milan Republican*, 1 November 1917.
36. A. J. Meyer to Saunders, 3 April 1918, *Papers*, folder 66.
37. Saunders to Mumford, 25 July 1918, *Papers*, folder 107; 31 December 1917, folder 90. See folder 136 for Buchanan County controversy.

schoolhouses to patriotic meetings, and the county council refused to force the issue. Nor would the council allow any patriotic speakers into their county.[38] As a result, members of the Gasconade County Council were able to point to participation on the council as proof of loyalty while using the council to protect the local community from state interference.

In many counties, regardless of ethnic composition, councils refused to act. Secretary Saunders drew up a list of eight that he believed were especially weak. These counties were either in the extreme north, along the Iowa border, and dominated by Republicans, or in the Ozarks, where transportation and communication were especially poor, and where traditions of aggressive isolationism had persisted for decades.[39] Arthur H. Fleming, of the national council, telegraphed the Missouri council to apply the whip in six additional counties along the Mississippi River. The chairman of the Miller County Council refused to do any work at all and ignored council exhortations, and evidently he was not alone.[40]

If the council had any doubts about the enthusiasm of its county councils, a questionnaire circulated a few days after the Armistice should have settled the matter. The questionnaire asked for information on the process of organization, on the progress of particular campaigns, and for comments. Only about half of the county councils bothered to respond. One chairman returned the questionnaire unanswered, but appended a note saying, "I resigned months ago and have written the fact over and over to headquarters."[41]

Of those who responded, only about a third indicated that they met regularly. Half met only when they believed there was something to do. Some never met at all. Most had organized their township councils, but few had bothered with community councils. Only about half had active committees. In general, however, those that responded were admirably active, and only a minority admitted doing nothing in the various war work campaigns. In the space for remarks, however, respondents made comments that shed light on local activities. "I will probably have to do it myself," complained one chairman, apparently surrounded by slackers. The Clay County chairman continued this theme: "I appointed township councils in all townships but got effective work out of only one . . . [and] was unable to find anyone who was willing to do as much as I did." The chairman in Vernon County found that in each township there were a few men he could rely on, but they generally worked alone. Another chairman made clear the extent of his commitment: "Some things I do, some I don't." In most urban areas, though,

38. Saunders to Herbert Hoover, 9 November 1917, *Papers*, folder 48; Saunders to Mumford, 26 February 1918, folder 94; 16 May 1918, folder 102; 2 August 1917, folder 75.

39. Saunders to Mumford, 18 February 1918, *Papers*, folder 94.

40. Fleming to Council of Defense, 27 April 1918, *Papers*, folder 14; Saunders to Mumford, 23 July 1918, folder 106.

41. See *Papers*, folder 594.

the work went well, especially Kansas City and St. Louis, where the population was concentrated and where local leaders had plenty of experience in this sort of activity, plus the means to carry out their programs. Often this meant nothing more than having policemen accompany campaign workers into certain ethnic neighborhoods, where the sight of a uniform carried more weight than an appeal to help Washington. But in populous St. Louis County and in Greene County (Springfield), the council had great difficulty even finding men who would serve as chairmen.[42]

Thus the council often proved unable to guarantee enthusiasm, or even compliance, within its own ranks. People had their own affairs to look after, or perhaps felt uneasy about going against their neighbors. In some rural parts of the state a man might think twice about voluntarily becoming a pariah. At the same time, many men and women did serve on the county councils, and they endured the pressure from state headquarters. Thus they were caught between a rock and a hard place and often resolved the issue by doing nothing, continuing to be listed as official patriots by remote superiors without having to antagonize their neighbors. Perhaps some even opposed the war but lacked the courage of those around them to resist. Serving on a county council may have brought satisfaction and prestige to some while bringing only trouble and despair to others.

The Armistice did not end the council's work. For some of its members the war had been too brief. They had not had a chance to consolidate their position, to demonstrate their effectiveness, nor to achieve their goal of an efficiently organized society. Further, they agreed that such leaders and such organizations would be needed, not only to see the country through the difficult period of demobilization, but also to enable the country to organize for the postwar world. For many on the council, America stood on the verge of the millennium, and they hoped everyone would step into the future together.

Word of a potential end to the war came from the federal government as early as 11 October 1918, when Franklin K. Lane, secretary of the interior, told all state councils that America had recently received word from Germany of that government's desire for peace. Lane asserted, "This should not in any way result in the slowing down of your war activities," and went on to stress the "absolute necessity" of continuing to support the war "with unabated zeal." Lane placed the safety of the country during peace negotiations squarely on Wilson's shoulders and indicated that Americans must support their president in this crisis. Others in government, including Josephus Daniels, Newton Baker, and William McAdoo, made similar appeals. The secretary of the Missouri Council of Defense was ordered not to let the peace note from Germany be used as propaganda: "Peace talk is dangerous," announced one telegram from Washington, for "America has just begun to

---

42. Ibid., folder 586; see Breen, *Uncle Sam at Home*, p. 171.

fight."[43] Clearly some on the council refused to let peace stand in the way of the war to end war.

The government had several reasons for wanting to continue the work of the state councils. Europe was exhausted and starving. The United States would have to provide food to prevent suffering "and resulting anarchy." Already there were signs of impending chaos in Europe, with the Russian Revolution as the outstanding example, and American policymakers wanted to prevent a recurrence elsewhere. If they could at the same time provide markets for American producers, so much the better. And with "famine and disorder" threatening, "every household" in America would have to rally to the cause. In addition, while the councils could prevent disorder abroad, they could also prevent it at home by aiding the armed forces in the apprehension of deserters. Evidently many soldiers still in camps in America simply headed home after 11 November, little knowing or caring about the impact their actions could have on a modern army. Missouri's adjutant general complained, "Desertions now cripple execution of plans for well regulated demobilization." And, worse, "unpunished desertions and violations of military law lead to civil disorder and lawlessness" among the general population. Russia proved that. The general asked the Missouri council to remind people that by helping the deserting soldier they were "assisting . . . in . . . aggravating a serious crime for which the extreme punishment is death."[44]

Other dangers threatened. An influenza epidemic had spread nationwide, and Grosvener B. Clarkson of the national council asked that the entire personnel of the state councils be placed at the disposal of public health authorities throughout the deadly winter of 1918–1919. Besides helping to cope with the epidemic, local councils could see to it that returning veterans stayed out of trouble. The government recognized that the country was "properly joyful and generous" now that peace had come, but it did not want people to go to extremes. Councils were instructed to see that "law enforcement both regarding liquor and vice be especially strengthened" to prevent anyone celebrating the end of the war in an improper manner.[45] This involved more than a moral question, for the government had expressed concern over possible civil disorder, and there was no telling what mobs of happy, drunken soldiers and civilians might do.

The point is that the federal government, for the brief period of the war, sought to extend its power over the daily lives of individuals, and established an elaborate structure, the councils of defense, to implement this effort. Now that the war was over, the people who had developed the system

43. Frank Reynolds to Robert Glenn, 11 October 1918, *Papers*, folder 41; 15 October 1918, ibid.; Breen, *Uncle Sam at Home*, p. 171.

44. Reynolds to Glenn, 14 November 1918, *Papers*, folder 141; Clarkson to Council of Defense, 18 November, 22 November 1918, folders 12, 13.

45. Clarkson to Council of Defense, 15 December, 20 December 1918, *Papers*, folder 13.

did not want to see it dismantled. "We in the Council of National Defense," wrote Secretary Lane in December 1918, "have been in intimate touch with all sections of the country through the organization of the state councils of defense. The government had just begun to make its influence felt. To return to the *status quo ante* would disturb that condition. The United States shall not disintegrate into so many individuals." Rather, "the organized effort which has been in existence throughout the war shall be maintained until we know that this war is over and its effects are passed."[46] Lane did not indicate when that might be, implying that the state councils might have to continue their work indefinitely, generating enthusiasm, suppressing dissent and individuality, overseeing mobilization for peace for many years.

Initially the Missouri council complied with federal requests to stay in business. A few days before the Armistice, and in accordance with a telegram from Lane, the secretary of the Missouri council prepared a telegram for all county chairmen. He referred to the "reported armistice" and pointed out that there was still much to do, asking the the counties to maintain their organizations. But soon after peace Mumford began to talk of "final termination." He had communicated with other state chairmen and seemed to believe that the end was near. He had not abandoned the idea that organization was valuable, however, and in a letter to Frank M. Robinson (Saunders's replacement), Mumford praised the idea of creating lasting community councils. He felt it was unjustified as a war measure, since there were already so many councils, but he suggested that some organization like the Council of Defense was necessary in peace time. The traditional institutions of government simply would not do. Robinson responded that he also hoped to "preserve and increase the efficiency" of the council. He was concerned lest Missouri "lose the great impetus for development, cooperation, and general knowledge which is essential to her progress."[47] As it turned out, the Farm Bureaus would attempt to fulfill a large part of this function (see Chapter 6).

Ella V. Dobbs, director of patriotic education for the Women's Committee, agreed on the need to continue the council's work. She was worried that an end to the council would leave the new communities without state support. In a letter to Robinson in late November she indicated that the rest of the women agreed with her. "It is the consensus of the Women's Committee that the organization of Community Councils should be pushed along the lines already used by the State Council." Her goal was "something permanent to build upon" for the betterment of Missouri's future.[48]

Certainly some local councils continued with war work as though there

46. Reynolds to Glenn, 18 December 1918, *Papers*, folder 142.

47. Minutes of meeting of 11 December 1918, *Papers*, folders 496–500; Mumford to Reynolds, 16 November, 18 November 1918, folder 114; Reynolds to Mumford, 19 November 1918, folder 114.

48. Dobbs to Robinson, 29 November 1918, *Papers*, folder 21; see other letters from Dobbs on the same issue in folders 20, 21; A. Ross Hill of the University of Missouri also urged

had been no armistice. The last Liberty Loan Drive, the name changed to Victory Loan, was conducted after the shooting had stopped. Herbert Hoover continued to appeal to Americans to conserve food. Mumford made one more effort: "The emergency is past. The war has been won," he announced. The council's patriotic work "not only saved this nation from the domination of a foreign power, but has saved the world from the terrors of an autocratic regime." But it was not enough. "It is hoped that you will maintain your organization. We may be permitted to express the hope that your organization so efficient in wartime may become equally efficient and successful in the peace activities which are to follow."[49]

The war represented only the beginning for people like Lane, Robinson, Dobbs, and Mumford. They shared a vision of the future that the war had confirmed. The overthrow of autocracy was the greatest reform campaign of all, and these people had played a large role in it. If the organization they worked to create remained intact, if all levels of government could cooperate harmoniously, and if some sense of emergency could be maintained, perhaps the people would go along as well. If not, some of those who served on the council at various levels understood the power of publicity, of orchestrated mass meetings, of lists of names and extralegal bands of armed men. If necessary, Americans would be brought into the modern era in spite of themselves.

Yet, with all the hard work by Mumford and his dedicated followers, the plan failed. True, Germany had been defeated. But modern, efficient organization of society at all levels had not developed in Missouri.[50] The Missouri council had even failed, perhaps through lack of time and trained people, to create an organized system to force people to participate in the war and stifle dissent. Or maybe their hearts just were not in the work. There were attempts to suppress dissent in Henry County, Cass County, Buchanan County, and elsewhere, and people went to jail and suffered other indignities for their failure to support the war. But such cases were localized and not the result of an organized system of oppression any more than they were the result of a hysterical majority driven wild by crusading zeal and war fever. Nevertheless, the Missouri council helped create a climate of fear with its rhetoric and its activities. And America did mobilize. The nation raised a giant army and billions of dollars, grew tons of wheat and made tons of weapons and sent them all, money, men, food, and weapons, to Europe in time to tip the balance against the German Empire. But for many Missourians the clue for action lay in the words of the local chairman who said, "Some things I do; some, I don't."

The following chapters will examine the level of participation by Missourians in several key mobilization campaigns of World War I.

---

retaining the council in peacetime: Hill to Mumford, 26 November 1918, folder 115.

49. Mumford to "All Members," n.d., *Papers*, folder 38.

50. Nor elsewhere, evidently. See the final reports of the councils of defense of Alabama, Arkansas, Illinois, Kansas, and Iowa in the New York Public Library.

Chapter 4

Conscripting Wealth

The demands of modern warfare required the federal government to try to influence the private lives of Americans as never before. In particular, the government needed billions of dollars for the war and decided that it could not rely on voluntary offerings or on taxation. Traditional revenue sources, which had provided for America's imperial ventures in the past, could not finance the sort of massive effort in which the nation was now engaged. True, the government had borrowed during the Civil War, but the results of that experiment did not encourage the men of 1917. Furthermore, they feared that people who were apathetic about the war in the first place would be reluctant to invest their money in it. Therefore, something new was called for. The result was a war bond campaign in which the government, working through its local agents, employed widespread publicity campaigns stressing the patriotic aspects of compliance, equating participation with support for the war. It claimed that majority participation was in fact occurring, thereby isolating nonparticipants and opponents. It threatened and engaged in coercion when persuasion failed. As a result it succeeded in raising the money needed to run the war. But insofar as it sought to use bond drives to generate support for the war, the government failed, for only a small minority of the population nationwide bought war bonds.

There was little overt opposition to bond drives in Missouri, and virtually no organized opposition at all. In this, as in other things, the nature of the mobilization campaign to a great extent determined the nature of resistance: the process of mobilization tended to fragment the community, breaking down old connections, driving wedges of suspicion between friends and neighbors; opposition therefore tended to be isolated, individual or family oriented as people remained quiet behind locked doors rather than organizing for political action or writing to leaders who no longer led. In the face of economic pressures combined with the government's mobilization campaigns, Missourians did what they could to hold on to their money. That the state in fact sent its full quota and more, that Missourians proved unable to protect themselves adequately, does not diminish the importance of their attempt. An examination of the dynamics of that struggle illuminates the relationship of people to their government in a crisis, and helps illustrate how America became a modern nation.

World War I severely disrupted the American economy in general and had an especially violent impact on the lives of individuals. During the first months of the war, European markets for American goods closed, production in this country fell off drastically, and the belligerents called home their gold. By 1915, however, Americans were doing a brisk business, especially with Britain and France, lending them money and selling them goods. This caused scarcity of both at home, and prices began a sharp climb. At the same time, the federal government needed funds. A large part of its revenues came from duties on goods imported from Europe, and this source had dried up. This meant that the American consumer and the American government were competing with the war for American dollars, commodities, and manufactured goods.

American mobilization only made matters worse, at least for the average citizen. During the war, individual corporations reaped huge profits, and corporate executives garnered both honor and power from their participation in the war effort. War production increased to $11.2 billion by the Armistice. Nonwar production, however, declined by $13 billion, so that between the first quarter of 1917 and the last quarter of 1918 the economy experienced an overall decline. Productivity per wage earner in manufacturing fell eleven points, while farm production fell five points. In the meantime, wholesale prices rose 29 percent between 1914 and 1916, and 78 percent between 1916 and 1920. Food was up 73 percent during the last year of the war, clothing rose 139 percent, and energy costs went up 58 percent. Wages rose as well, but they could not keep up, and the American consumer paid the bill.[1]

The federal government initially tried to raise money in the usual ways. In 1915 it raised taxes on toilet articles, chewing gum, and telephone and telegraph use. It imposed special licensing taxes on tobacco products and dealers and on amusements and placed a stamp tax on playing cards, promissory notes, and deeds. Liquor taxes were raised. In 1916 the Emergency Revenue Act doubled the income tax and raised estate taxes. It placed taxes on munitions manufacturers and an excise tax on corporations. These programs and others during the war failed to raise enough money while angering taxpayers. Missourians noted with scorn that congressmen had exempted themselves from the tax hikes. And despite stiff war profits taxes, the new Internal Revenue Service reported that munitions makers cheated on their taxes to the tune of $12 million in 1917 alone. As a final insult, local mobilization agencies helped the government collect from private citizens: the Missouri Council of Defense offered to put its people to work gathering data on those eligible to pay, especially those in the lower tax brackets who were, according to the council, notoriously poor record keepers.[2]

1. For a discussion of the impact of the war on the American economy, see Charles Gilbert, *American Financing of World War I*, esp. pp. 20–27, 50–51, 53–54, 77–79, 203–304.

2. *St. Louis Post-Dispatch*, 1 September 1917, p. 1; 9 October 1917, p. 22; *Missouri on Guard* 1 (February 1918): 8; *Springfield Republican*, 19 June 1917.

While Americans thus accustomed themselves to new experiences in taxation, corporations gathered a windfall. Businessmen in Missouri called the war a "Godsend." Meatpackers in Kansas City and St. Louis flouted antitrust laws and announced that they were uniting "in a voluntary and officially sanctioned" combination in order to "solve the meat problem." And with the War Industries Board and the U.S. Food Administration, among others, encouraging such activities, smaller firms seized the opportunity to wrap profiteering in the flag. St. Louis milk retailers combined and immediately boosted prices. Bakeries followed suit. Some went too far, however, and four grocery firms were actually fined for profiteering. Most companies, however, escaped official action, suffering only the slings and arrows of outraged consumers, something they were at least used to.[3]

Profiteering during the war attracted attention because it was so blatant. It was usually characterized as a patriotic war measure, but some firms simply blackmailed the government, threatening to withhold necessary goods unless allowed to carry on unimpeded. Meatpackers threatened to halt production if the Federal Trade Commission did not stop prying into their business. In fact, such investigations, including some by Congress, continued throughout the war and regularly turned up corrupt deals between military purchasers and corporate suppliers, but little was done. In mid-1918 the FTC informed Congress that major corporations, motivated by "inordinate greed" and operating on "barefaced fraud," were using the war as an excuse to monopolize, drive out competitors, corner markets, increase profits, and pay huge salaries to executives. But if profiteering in military contracts angered many, it was also widely recognized as virtually an essential element in war. It was the profiteering in such consumer essentials as food, clothing, and fuel that enraged the average citizen. Profits in consumer goods had grown from 100 percent to 1000 percent during the war.[4] Transportation costs skyrocketed. Both the St. Louis and Kansas City transit companies requested, and received from the public service commission, substantial rate increases. In pleading his company's case, the attorney for United Railways of New York, which owned the streetcars in St. Louis, said, "It has been urged that the first interest to be considered is of the public who buys the service. I dispute that on the grounds . . . that a fair return on a just investment must be assured before the service to the public must be considered."[5]

In theory, at least, this position is arguable, since capitalism means that when profit is placed before anything else, people will benefit. In practice, large numbers of Missourians disagreed, for the simple reason that they

3. *Springfield Republican*, 3 January 1918; *St. Louis Post-Dispatch*, 8 September 1917, p. 1; 21 September 1917, p. 1; 1 January 1918, p. 2.

4. *St. Louis Post-Dispatch*, 29 June 1918, p. 3; 17 August 1918, p. 1.

5. Ibid., 22 April 1918, p. 3.

were suffering. Consumer buying power was half what it had been before the war. Grocery stores halted charge accounts and ended home delivery. Laundries operated on a cash-only basis. Physicians raised fees by as much as 50 percent to cover the increased cost of drugs. The City of St. Louis, after the streetcar companies got their rate increase, eliminated hundreds of stops to conserve energy, thereby guaranteeing that consumers got less while paying more. No new telephone hookups were available because the government needed all the communications wire it could get. And phone rates increased as soon as the government began setting them. Shoes rose 75 percent. Thanksgiving dinner in 1917 cost 20 percent more than it had in 1916.[6]

Indeed, the war seemed in almost every way to mean higher costs to consumers, especially if the government intervened. Fuel is an example. Coal heated most homes in Missouri, but it was also vital for transportation, manufacturing, and generating electricity. The federal government attempted to deal with the problem through a federal administration. The Lever Act of August 1917, which created the Food Administration, also created a Fuel Administration with broad powers of regulation, including supervision of labor-management relations and the right to set prices. However, despite considerable cooperation in Washington among unions, mine owners, and the government, chaos reigned at the local level. As one Missourian said, "While the government is fixing the price of coal at the mine, it might go a little further and say what it will be at the consumer's chute."[7]

The problems were scarcity and high prices. Coal dealers in Missouri joined to fix prices, often at three times the federally approved rate, then covered their actions by doctoring their books. A bitter strike in the Illinois coal fields, which supplied St. Louis, resulted in higher wages for workers; but the companies passed the increased costs along to consumers, while raising prices in company stores by as much as 39 percent. Local retailers raised prices still higher and made large profits.[8]

Strikes caused scarcity, as did snarled transportation lines and the added demands of war industries. Coal companies held back output in hope of still higher prices. In January 1918 federal fuel administrator Harry A. Garfield, son of the murdered president, ordered coal-fired steam plants east of the Mississippi River to shut down for five days and called for "fuelless" Mondays until winter and the shortage had passed. Places of amusement in Mis-

6. Ibid., 27 November 1917, p. 3; 12 December 1917, p. 23; 16 December 1917, p. 1; 28 March 1918, p. 1; 16 September 1918, p. 1.

7. Eighty-fifth Cong., 2d sess., House Documents, vol. 96, *Food and Fuel Administration Reports*, 1917 (Washington: 1918); Watson, *Development of National Power*, pp. 245–59; Kennedy, *Over Here*, pp. 116, 123–25, 251; Hawley, *Great War and Search for Modern Order*, pp. 23–26, 47; *Springfield Republican*, 1 July 1917.

8. *St. Louis Post-Dispatch*, 26 November 1917, p. 18; 8 April 1918, p. 3; 31 October 1917, p. 2; 19 December 1917, p. 2; *Springfield Republican*, 8 January, 10 January 1918.

souri closed. Electric signs were prohibited. As cities darkened, people began burning furniture and cutting down shade trees for kindling. Municipal governments purchased coal and firewood and sold it, usually at cost, to the poor. Corporations hoarded huge stocks of coal. A Kansas City fuel committee seized twenty-four carloads from a "local packing company." Railroads hoarded coal as well, and shivering Missourians grew angry looking at laden cars in the depots. The mayor and city marshal of Ash Grove, tired of begging the Frisco to sell the town some coal, commandeered a car, sold its contents to the townspeople, and gave the money to the stationmaster.[9]

Thus federal regulation may have been a boon to the war effort and the mineowners, but it did little for union miners, and it left the average Missourian cold. "By the time the producer, the middleman, and the retailer get through," complained one citizen, "about the only thing left for the consumer is the bill."[10] But people found ways of dealing with shortages and high prices that did not necessarily involve commandeering railway stations. The bitter humor that attended the advent of war was also applied to the effects of war. There was a story going around in 1917 of a man in Lamar, Missouri, who wore a baby onion in one lapel and a potato in the other: he claimed to despise "cheap items" like rubies and diamonds. People in urban areas used vacant lots to grow truck patches. Municipal governments approved this activity, and state agricultural experts gave advice on the best crops to grow and how to grow them. Cities revived farmers' markets, calling them "consumers' markets," in which farmers brought extra produce to town and sold it directly to consumers. With food prices and anger at middlemen running especially high among both groups, these markets were popular, and at one point St. Louis had eight going simultaneously.[11]

The problem was simple. Wages may have been unusually high, but prices were higher: "Everybody seems to be getting more money, but not more to eat or wear." Many blamed federal tax policies, which seemed to hit average citizens especially hard. And to some extent the crisis revived old city-country animosities, as consumers blamed farmers for high food prices and farmers blamed consumers for demanding fancy packaging and other frills that raised prices while gaining the farmer nothing. In most cases, however, corporations were the targets of choice, especially those involved in processing and marketing food products. The term "I Won't Work," usually reserved for the members of radical labor organizations, came to be applied to food dealers, and even those who supported the war insisted that

9. See *Springfield Republican* throughout January 1918; *St. Louis Post-Dispatch*, 18 October 1917, p. 1; 4 April 1918, p. 1.

10. *Milan Republican*, 3 May 1917.

11. *Slater Rustler*, 8 March, 29 March 1917; *Springfield Republican*, 15 August 1917; *St. Louis Post-Dispatch*, 4 October 1917, p. 9; 6 October 1917, p. 2.

the government's failure to check these "ghouls and traitors" could lead to dangerous unrest, as had occurred in Russia.[12]

In addition to suffering considerable economic hardship while witnessing the outlandish behavior of war profiteers who cloaked their greed in patriotism, people also had to undergo seemingly endless appeals for money. Many of these appeals came from private organizations engaged in war work. The Salvation Army and the YMCA, for instance, provided various services for American soldiers, specializing in a clean and wholesome environment for American fighting men during their off-duty hours. These dedicated volunteers, widely regarded as draft dodgers by servicemen, strove to protect the souls of the "Sammies" so their bodies could face shot and shell unweakened by the evils of French or American fleshpots. They ran canteens near training camps in the United States and tried to provide hot coffee and doughnuts, cigarettes, and someone to talk to, preferably an American girl, when the men came off the line. Their work required a great deal of money, and the Salvation Army and the YMCA conducted several fund drives during the war, with workers going door to door soliciting money and with the newspapers urging compliance.[13]

The Red Cross led the other private agencies in the vigor of its fund-raising campaigns. It enlisted women to make surgical dressings and to knit clothing for the poorly equipped soldiers. It also taught first aid and sent health care specialists and other volunteers to France. The Red Cross conducted two fund drives and a "monster" membership drive during the war in support of these efforts. Through extensive advertising, much of it depicting the hardships its volunteers underwent, the Red Cross identified itself with patriotism and the war to defeat tyranny. It flooded neighborhoods with campaign workers. It enlisted Boy Scouts to hand out leaflets on street corners, pretty girls to solicit contributions on streetcars, and volunteers to enter factories during lunch to get money from workers.[14]

The Red Cross felt free to employ whatever methods it thought appropriate in its great work. It promised to publish an honor roll of all who donated money, thereby also publicizing those who had not. It proclaimed itself a "governmental agency" that "represents you." This meant that anyone who refused to contribute could be called a traitor. The Red Cross wanted every woman who knitted for civilian use alone named a slacker. Red Cross headquarters ordered that new membership be voluntary, but local war workers

---

12. *St. Louis Post-Dispatch*, 18 August 1918, p. 2; *Springfield Republican*, 1 November 1917; *Savannah Reporter*, 6 March 1917; *Missouri Farmer*, 15 May 1917, 15 December 1918; *Milan Republican*, 26 April, 3 May 1917; *Missouri Ruralist*, 15 July 1917.

13. *Springfield Republican*, 1 February, 1 September 1918; *St. Louis Post-Dispatch*, 11 November 1917, p. 11; Breen, *Uncle Sam at Home*, p. 68; Ferrell, *Woodrow Wilson*, p. 63.

14. *St. Louis Post-Dispatch*, 14 December 1917, p. 1; *Springfield Republican*, 17 June 1917; *Slater Rustler*, 24 January 1918.

exceeded their orders. Workers were told, "Report every slacker to the department of Justice. Get every man and woman listed as disloyal who refuses to donate what they can to the Red Cross." Anyone who would not give to the Red Cross was "a TRAITOR and his case should receive immediate attention." During the second fund drive, policemen had orders to call on all houses not displaying a Red Cross window flag and urge the inhabitants to donate.[15]

Such activities met with only limited success. Thousands of Missourians responded to pressure to join and donate, but every drive was a struggle. Only at the last minute, and after extreme measures had been imposed, did communities meet their quotas of money and members. Quotas for funds, in fact, were usually met by local philanthropists rather than by average citizens with little money to spare. Merchants, for instance, would donate a percentage of one day's receipts to the Red Cross. The Springfield Transit Company donated all of one day's fares. And almost all the donations in a ten-county area in southwest Missouri came from various business groups. Clearly, sending policemen to the door and calling people names could have only limited effect.[16]

During the war, anyone who failed to support the war vigorously could count on being called a traitor by someone. The government's policy of lending its authority rather carelessly to local war workers and private agencies claiming to support the war meant more charges of treason and a consequent tendency to redefine such things as patriotism and charity. If you could identify your particular private interest with the war, then you could designate opponents, or even people who did not happen to share your private interests, as traitors. Fairly quickly, in fact, Missourians were being accused of treason if they failed to deposit money in one particular local bank or other, if they did not support increased barge traffic on the Mississippi River, or if they did not buy an automobile.[17]

Definitions of charity also changed. In addition to the Salvation Army and the YMCA and the Red Cross, there were Knitting League drives, YWCA drives, Knights of Columbus drives, and Boy Scout drives.[18] Support for such organizations, which had been voluntary before the war, now became a measure of patriotism in the eyes of their leaders. At the same time, members of such organizations might find themselves listed among supporters of the war whether they actually were or not. Giving became virtually compulsory as the role of fairly ordinary voluntary associations

15. *Slater Rustler*, 30 May 1918; *Springfield Republican*, 4 July, 3 June 1917, 23 May 1918; *St. Louis Post-Dispatch*, 30 October 1917, p. 13; 15 December 1918, p. 1; 19 December 1918, p. 3.

16. *Springfield Republican*, 23 June, 24 June, 17 November 1917.

17. *St. Louis Post-Dispatch*, 25 April 1917, p. 15; 10 April 1917, p. 16; *Springfield Republican*, 4 August 1918.

18. *Springfield Republican*, 26 May, 1 August 1918.

and charitable organizations became confused by the war crisis and by identification with the federal government.

Clearly, however, the war was an expensive business. By 1918 it was costing the government one billion dollars a month, and of this only one-sixth came from traditional revenue sources.[19] The rest was borrowed from the American people in the form of interest-bearing bonds. Thus all the worst fears of the opponents of war were coming true: while the people, and future generations, paid in money and blood, the corporations profited in money and power; and hard-pressed citizens found themselves pressed still harder by a federally approved committee that wanted still more of their hard-earned dollars.

Treasury Secretary William Gibbs McAdoo decided to borrow from the people by appealing to sentiments patriotic rather than economic. McAdoo believed that Salmon P. Chase, Lincoln's secretary of the treasury, had failed by not appealing directly to the public in Civil War bonds issues. Such an appeal, McAdoo felt, could generate public support for the war by getting people to invest in it. Perhaps they would then be as anxious about the outcome as J. P. Morgan. McAdoo also hoped to save the government some money. The bonds he proposed would be of such low interest that the usual investors in government securities would not be attracted by them; an appeal to the public would be essential. It also meant the government would not be too out of pocket when the time came to pay off the bonds. The bond issues also promised to solve the problem of competition for goods. McAdoo hoped to impose habits of thrift on people, getting them to divert funds into long-term investments instead of buying clothing, food, and fuel, all of which put a strain on the government's efforts to equip and feed itself and its allies. Most important, bonds could be used as a measure of support for the war because, according to McAdoo, patriots would buy them eagerly while the disloyal would refuse. The latter then could be singled out and dealt with.[20]

The federal government conducted five bond drives connected with the war: summer 1917; fall 1917; spring 1918; fall 1918; and spring 1919. They were called Liberty Bond drives, except for the last one, called the Victory Bond drive since the war was over. Each of the five offerings was greatly oversubscribed, enabling the government, the press, and the bond salesmen to claim popular support for the war.[21] But if the dominant theme was optimistic, praising the public's patriotism with the success of each drive, there ran a counterpoint of mutterings about possible failure, complaints about slacking, and a program of persuasion coupled with coercion beside which the Red Cross campaigns paled in comparison.

19. Ibid., 2 March, 5 April 1918.
20. Gilbert, *American Financing of World War I*, pp. 117–18, 126.
21. Ibid., p. 120; Watson, *Development of National Power*, pp. 229–31.

Courtesy Western Historical Manuscripts Collection, Columbia, Missouri.

The people in charge of bond sales in Missouri wanted to sell one to every man, woman, and child in the state. Missouri bankers asserted that bonds would be especially popular with workers and farmers. Throughout the war, bond boosters claimed that bonds were being snapped up by the small subscriber. The First Liberty Loan was hailed by war supporters as a great success because Americans "of small means hastened to do their part." The government announced as proof of this the fact that every fifty-dollar bond (the smallest denomination) had been purchased. The Second Loan Drive opened with a ringing of bells and a blowing of factory whistles nationwide, amid predictions that Americans would gladly cut back on necessities to buy bonds for the war. To help sales, Gov. Frederick D. Gardner, on orders from President Wilson, proclaimed 24 October 1917 as Bond Day. Speakers at rallies spoke enthusiastically about the awakening seriousness of the people regarding the bond drives. The *St. Louis Post-Dispatch* announced, "The outstanding feature is the fact that bonds have actually been sold to the public." And from around the state came reports of "a torrent of buying."[22]

The following year the *Kansas City Journal* announced that the Third Liberty Loan would "be welcomed by the people," who were at last becoming aroused to the importance of buying bonds to win the war. In response to some complaints, the *Missouri Ruralist* insisted that farmers did indeed buy bonds, even those who were hard up. A loan official in St. Louis agreed, writing to Eighth Federal Reserve District president Rolla B. Wells that success in rural areas should "answer for all time the question as to whether rural communities will not respond to our government's need, when the proposition is properly presented."[23] The Fourth Liberty Loan a few months later was touched off by a national moment of silence at nine o'clock one morning. Everything stopped and people were asked to face east, toward the fighting, for two minutes. And, although the flu epidemic and rumors of peace caused a slowdown in sales, the Fourth Liberty Loan was also oversubscribed.[24]

The bond boosters hoped to use optimistic reports as a means of getting people to buy bonds. The goal, as in other mobilization campaigns, was to isolate anyone who had not participated, to make him or her feel alone amidst a great wave of patriotism. There can be no other explanation for so many rousing claims of success by men who must have known better in the face of such negative facts as actual sales figures reveal. In practice bond salesmen tried to sell to crowds, relying on group pressure and fear of being

22. *St. Louis Post-Dispatch*, 26 March 1917, p. 2; 2 April 1917, p. 6; 29 September 1917, p. 10; 1 October 1917, p. 1; 28 October 1917, p. 1; *Slater News*, 28 June 1917; *Springfield Republican*, 16 June 1917; 17, 23, 25 November 1917.

23. *Kansas City Journal*, 6 March 1918, p. 4; *Missouri Ruralist*, 5 May 1918; Tom K. Smith to Rolla B. Wells, n.d., in World War I Papers, Liberty Loan Folder, Missouri Historical Society, St. Louis, Missouri.

24. *Springfield Republican*, 27 September 1918; 9, 10, 11, 15 October 1918.

singled out to persuade people to buy when they otherwise might not. Specially designated speakers, called "Four-Minute Men" because of the length of their talks, spoke on the importance of bonds during intermissions at movie houses, athletic events, or anywhere there was a crowd. Soon attendance at such events declined as people stayed home, where presumably they were safe from the blandishments of bond boosters.

It was hard to avoid them, though, since the government made it easy to buy bonds and local dealers flooded the countryside with salesmen. "Flying squads" visited schools with purchase blanks for students to take home to their parents. Businessmen entered into competition among themselves to see whose employees could buy the most bonds, thus putting great pressure on workers to subscribe. Rural Free Delivery carriers in the country and letter carriers in town carried purchase forms. So did policemen: speeders apprehended in St. Louis, for example, were let off if they subscribed to a bond on the spot. In addition, bonds could be purchased on time from the bank, or helpful employers would simply deduct the price of bond payments from a worker's paycheck. Farmers who sold wheat at local mills were often paid partly in money and partly in bonds, whether they wanted the bonds or not. Groups holding raffles gave bonds as prizes. Companies gave them as Christmas bonuses in 1917. Boy Scouts and Campfire Girls stopped people on the streets and tried to sell them bonds. In some cities, Home Guardsmen went door to door selling bonds. Women also went door to door trying to sell a bond for every family member per household. Businessmen armed with data on what employees were paid canvassed each other's businesses. Preachers gave sermons on "A Liberty Bond in Every Home" on Liberty Bond Sunday. Bond salesmen insisted that rumors of peace in 1918 were nothing but Hun propaganda and that the flu was just another Hun atrocity, both efforts aimed at keeping Americans from buying bonds.[25]

Although the First Liberty Loan passed virtually unheralded because McAdoo regarded advertising as too expensive, by the time of the Victory Loan, bond boosters had inundated the public with various forms of persuasion and publicity. Vice-president Thomas Marshall spoke in St. Louis, and John Philip Sousa's band played around the state. Movies like *The Kaiser—The Beast of Berlin* played in theaters. Posters showed a "slim, young, modernized goddess of liberty" urging bond purchases. Movie stars Mary Pickford and Douglas Fairbanks toured the state and drew large crowds at bond rallies. Advertisements in the press showed spiked clubs used by the Germans and appealed to Missourians to save civilization from the kind of

25. Ibid., 17, 18, 19 October 1917; *St. Louis Post-Dispatch*, 28 October 1917, p. 2B; 18 April 1918, p. 3; 19 April 1918, p. 1; 20 April 1918, p. 4; 29 May 1918, pp. 2, 3; 30 September 1918, p. 1; 10 October 1918, "Women's Page"; *Springfield Republican*, 15 October 1918; Vincent L. Price, *Third Liberty Loan, County Sales Plan*, Eighth Federal Reserve District, p. 27, in Liberty Loan Folder, Missouri Historical Society.

Courtesy State Historical Society of Missouri.

men who would use such weapons. Another showed a German soldier about to bayonet an American. "Don't let the SON go down," begged the ad. Wounded soldiers fresh from the front gave speeches and sold bonds.[26] Schoolchildren learned the following song:

> What are you going to do for Uncle Sammy?
> What are you going to do to help the boys?
> If you mean to stay at home
> While they're fighting o'er the foam,
> The least that you can do is buy a Liberty Bond or two.
>
> If you're going to be a sympathetic miser
> You're no better than one who loves the Kaiser.
> It makes no difference who you are
> Or whence you came or how,
> Your Uncle Sammy helped you then, and you must help him now.[27]

Coercion supplemented the propaganda. In early 1918 the press in Missouri reported that the federal government was asking for information on every American's financial contribution to the war, whether it was by bonds, Red Cross contributions, or some other method.[28] This percolated down through the mobilization machinery. The Boone County Council of Defense sent out letters to teachers, editors, and "prominent men" asking for information on bond slackers. War boosters called for a special sedition law to deal with anyone who spoke out against buying bonds. The state council received letters complaining of coercion in the selling of bonds, but it merely passed along the federal government's assertion: "We are not trying to force any man to buy a bond."[29]

They were, of course. Bond boosters in Missouri warned people to buy bonds immediately or face the consequences. Those who failed to do so threatened the safety of Americans overseas, threatened the entire war effort, threatened to permit Prussian barbarity to sweep across the world. Such people were slackers, traitors, un-American, since a bond was "a certificate of citizenship." "Don't wait for the 'Committee' to come after you," was the warning. And war loan committees, usually headed by local bankers whose banks sold bonds, did make periodic checks on people's ability to subscribe; those who had not were called in to explain their failure. The ever reliable Boy Scouts went on "slacker hunts," and life insurance agents went

26. *St. Louis Post-Dispatch*, 1 April 1918, p. 14; 18 March 1918, p. 1; 7 April 1918, p. 1; *Springfield Republican*, 10 March, 7 April, 1 May 1918.

27. *St. Louis Post-Dispatch*, 3 April 1918, p. 5.

28. *Springfield Republican*, 3 May 1918.

29. *Missouri on Guard* 1 (March 1918): 5; 2 (May 1918): 4; *Milan Republican*, 9 May, 27 June 1918; *Springfield Republican*, 19 October 1917, 3 May 1918; *St. Louis Post-Dispatch*, 1 October 1917, p. 1.

door to door to "induce" people to buy bonds. Two Missouri Pacific employees in St. Louis were fired, not for failing to buy bonds, but for buying them at home rather than at work where they could have helped their employer meet its quota. An employee of the Brown Shoe Company confirmed the rumor that those who did not buy bonds would be let go: she did not and she was. A bond committee visited every worker in the Frisco shops in Springfield, and the fate of any who would not buy was suggested by the mock burial of a bond slacker outside the entrance.[30]

During the bond drives, Missourians were confronted on all sides by bond salesmen: stopped on the streets, cornered at work, besieged in their homes. At the movies, from the pulpit, in the press, from the walls of buildings, someone begged or ordered them to buy a war bond, usually under pain of some sort of punishment, implied or stated. But despite all this, Missourians in large numbers failed to respond.

Economic conditions during the war worked against widespread bond purchases by the so-called "small subscriber." Wages had not risen as fast or as high as prices. Interest rates on deposits were higher than the return on bonds, so anyone with a little extra cash to invest was better off banking it. Besides, people with a little extra money tended to take care of immediate needs first. They supported their families and paid old debts, and the purchase of war bonds tended to end up well down the list of priorities. In addition, the people at whom the bond drives were aimed had not really acquired the investment habit. They were not thriftless, as McAdoo implied, but usually they could not afford to tie up their assets in long-term bonds, regardless of the yield. Few farmers or workers were comfortable enough with the growing market system to be able to make their money work for them. When they had money they bought things; when they didn't have any, they tried to get it. Their economic lives were day-to-day affairs in which survival was paramount. They did not hover constantly on the verge of poverty. They worked as hard as necessary and expected to reap the benefits when they needed them, which was right now. Investment, buying bonds that would pay off some day in the future, was not a character trait of many Missourians in 1917, even if they could afford it.

None of which is to imply that Missourians would have bought bonds had they been able to do so. The issue was popular attitudes toward the war. War boosters made the purchase of bonds a measure of war support. When they praised the small investor for buying bonds, they were praising him for supporting the war. When they criticized people for failure to subscribe, they did not harp on their failure to take advantage of a good investment opportunity, nor did they excuse it by blaming inflation; they accused peo-

30. *Missouri Ruralist*, 15 May 1917; *Missouri Farmer*, 15 October 1917; *Springfield Republican*, 12 February 1918; 24 May, 16 October 1917; 30 April 1918; *St. Louis Post-Dispatch*, 24 February 1918, p. 9B; 9 October 1918, p. 2; 11 April 1918, p. 1.

ple who did not buy bonds of opposing the war. And it is likely that to a great extent this assessment was correct.

There is plenty of anecdotal evidence to suggest that Missourians did not buy bonds in the numbers claimed by optimistic reporters. Depositors in some areas, for instance, threatened to withdraw their money from banks dealing in bonds. A St. Louis grocer had to take down his patriotic bond posters because his customers threatened to boycott him if he did not. Tom McNeal confessed in his *Missouri Ruralist* column that he was tired of hearing people complain about being forced to buy bonds. In Springfield the publicity director of the war loan committee announced that at future bond rallies there would be none of the usual soliciting. Perhaps he was having attendance problems and sought in this way to remedy them. St. Louis banker Festus Wade complained that rural banks were not doing their part in selling bonds to farmers, and Missouri's farm press reluctantly agreed that farmers had bought few bonds voluntarily. The *St. Louis Post-Dispatch* claimed that the urban middle classes had not purchased as many bonds as they could afford. And a Springfield editor summed it all up by saying, "The indifference of the general public in the Liberty Bond issue bespeaks anything but a deeply aroused nation on the war."[31]

Further data reveal that the bond issues failed to achieve widespread support. During the First Liberty Loan only 4 percent of the population nationwide bought bonds. Thereafter the percentage increased until the end of the war: in the Second Liberty Loan, nearly 10 percent participated; in the Third, 18 percent; in the Fourth, 21 percent of the American people bought bonds. Participation in the Victory Loan dropped to 11 percent.[32]

Missourians participated at a lower rate. (The evidence here is for the 96 of Missouri's 114 counties lying in the Eighth Federal Reserve District; excluded are the counties along the western border of the state plus Kansas City.) During the Second Liberty Loan Campaign, only 11 counties showed over 5 percent participation. In 21 counties fewer than 100 people bought bonds, and in only 17 did more than 1,000 subscribe. On the Third Liberty Loan, fewer than 18 percent participated. The table below shows the distribution of bond purchases in fourteen counties around the state for the Second and Third Loan Drives.[33]

31. *Springfield Republican*, 16 May, 14 June, 29 October 1917, 27 September 1918; *St. Louis Post-Dispatch*, 13 April 1917, p. 4; 25 October 1917, p. 2; 11 June 1917, p. 2; *Missouri Ruralist*, 15 April 1918.

32. Gilbert, *American Financing of World War I*, pp. 126–28, 129–32, 139, 234.

33. Treasury Department, Bureau of Publicity, War Loan Organization, *Results of Victory Liberty Loan Subscriptions* (Washington, 1919); *St. Louis Post-Dispatch*, 21 April 1918, p. 3.

COMING

A REAL BATTLE TANK

One of the Thousands Built by the
Government to put the Hun on the Run

VICTORY LIBERTY LOAN

Come and see the Tank in Operation
on Our Streets and Roads

COLUMBIA, MO.
7:00 a. m. to 10:30 p. m.   **APRIL 18**

Courtesy Special Collections, Ellis Library, University of Missouri–Columbia.

COUNTY	% Subscribing 2d Loan	% Subscribing 3d Loan
Barry	2	8
Cape Girardeau	4	8
Carroll	5	11
Cooper	3	10
Douglas	3	12
Jefferson	2	14
Linn	2	16
Livingston	6	15
Moniteau	4	7
Ralls	8	11
Ray	3	20
St. Charles	5	13
St. Francois	1	5
Shannon	4	6

The table reveals a substantial increase between the Second and Third Liberty Loans: average participation in the Second Loan was 3.8 percent, in the Third Loan almost 11 percent.

None of the counties in the above table contains a major city, where participation in bond drives was slightly greater than in the rest of the state. In those counties with large towns, the bulk of the purchases probably came from townspeople. During the Second Liberty Loan, for example, 1,975 people in Saline County bought bonds, or about 7 percent of the population. Of that total, 974 purchasers lived in Marshall and 334 lived in Slater, the two big towns. All of which may simply reflect the fact that townspeople were more accessible to bond salesmen than widely scattered farm families. Certainly Cape Girardeau County and St. Charles County, containing the major towns of Cape Girardeau and St. Charles, showed fairly high rates of participation, while remote Ozark counties like Shannon and Barry showed relatively low participation.[34]

Since every bond issue in Missouri was oversubscribed, somebody must have participated. The evidence suggests that bond purchasers came from the same ranks as those who staffed the county councils: middle- and upper-income individuals, plus wealthy institutions, with money to spare and the inclination to invest. By the First Loan, for example, J. Ogden Armour, the packing millionaire, had subscribed for $1 million in bonds. United States Steel had purchased $50 million. Augustus Busch, the wealthy St. Louis brewer, bought some $2 million in bonds by the end of 1917 and another $1 million in 1918. Thomas May, St. Louis dry-goods merchant, bought $200,000 in bonds during the Third Liberty Loan, and Jackson Johnson of International Shoe bought $50,000 worth. Arch MacGregor, Springfield banker and member of the Greene County War Loan Committee,

34. Treasury Department, *Results of Loan Subscriptions; Slater Rustler,* 28 March 1918.

bought a $100,000 bond in late 1918. A prominent Springfield jeweler bought nine $50 bonds and three $100 bonds. (At least they were among the loot recovered after his store was robbed.) In Walker, Missouri, at the end of the Fourth Liberty Loan Drive, the president of the bank was the leading subscriber, the bank itself came in second, and two others among the top ten purchasers in town were bank directors.[35]

Business and financial institutions bought bonds, as did city governments and fraternal orders. Mississippi Valley Trust of St. Louis bought $5 million by late 1917. International Shoe bought $500,000, Brown Shoe $150,000, Southwestern Bell $350,000. Laclede Gas Company bought $250,000, as did Wagner Electric. Missouri State Life Insurance Company bought $25,000, Mercantile Trust $4 million, International Fur $155,000. The Knights Templar of Missouri subscribed to $55,000. Springfield banks together bought over $500,000. The City of St. Louis bought $100,000.[36]

The efforts of employers to persuade their workers to buy bonds enjoyed a measure of success. Confronted by "the Committee" or faced with possible dismissal, many workers dutifully bought bonds. During June 1917, 718 employees of the Frisco Railroad bought $60,000; employees of a Springfield saddler with war contracts bought $10,000 in bonds, as did employees of Springfield Gas and Electric. No doubt other workers in other parts of the state also bought bonds when faced with similar pressure, but there is also some evidence that many "small subscribers" almost immediately sold their bonds back to the government, thus getting the war boosters off their backs and saving their money at the same time.[37]

In the words of William Gibbs McAdoo, "Purchasing government securities was to be the expression of fundamental patriotism."[38] Obviously only a few Missourians achieved McAdoo's standard. While inflation and unfamiliarity with investing must be taken into account in explaining low levels of participation, popular nonparticipation in the bond drives, combined with the extreme pressure exerted by bond salesmen, added to the evidence noted above (in Chapter 2) of Missourians' opposition to the war, together lend powerful meaning to McAdoo's words. Missourians suffered

35. *Springfield Republican,* 23 May 1917, 28 September 1918, 10 October 1919; *St. Louis Post-Dispatch,* 14 October 1917, p. 1; 9 April 1918, p. 1; 21 April 1918, p. 3; 11 April 1918, p. 4; *Green City Press,* 2 November 1918; *Walker Herald,* 17, 24, 31 October 1918 (brought to my attention by Larry Gragg); Gilbert, *American Financing of World War I,* pp. 120, 136, emphasizes McAdoo's failure to achieve his goal of wide distribution of bonds. By the Fourth Liberty Loan, according to Gilbert, "Bonds were still being sold primarily to the large subscribers who represented . . . an infinitesimal part of the population" (p. 136).

36. *St. Louis Post-Dispatch,* 9 June 1917, p. 1; 1 October 1918, p. 9; 3 October 1918, p. 3; 25 October 1918, p. 2; 11 April 1918, p. 11; *Springfield Republican,* 24 May, 14 June, 14 October, 19 October 1917.

37. *Springfield Republican,* 17 June, 26 July 1917; 16, 24, 25, 28 October 1917; 26 April, 8 May 1918.

38. Gilbert, *American Financing of World War I,* p. 117.

from scarcity and the high prices of necessities caused by a war they opposed. While they watched profiteers blatantly fattening off the nation's misery, Missourians found themselves set upon by private and public fundraisers demanding money for this activity or that organization, all in the name of the war. Too often the very people who instructed Missourians to buy war bonds were the same ones soliciting for the Red Cross, the people with the local war contracts, the holders of mortgages, the retailers who raised prices, the council of defense members who called people slackers and traitors. Missourians cannot have liked these people well enough to buy war bonds from them, and they did not support the war to the extent of investing their money in it. Nor, as the next chapter demonstrates, did they want to invest their young men in it.

Chapter 5

Conscripting Men

While Missourians resisted investing their money in war, they were even less willing to send their young men. In March 1918, when they were begging the United States for help, the hard-pressed British and French claimed that American money, material, and perhaps a few volunteers would suffice to win the war. They knew, however, that the American people opposed entry into the war; and they also knew that their own condition was growing desperate, with British supplies running low and the French army on the verge of mutiny.[1] Few Americans were aware of this, and even after the declaration of war many in this country hoped that the fighting would soon end, or that American soldiers would not actually have to participate in it. "We could send munitions to the allies," wrote one Missourian, "and give them our moral and financial support." Another assured his mother, "I do not think this country will have to send any soldiers to Europe. I believe the war will be over in six months." And a third revealed a full range of attitudes. While lamenting that "the fires of patriotism are not burning very brightly" in America, he nevertheless argued that the war had to be fought and German militarism defeated. At the same time, while "fortunate is the man who loses his life in a good cause," it was obvious that the war would be over in a few months, long before any Americans could get into danger.[2] Such attitudes may have reassured some of those who supported Wilson and the war, but they faded quickly in the face of conscription.

Actually, many supporters of the war were prepared, psychologically at least, for the necessity of a draft. This was a result of the belief that war was in itself a good thing, a belief that arose partly from the fact that few who held it had ever been in a war, certainly nothing like the one then raging in Europe. Many in America had grown up with romantic notions about the actual nature of warfare based on the mythology of America's past conflicts.

1. Daniel R. Beaver, *Newton D. Baker and the American War Effort, 1917–1919*, p. 39; see also the bibliographic essay in Arthur Link's *Woodrow Wilson and the Progressive Era*, p. 310: "The keenest analyses of American opinion . . . were made by British observers, most of whom never deluded themselves into believing the American people wanted to enter the war."

2. Undated transcript, p. 2, in Robert Davidson Papers, WHMC Collection no. 3154, folder 9; *St. Louis Republic*, 4 August 1914, p. 6; Ewing Y. Mitchell to Mrs. Corrinne Mitchell, 14 April 1917, in Ewing Y. Mitchell Papers, WHMC Collection no. 1041, folder 1545; *Missouri Ruralist*, 20 August 1917.

The Civil War especially served as a model for some young men who in 1917 formed local companies and began drilling in the hope that they would be taken into federal service. R. P. Dickerson of Springfield, evidently not aware of the fate of cavalry on the Western Front, announced plans for a regiment of "Ozark Rough Riders," to be made up of cowboys, sportsmen, athletes, and veterans. Dickerson headed for Washington to plead his case, but in New York he was robbed by two prospective recruits. The New York press ridiculed him, the government rejected his proposal, and Dickerson returned to Springfield. Others had similarly outdated notions. Governor Gardner, who believed that modern warships were made of wood, was highly offended when the federal government proposed joining the Missouri and Kansas national guards into a single division. State identity was an important tradition, and Gardner was ready to go to Washington to fight for it, though he ultimately lost. Finally, in a tradition as old as warfare in America, leading Missourians proposed selling state land to returning veterans at cost. They could then farm the land and go back to being the backbone of America. As it happened, the land in question was cut-over hill country or swamp, and most of the boys who went to fight were from Missouri's towns and cities anyway and were not interested in farming.[3]

Other notions persisted. Even after watching the slaughter in Europe for two or three years, jingo editors feared the war would end "before the United States gets far enough into [it] to get any glory out of it." Many agreed with the assumption that Missourians would send their sons "with joy, because we realize that they are going into the greatest adventure in behalf of mankind that it has ever been the lot of freemen to undertake." A Red Cross advertisement promised a clean battlefield with equally clean young men lying about casually, as though resting, barely noticeable bandages on arm or leg. They were attended by a lovely Red Cross girl in a pristine uniform who seemed able to cure by the laying on of hands, as she carried no medical equipment. But such views accorded well with reports like the one filed by a correspondent who asserted, "U.S. Troops Like Life in Trenches."[4]

One prevalent attitude expressed by war supporters was that war was an agent of progress. It was not only good for the individual (in the Roosevelt sense), but it was also good for the nation, indeed for the world (in the Wilsonian sense). Thus conscription was a good idea because so many young men were unhealthy and inefficient workers: "the stoop-shouldered, sallow clerk has returned from [training camp] bronzed, sturdy, and straight." War was good for the soul, causing it to strive to succeed, leading "our citizenship [to] assume a higher plane and [to] think in international terms"—

3. *Slater News*, 29 March 1917; *Springfield Republican*, 23 May, 21 April, 1 May, 5 May 1917; 8 May 1919.
4. *Springfield Republican*, 22 April, 21 November 1917; *St. Louis Post-Dispatch*, 1 September 1917, p. 10; 21 December 1917, p. 15.

which led directly from Wilson's argument that America had entered the war to improve the world. One Missouri journalist, in a spasm of alliteration, believed that the war would lead to "a Protocol of Perpetual Primacy for the People against Privilege—whether of Press, Place, Power, Plutocracy, Politics, Patents, Predacious instincts, Primogeniture, or Pedigree." War would bring the trusts to heel and protect the poor, he insisted, finally breaking into rhyme:

War is the oath of souls that swear
Eternal overthrow of Vested Wrongs
Against Mankind! Ah, let us not despair
While men sing battle songs.[5]

Attitudes like these led war supporters to some remarkable conclusions. A scholar promised the rewriting of history to tell the truth of the American Revolution: that it was really a war waged by England and America against George III's Germanism. And if Wilson claimed that we were at war with German militarism and not the German people, if he saw the war primarily as a conflict of ideas, there were people in Missouri who knew that Germans, and Americans, would be killed and maimed in the process. And despite the rhetorical nature of Wilson's assertion, in a letter to the troops, that "I should like to be with you on the field and in the trenches," there was little likelihood that grim reality would challenge the president's carefully reasoned conclusions on the meaning of war.

Others held images of war that seemed to exist blithely in defiance of clear evidence from the Western Front. A Missouri editor commented on two books by men with long experience in the trenches. War as portrayed by these men, he wrote, was indeed horrible, "with its daily grist of maimed and dead, its filth and fury, its meanness and barbarism." This, however, applied only to men from other lands; "there is another view, which we must hold to the end," because nothing less would justify our decision to go to war. It was of brave Americans "going to battle for the salvation of the world . . . [with] joy in their work, even in the most terrifying environment and the imminence of death . . . [where] their wit and cheerfulness relieve the otherwise universal sordidness and gloom of the battle area." Regardless of the war that others might be fighting, the war that America would fight "has the sanction of heaven and earth. Those who fight it have a right to step high and smile as they go forward."[6]

One can only conclude that such a view was not grotesque hypocrisy, but

5. *St. Louis Post-Dispatch*, 18 August 1917, p. 11; *Kansas City Journal*, 10 March 1918, p. 3; *Warrensburg Star-Journal*, 3 April 1917; *Reedy's Mirror*, 28 August 1917, p. 3; 4 September 1917, p. 4.

6. *St. Louis Post-Dispatch*, 23 June 1918, p. 1; 4 October 1918, p. 14; 30 May 1918, p. 16.

instead comforted those who were about to send Americans into a war that was immeasurably more horrible than their blackest nightmares.

Conscription had had powerful and important advocates for years, including Theodore Roosevelt and his favorite regular army general, Leonard Wood. In 1915 Wood and his adherents began a training camp for future officers at Plattsburg, New York. The National Association for Universal Service, a private preparedness organization, boasted among its members such men as Elihu Root and Henry Stimson, both former secretaries of war. Wilson's secretary of war, Lindley Garrison, was himself a preparedness advocate, and shortly after the fighting began in Europe he asked the army staff to prepare a report on American military strength and on the future possibility of a large national army based on conscription to replace the national guard as the nation's primary defense. Garrison's advocacy of conscription brought a storm of protest from Congress, many of whose members did not oppose preparedness so much as they preferred to reserve a major role for state troops. And Wilson, as yet unwilling to take a stand on preparedness, forced Garrison out of office.[7]

Wilson sought to appear more moderate on the question. He replaced Garrison with Newton D. Baker, a man with a reputation as a reformer and an antimilitarist. But the sinking of the *Sussex* in 1916 led to the passage of the National Defense Act, which called for increased military spending and an increase in the size of the army and the national guard. In addition, national guardsmen would, upon mobilization, pledge allegiance to the federal government as well as to their individual state governments. The federal government would pay for forty-eight training sessions a year, and standards for officers and enlisted men would be raised.[8]

American intervention in the Mexican Revolution overcame much of the opposition to conscription by demonstrating the weaknesses of the national guard system. Baker's calls for increased enlistment in the regular army met widespread apathy, and Wilson was forced to call out several national guard units, including Missouri's, for patrol duty along the border. The intervention was a disaster. Not only did the Punitive Expedition flounder helplessly in the desert in its pursuit of Pancho Villa, but state troops proved themselves inadequate even for border patrol. "We have no National Guard troops really fit for the first line of defense," admitted the War Department. State militias were too often the playthings of state politicians, with commissions going to allies and friends while the ranks were filled with the poor. Officers were ignorant of strategy and tactics and unable to discipline their troops. The men were poorly trained and motivated and received no support from home; men with jobs lost them to civilian applicants while

7. Russell F. Weigley, *History of the United States Army*, pp. 342–45.
8. Beaver, *Newton D. Baker*, pp. 1–8; Weigley, *History of the Army*, pp. 348–50.

they were away on duty, and the general public regarded them as fools for going in the first place.[9]

By the time of America's declaration of war on Germany, even Newton D. Baker had become an advocate of conscription. He began to agree with those who argued that volunteering was inefficient and unreliable, removing men from crucial sectors of the economy and placing them in the military while the inefficiently employed and the idle avoided service entirely. By April 1917 Baker had bowed to the urgings of the Council of National Defense and leading military experts and authorized the War Department to begin planning for a draft.[10]

The problem the government faced was how to have compulsory military service while avoiding the appearance of compulsory military service. The experience of the Civil War draft loomed large in the minds of military and civilian leaders, and they feared that the current war's lack of popularity would lead to unrest. Yet the need for a draft was clear from the start. The Allies required large numbers of American soldiers to save them from defeat. The national guard could not fight without a massive program of reorganization, retraining, and refitting. Besides, few in the War Department had any faith in the guard. Recruiting was not only inefficient, it was unsuccessful. During the first few weeks of the war, thousands of enthusiastic young men rushed to enlist. But the government needed millions, and conscription was the only way to get them.[11]

A Missourian, Provost Marshal General Enoch Crowder, had in fact devised a plan to remove the sting of conscription, or at least put a buffer between the drafted men and the government, well before the declaration of war. Not only did Crowder's plan do away with enlistment bounties and the purchasing of substitutes, which had caused so much trouble during the Civil War; he based his conscription plan on a fundamental aspect of American life. America, Crowder noted, was a nation dominated by localism. Consequently Americans were more comfortable with their own local leaders than with outsiders from Washington. They would especially resent the spectacle of uniformed press-gangs in their towns rounding up young men. Under Crowder's system, conscription was to be based on civilian control at the local level. Plans were being drawn up even as the Senate debated Wilson's armed-ship bill. And as soon as the plan was completed, Crowder

9. Weigley, *History of the Army*, pp. 348–51; War Department, Militia Bureau, *Report on the Mobilization of the Organized Militia and National Guard of the United States* (Washington, 1916), pp. 143–54.

10. Militia Bureau, *Report*, pp. 143–44; Beaver, *Newton D. Baker*, pp. 11–15.

11. Beaver, *Newton D. Baker*, pp. 23–29, 40–49; Weigley, *History of the Army*, p. 357; War Department, Provost Marshal General's Office, *Second Report of the Provost Marshal General to the Secretary of War on the Operations of the Selective Service System to 20 December 1918* (Washington, 1919), p. 13.

sent bundles of forms, with instructions and cautions of secrecy, to local law-enforcement officials well before Congress made conscription the law.[12]

Congress, after much debate, did pass the conscription law on 18 May 1917. The law established that on 5 June every male between twenty-one and thirty-one would register at one of over 4,000 local boards around the country. About 12,000 board members, aided by 125,000 clerical personnel, assembled on that date and registered for conscription just under 10,000,000 men. Throughout the registration process the government relied on local agencies and individuals. Not only did the government lack the time to create an entire federal draft structure, but such local participation helped maintain the fiction that it was their neighbors who were drafting these men, not the government—which was exactly what Crowder had intended.

The governor of each state, assisted by the state adjutant general, supervised the process. Each county, or each ward in large cities, was a registration unit, and the whole system relied on voting registration machinery. The federal government sought to have local officials serve on local boards, usually a county medical officer to examine anyone claiming physical disability, an attorney to deal with legal questions, and a law-enforcement official to lend an element of coercion should it prove necessary. The government hoped board members would serve voluntarily, but stood ready to pay if it had to. This system was in place and ready to operate by the end of May, thanks to advance preparation by Crowder's office. Registration went fairly smoothly.

Young men who registered could claim exemption from military service on various grounds, including physical disability, occupational requirements, and dependency. Local boards determined exemptions, with appeal to a district board, and ultimately to President Wilson, permitted. Crowder and Baker agreed that local draft boards, which were to succeed the registration boards, should include representatives from labor, agriculture, and industry to provide the appearance of representing all segments of society. In practice the registration board usually became the draft board with little change in personnel. At Crowder's recommendation the local councils of defense, also being formed at this time, were pressed into service in such matters as publicizing information about the draft and rounding up the reluctant.

The actual process of conscription, of choosing who was to go and who was to stay home from among those who had registered, got underway in July. Each man had been given a number when he registered. A drawing was held in Washington to determine the order in which the numbers would be called. The results of the drawing appeared in the press. The army

12. War Department, Provost Marshal General's Office, *First Report of the Provost Marshal General to the Secretary of War on the Operations of the Selective Service System* (Washington, 1918); and Crowder's *Final Report* (1920).

needed 687,000 men in the first group, in addition to the 164,000 who had joined the national guard and the 183,000 who had enlisted in the regular army and other branches. Each state and each county had a quota based on population and the number of men already in service, and counties that had filled their quotas with voluntary enlistments did not have to draft men. However, only a handful of counties were able to take advantage of this; the three in Missouri, for example, were small and sparsely populated.

By September, men began leaving home for training camp, despite the fact that facilities and equipment could not be assembled quickly enough for them. There were problems of overcrowding, and thousands trained without weapons and in their civilian clothes. But 180,000 men had gone into camp and more were on the way. In June 1918 all men who had reached twenty-one in the preceding year had to register, and on 24 August all who had reached twenty-one since June registered. Still the army called for more men. By a law of 31 August 1918, the pool was enlarged: all men between eighteen and forty-five who had not registered were required to do so on 12 September. By that time the government had devised a classification system to organize the nation's manpower. Class I included those most eligible by age and occupation; Class V included those not draftable at all. The classes in between contained those deferred for various reasons, but who could be called up if necessary. Under this law, in order to satisfy the proponents of conscription who now had a successful example to point to, voluntary enlistment by registrants was halted.

Ultimately 23,000,000 men registered for the draft, or about 44 percent of the males in America. By the end of the war some 2.7 million had been drafted into service, mostly between the ages of 19 and 36. The draft accounted for 67 percent of American military manpower during the war, and a much higher percentage of soldiers, since the navy and marine corps filled their ranks through enlistments. Almost 800,000 Missourians registered. Approximately 92,000 Missourians were drafted into service. Draftees made up almost 60 percent of the Missourians who served in all branches of the military during the war; thus enlistments in Missouri were slightly better than nationwide.[13]

Missouri furnished 3.42 percent of the nation's army (including its commander, John Pershing) and thus ranked eighth among the states. Missouri's draftees joined men from Kansas, Nebraska, and South Dakota in the 89th Division. The national guards of Kansas and Missouri were united in the 35th Division. After approximately six months at either Camp Doniphan, Oklahoma (35th Div.), or Camp Funston, Kansas (89th Div.), Missouri

---

13. Secretary of War, *The Official Record of the United States in the Great War* (Washington, 1920); Leonard P. Ayres, *The War with Germany, A Statistical Summary* (n.p., n.d.); and Walter Williams and Floyd Shoemaker, *Missouri, Mother of the West* (Chicago and New York: American Historical Society, 1930), 2:583–96.

troops spent an additional two months training in France before being sent to a quiet sector of the line for one month. After that they were judged ready to face the enemy.

The Missourians arrived in Europe in May and June 1918. The 35th Division spent about 135 days in the line, the 89th Division about 90 days. The two divisions participated in the Allied fall offensive, and Missourians fought in the battles of St. Mihiel and the Meuse-Argonne. The 35th Division advanced some 8 miles and captured 781 prisoners. It suffered 1,067 dead and 6,216 wounded, and members were awarded 2 Congressional Medals and 85 Distinguished Service Crosses. The 89th Division advanced more than 25 miles and took 5,061 prisoners. It suffered 1,433 dead and 5,858 wounded and was awarded 5 Congressional Medals and 165 Distinguished Service Crosses. During the war 2,644 Missourians died of all causes; 1,270 were killed in action, and 7,000 wounded. This was approximately 3 percent of all American casualties suffered in the war.[14]

The draft that brought the majority of these men into national service worked quite efficiently, providing the necessary men without causing organized rebellion against the government. The federal officials who supervised the draft could scarcely conceal their delight. The whole system, said Crowder, rested on faith in the people, who "instantly responded to the first call of the Nation with a vigorous and unselfish cooperation that submerged individual interest in a single endeavor toward the consummation of the national task." All this was done without friction "and without the slightest manifestations of antagonism on the part of any disturbing element." The result was the "cheerful and eager submission of the nation." Woodrow Wilson agreed, announcing that the nation had "volunteered in mass."[15] Missouri seemed to fit this pattern, according to a poll taken by the *St. Louis Post-Dispatch*. The paper asked one hundred correspondents around the state each to question ten men on the draft. The correspondents naturally sought out "spokesmen" and "opinion makers," including bankers, businessmen, professionals, and others, most of them undoubtedly over the draft age. They supported conscription five to one.[16]

Crowder admitted that the government had expected trouble. The war's unpopularity was no secret. But patriotism and the desire to preserve democracy, according to Crowder, overcame popular opposition. Crowder spoke of the "universal interest in many aspects of community life" which

14. Edward M. Coffman, *The War to End All Wars: The American Military Experience in World War I*, pp. 275–76, 278, 280, 286, 304–5, 314, 333, 343–46, 355, and especially pp. 311–12, which recount the 35th Division's disintegration during the Meuse-Argonne Offensive and offers an explanation for the unit's poor performance.

15. Office of the PMG, *Report*, 1918, p. 6; Ferrell, *Woodrow Wilson and World War One*, p. 18; Beaver, *Newton D. Baker*, p. 37.

16. Office of the PMG, *Second Report*, 1919, p. 2; *St. Louis Post-Dispatch*, 25 March 1917, pp. 1, 2, 4, 8; 26 March 1917, pp. 1–3.

the draft stirred up. This in turn educated people to the problems of the nation at war. Crowder praised the impact of the draft on society, noting that conscription tended to organize the population for national service in the same way that other war measures organized business and industry. The draft, promised Crowder, would have a lasting effect on America.

But Crowder's optimism, echoed by the War Department and the jingo press, sounds like the praises sung of the "small subscriber" during the bond drives, and it masks the reality of popular attitudes toward conscription. As Crowder noted, the draft worked largely because it was local and civilian in operation, thus placing a buffer between the draftees and the government, attracting and diverting resentment "like local grounding wires," in Crowder's phrase, dissipating the force of discontent and "enabling the central war machine to function smoothly without the disturbance that might have been caused by the concentrated total of dissatisfaction." In other words, Crowder denied and admitted the existence of dissatisfaction in practically the same breath: it existed but had been diverted by the machinery of conscription.

Crowder was correct. The government encouraged local interest in the draft and praised the willingness of some people to inform on their neighbors who spoke out against it or sought to avoid service. With the draft based in local communities, small towns, or neighborhoods, it was hard for a young man to avoid the investigations of self-appointed vigilantes, much less the police and the council of defense. State and federal officers were empowered to arrest draft evaders and were offered a fifty dollar bounty for each one they brought in. The Justice Department's Bureau of Investigation proved especially adept at this sort of work. Duly appointed law-enforcement agents, aided by local allies, including home guards, conducted periodic "slacker raids," stopping young men in the street, sweeping through places where they gathered, demanding proof of military service. And if some of these people were beaten or improperly imprisoned, Crowder could only regret what he called "confusion and lack of judgment" on the part of local officials.[17] However, legal or not, such activities received wide publicity, as did the government's announcement that draft dodgers would be inducted into the army, whereupon they would be treated as deserters and hence liable to court-martial and execution. Obviously draft resisters would have to give serious thought to opposing the government's program.

Yet the evidence suggests that the nation did not volunteer in mass for military service; certainly they did not submit cheerfully. On the contrary, there is considerable evidence of friction and "manifestations of antagonism." Antidraft uprisings occurred in Texas, Oklahoma, Montana, North Carolina, Georgia, West Virginia, Virginia, Utah, Arizona, and Arkansas. Civil disturbances coincided with registration in Missouri and Illinois and in

17. Office of the PMG, *Second Report*, pp. 13, 277, 202, for Crowder's comments.

the Pacific Northwest. Outspoken draft opponents, including Wobblies and socialist Eugene Debs, were harassed and imprisoned. And if most young men did not rebel or riot, many did what they could legally do to avoid service. Between 60 and 70 percent of *registrants* nationwide applied for exemption. The government estimated that an average of sixty-nine men in every local draft board in the country married to avoid service before the government made it illegal after 18 May 1918.[18]

An examination of the workings of conscription in Missouri indicates the nature and extent of attempts to avoid service and of enforcement measures taken at the local level. During the early stages of conscription, those men who had not rushed to the altar sought to avoid the draft through occupational deferment. State and national farm spokesmen, including the leaders of the Missouri Council of Defense, sought occupational deferments for farm boys, arguing that they were needed at home to grow food essential to the war effort. Some went so far as to assert that, while supposedly healthy rural lads should not have to go, sickly town boys were good enough for a conscript army. In Joplin, leaders of the Anti-Horsethief Association of Missouri, Kansas, Arkansas, and Oklahoma tried to find farm work for young men, which would not only provide much-needed agricultural labor, but might protect them from the draft as well. Draft boards in Missouri investigating claims for agricultural exemption often discovered that farmers beyond the draft age had turned control of their property over to their young sons to help them claim deferments.[19]

Young men sought refuge from conscription in other fields as well. A local press association in southwest Missouri tried to claim a group exemption for journalists on the grounds that they were essential to war work. Letter carriers requested group exemption on the same grounds. Young men sought teaching positions in the hope that teachers would be exempted. And once it became clear that shipbuilding would turn out to be a truly essential war service, hundreds of Missourians sought construction work in shipyards on both coasts. In some parts of the state, in fact, so many applied that recruiters ran out of application forms.[20]

Missourians also claimed physical disabilities as grounds for exemption from service. In Springfield "the bad back was all the go." In central Missouri an observer commented, "There are a whole lot of young men in this community who have been visiting local physicians to see if some physical infirmity cannot be found which will free them from the draft." Local physicians received warnings from draft boards about the dangers of aiding draft dodgers. A man in Mexico, Missouri, was arrested for providing young

18. Ibid., pp. 121, 158, 212.

19. *Missouri Ruralist*, 20 April 1917; *Missouri Farmer*, 15 April, 15 July 1917; *Saline Weekly Citizen*, 28 April 1917; *Springfield Republican*, 2 May 1917.

20. *Springfield Republican*, first week of May 1917; 14 July 1917.

men with chemicals to put into their eyes to make them fail the eyesight test. In northwest Missouri federal agents uncovered a scheme whereby officials on the St. Joseph draft board sold physical exemptions to registrants; as many as 75 percent of those found physically unfit by the St. Joseph draft board had purchased their exemptions. Indeed, the government evidently decided that too many young men nationwide were failing the physical, so it lowered the standards and ordered reexamination for all. In that way thousands who thought they were safe got caught.[21] Other young men resorted to forgery and fraud to avoid service, and an attorney in Dade County was arrested for counseling young men on the best ways to evade the draft. Some mutilated themselves to guarantee physical exemption.[22] Indeed, the draft had caused panic in some quarters. Observers noted a wave of fear through ethnic neighborhoods as men who had fled militarism in Europe tried to avoid it here. Jess Tollerton wrote Herbert Hadley that during the summer of 1917 "everybody who is within the draft limit is trying to claim exemptions from going to war." The head of the district board in Joplin, supervising one-fourth of Missouri counties, complained, "I am convinced that the young men of draft age are not awake to the seriousness of the war and the need for personal sacrifice." (Obviously they were.) And an editor admitted, "What with the flat feeters and the cold feeters, Uncle Sam will have a dickens of a time getting his army up to the two million mark."[23]

Hints of cowardice did not deter those intent on dodging the draft. Over 60 percent of Missourians who registered applied for exemptions, and the percentage was higher in some parts of the state. In St. Charles County only one-third did not apply for exemption. In Springfield only 59 of 368 men who had been called by August 1917 had been found physically fit or had made no exemption claim. The *Milan Republican* reported that applications for exemption were running over 50 percent in the northern part of the state, but in only four of St. Louis's twenty-eight wards did a majority of registrants fail to claim exemption. And majorities claiming exemption in the other twenty-four wards ran as high as 75 percent.[24]

Conscription drove some Missourians to the wall. Several young men committed suicide, while thousands risked imprisonment, perhaps execution, by fleeing. In August 1917 the Springfield draft board began receiving threatening phone calls. They were called murderers and worse and threat-

21. Ibid., 9 June, 20 July 1917, 1 March 1918; *Slater Rustler,* 5 July 1917; *St. Louis Post-Dispatch,* 9 August 1917, pp. 1, 2; 13 August 1917, p. 1; 14 September 1917, p. 1.

22. *Springfield Republican,* 19 August 1917, 4 June 1918.

23. *St. Louis Post-Dispatch,* 1 June 1918, p. 1; "Jess" to Hadley, n.d., Hadley Papers; *Springfield Republican,* 1 August, 30 September 1917.

24. *St. Louis Post-Dispatch,* 6 June 1917, p. 2; 13 June 1917, p. 1; 10 August 1917, p. 1; 1 August 1917, p. 1; 2 August 1917, p. 1; *Springfield Republican,* 10 August 1917; *Milan Republican,* 28 June 1917.

ened with death themselves if they did not resign. By late September the board had received so many such calls that they no longer bothered reporting them to federal agents. A board member in Dallas County angered so many people with his decisions that his barber shop was painted yellow.[25] All of which simply demonstrates the accuracy of Crowder's assessment about American life. In their opposition to the draft, people either turned against themselves, or against each other, exhausting themselves in personal or social self-mutilation rather than directing their attacks at the government.

But regardless of their inefficiency in dealing with the problem, large numbers of Missourians clearly opposed conscription, and they often opposed it for the same reasons that they opposed the war. As one man shouted at a member of his local draft board: "Is Pierpont Morgan paying you for this kind of work?" Some feared that the draft would become a political tool, or a social one, with the rich hustling the angry masses off to war. For others conscription meant the militarization of American life and the end of freedom. Fundamentally, however, the draft attacked the family. A Missouri woman wrote to President Wilson that the draft would conscript young men, "tearing them from their wives and babies" and sending them to die in France. The poet who wrote that the "laughing, crowing baby boy" little knew that the war "would make him fatherless" made a powerful comment on the impact of conscription on the lives of Missourians. Mrs. Walter Miller, a leading member of the movement to mobilize women for war, wrote a friend, "I am glad for you . . . that your lads are not old enough to find a duty outside of a school room." Wives and parents besieged draft boards, begging that their young men be spared. One woman dropped dead on hearing that both her sons had been drafted. And young draftees in Springfield asked that the city not give them a big patriotic party honoring their sacrifice; they said they would rather spend as much time as possible with their families before going off to training camp.[26]

The fact that the vast majority of young men who claimed exemption did so on the grounds of dependency underscores the importance of the family. The government allowed such exemptions primarily to avoid burdening the state with a lot of dependent women and children. The government hoped to get around this with the proposed military insurance program, but at the local level many draft board members agreed with their neighbors that the family was a good reason for exemption, and many who claimed dependency exemptions received them. There were local exceptions, like the Dade

25. *Springfield Republican*, 11 August 1918; 19 August, 20 September, 22 September, 21 October, 27 November 1917.

26. *St. Louis Post-Dispatch*, 8 September 1917, p. 2; 16 September 1917, p. 1; Sarah Koehler to Woodrow Wilson, 22 August 1917, copy to Robert M. La Follette, La Follette Family Papers, Series B, Manuscripts Division, Library of Congress; Mrs. Miller to Mrs. Hugh Wood, 26 July 1917, Papers of the Missouri Council of Defense, WHMC, folder 408.

County board, which drafted men with wives and children, as well as those who had rushed to the altar as soon as a draft became law. But it must have rankled draftees with families to support to read about millionaire Jay Gould's grandson receiving an exemption because he had to take care of his mother. Thus the assertion that "the government's net takes everyone in" was not entirely accurate.[27]

The war boosters, who usually were not going overseas themselves, took particular delight in forcing the unwilling—indeed, the unfit—to serve. One editor gloated when the government forbade marriage as grounds for deferment. "Patriots will register—OTHERS MUST!" shouted a Council of Defense headline during the September 1918 campaign, though the accompanying story did not explain if the council wanted traitors in the military. At the same time, for all their claims about the loftiness of the sacrifice and the eagerness of Missouri's glowing young manhood to suffer and die for democracy, many still regarded military service as punishment for criminals, or as a refuge for the lazy. This was certainly a traditional attitude, and it was not incompatible with the belief that war was good for the individual, and thus it may explain why judges often ordered guilty men to join the army or go to jail. Railroad police ordered men caught riding the rails to sign up or go to prison. Policemen used the draft as a weapon against hoodlums and loafers, since the prospect of trench warfare was perhaps more frightening than a jail term.[28]

While local boards did grant exemptions generously in some cases, even to the extent of drawing fire from federal officials, and local groups proved willing, either voluntarily or for a price, to help men dodge the draft, those who did work for conscription were ready to resort to coercion when necessary. The attorney general of the United States announced early that anti-draft activity was illegal, and the press reminded readers of the fate awaiting draft dodgers. The government announced that there would be no class exemptions, and that each case would be decided individually. It ordered the reclassification of certain married men as a means of rounding up slackers. Finally it stopped sending exemption application forms to local boards. Federal agents surfaced in Missouri communities on registration day and made it clear that troublemakers took great risks if they sought to disrupt the proceedings. The Bureau of Investigation began its long history of tracking down dissenters with its searches for draft resisters, and the government constantly prodded local boards to be stricter and more efficient.[29]

27. *Kansas City Journal*, March 1918, p. 4; *Springfield Republican*, 16 June 1917; 22 June 1918; 17 August, 18 August 1917; 8 September 1918; *St. Louis Post-Dispatch*, 15 August 1917, p. 1; 23 October 1918, p. 1.

28. *Council of Defense Letterbook*, 5 September 1918; *Springfield Republican*, 12 May 1917; *St. Louis Post-Dispatch*, 4 September 1918, p. 1.

29. *St. Louis Post-Dispatch*, 28 May 1917, p. 1; 2 July 1917, p. 1; *Springfield Republican*, 10, 11, 21 August 1917.

State and local officials responded to the government's urgings. The day after Wilson announced that failure to register would have grave consequences, Kansas City police began arresting anyone who spoke out in public against conscription. After 5 June 1917, the government ordered the arrest of nonregistrants, and police redoubled their efforts. After registration was over and the federal government stopped sending out exemption application forms, local boards in Missouri had them printed up and charged applicants $1.25 apiece for them. Some local boards read applicants the penalty for false exemption claims; some simply told men not to bother to apply, since they probably would get drafted anyway. Some district boards refused to consider any appeal for agricultural exemption; others refused all claims for medical exemptions (leading in one case to a retarded boy being drafted). Finally, when the government halted industrial exemptions, applications slowed to a trickle.[30]

In some areas stringent methods were applied throughout the war. Local police all over the state indiscriminately harassed men within the age limits. During the summer of 1917, the deputy mayor of St. Louis (his boss, a prominent German-American, left town for the season) ordered police to make a house-to-house canvass prior to registration to locate all eligible men in the city. By late May some 90 percent of the city's policemen were engaged in the draft canvass, and the city government issued a public statement asking people to refrain from criminal activity until the canvass was over. Then, after registration was over and call-ups had begun, the police again went house-to-house to find draft dodgers. In one week they netted one thousand in only four wards. As many as four hundred fifty were arrested in one week in late 1918, with ninety-two caught in one day.[31]

The strictest measure the government took was the "Work or Fight" order of early 1918. The intent was to force every able-bodied male into war service on pain of conscription. In order to "destroy idleness," every man would have to become either a soldier or an effective war producer. The order made deferments due to dependency, or even to a lottery number not yet called, conditional upon employment in a productive occupation. The government felt that too many men who could help in the war effort were wasting their energies in nonproductive jobs. Such jobs were defined as those that could be performed by women, children, or old people, or which perhaps should not be performed at all. They included waiters and bartenders, elevator operators, doormen, and bellboys; ushers and attendants at sporting events and in theaters were included, as were sales clerks and office clerks, gamblers, fortune tellers, and race track attendants; even men in professional sports came under the order, which proved highly unpopular with

30. *St. Louis Post-Dispatch*, 1 June 1918, p. 2; *Springfield Republican*, 1, 23, 28 August 1917; 8 July 1917.

31. *St. Louis Post-Dispatch*, 25 May 1917, p. 1; 30 May 1917, p. 2; 19 June 1917, p. 2; 7 August 1917, p. 1; 9 August 1917, p. 3; 4 September 1918, p. 1; 21 September 1918, p. 3.

baseball fans. In all, the order netted over one hundred thousand men, but baseball was granted a special dispensation and allowed to continue until the 1918 World Series was over; by then, of course, the war was in its last innings as well.[32]

The implications of the work or fight order were not lost on its advocates. "The possibilities of this principle," said Crowder, were limitless. "As time went on more and more occupations were to be catalogued as non-productive." Soon all healthy men would be serving the state. But despite the best efforts of the war supporters, the program suffered certain inadequacies. The press pushed the order fervently, and councils of defense did their best to round up slackers. The police seized yet another opportunity to stop anyone on the street who looked suspicious to them. But young men insisted on staying in nonproductive but temporarily unclassified occupations. And just because the government sought to force men into productive work did not mean it could distribute them effectively throughout the economy. Severe labor shortages occurred in agriculture and other areas, and employers raided each other for workers. Men in productive fields often refused to work hard enough to satisfy the government, and organized labor exhibited a tendency toward "conscious and willful avoidance of full and fair measures of exertion." The government contemplated new regulations to correct these abuses, but peace intervened. Thus, while the evidence of the order's impact on Missourians is limited, it seems that few people actually changed jobs in compliance. Clearly individuals were harassed, some arrested, still others left bitter and angry by the experience.[33]

In the end, thousands of Missourians did enter the military, willingly or otherwise; and Missourians served with distinction in battle. Men enter the military for all kinds of reasons. Obviously an important reason in 1917 was the lack of alternative choices. Despite the fact that word began to filter back that life at the front was not as the press said it was, over fifteen thousand Missourians had volunteered by the end of 1917. Whether in volunteering or in submitting to the draft, there was always pressure, the subtle pressure of peers and of popular images of manhood, the not-so-subtle pressure of the government and its local helpers. One Missourian said after the war that when he enlisted, "I felt like a hero. Everyone praised me for my patriotism, but seemed to infere [sic] that I had done a very foolish thing." And there was another kind of pressure. "I can't say I wanted to go," another said. "I'm not much on this killing business. But the more I thought about it, the more I felt I didn't want to spend the rest of my life explaining why I wasn't there."[34]

32. Office of the PMG, *Second Report*, 1919, pp. 79–85; *St. Louis Post-Dispatch*, 23 May 1918, p. 1; 21 September 1918, p. 3; *Springfield Republican*, 21 July 1918.

33. Office of the PMG, *Second Report*, 1919, pp. 17–18.

34. Undated transcript in Robert Davidson Papers, Collection no. 3154, folder 9, WHMC; *Springfield Republican*, 10 January 1918.

The point, however, is that all of this is a long way from the upsurge of patriotism that Wilson, Crowder, and others at the time, and since, have claimed occurred during the war. Missouri seems to have been about average in the level of claims of exemption from military service, but in some parts of the nation claims ran as high as 80 percent. However this is characterized, it cannot be considered a nation volunteering in mass. People did buy bonds; men did enter the military. But patterns of oppression and resistance begin to emerge. The basic design is one of widespread opposition as demonstrated by resistance to bond drives and to conscription, contrasted with the strident utterances of the jingo press and other war supporters, plus the hard work of many members of local councils of defense, war loan committees, and draft boards, to say nothing of police at all levels, plus amateur and volunteer spies and agents. The popular response was not an upsurge of organized antiwar groups, but a kind of turning inward on basic resources, defending one's pocketbook from the bond salesman and one's family from the draft in primarily individual ways, though sometimes with help from the very people who were supposed to be carrying out the government's programs but who in fact hindered mobilization either intentionally or through inaction and inefficiency. There were still enough who eagerly pressed the war upon their neighbors so that the job got done, just as there must have been many, in remote areas, backwoods or back alleys, who simply stayed very quiet while the storm passed over. But divisions within society must have been sharpened as a group emerged with clear ties to Washington: bankers, attorneys, businessmen, and others who skirted local institutions and loyalties and forms of behavior and looked instead directly to the growing center of power in America, the nation's capital, and received in turn official sanction from men like Herbert Hoover and Enoch Crowder as leaders, spokesmen, indeed, as representatives of popular opinion. The majority was left increasingly voiceless, isolated from the new powers, branded as unpatriotic, regarded as dangerous by the new leaders.

This pattern was reinforced in the government's efforts to solve the food crisis brought on by the war.

Chapter 6

Food Production and Food Consumption

Shortly after America's entry into the war, it became evident to leaders in Washington that in addition to men and money, the Allied war effort would have to rely heavily on food produced in the United States. The drain of men to industry and to the trenches had reduced agricultural production in Britain and France, and German submarines had slowed shipments from abroad. Women, children, and the aged had struggled to maintain output, but by 1917 the food crisis posed as severe a threat as the German armed forces. In addition, although food dealers in the United States had been sending foodstuffs to the Allies for years, America's entry into the war threatened to lessen those food shipments, for the war would now take American farmers from the fields and workers from the processing plants and send them into battle. In order to feed the fighters and civilians both here and abroad, the federal government sought to mobilize the American people to increase production of certain basic foods and to engage in a nationwide campaign of food conservation. The government's steps were halting. There was rationing in fact but not in law, nor was it especially systematic, and at times chaos resulted. The government made only hesitant moves to grant farmers price supports to encourage production, and farmers sometimes protested what they saw either as unwelcome interference or profit ceilings in a booming economy. At the same time, while promising to curb the excesses of food profiteers, the government seemed mainly interested in restricting the activities of small retailers while giant corporations reaped huge profits. In Missouri, at least, people were reluctant to produce more, or to conserve more, for a war they did not support in the first place, and the efforts of the federal government and its local agents only served to alienate people further.

The creation of the United States Food Administration in August 1917 indicates the importance the government placed on food. President Wilson appointed as head of this new agency Herbert Hoover, a wealthy mining engineer who had supervised war relief in Belgium early in the war, and who had been advising Wilson on food for some time. Hoover in turn appointed state food administrators who appointed county food administrators. In Missouri, Frederick B. Mumford served as food administrator as well as chairman of the state council of defense. This duplication occurred at the lower levels of the food administration as well.[1]

Herbert Hoover wanted the Food Administration to mobilize people as producers and as consumers, to educate them "to bring about an intelligent understanding of the foodstuffs most needed for export and substitutes therefor and methods of reducing waste."[2] As usual, though, many war boosters at the local level could not rest content with simply increasing the nation's food supply. They measured increased production and conservation as support for the war. Consequently, the goal of increasing the food supply was reached, but the program of enlisting support for the war achieved only limited success. Food production increased dramatically, consumption declined, and America successfully fed herself and her allies during the war and for some months thereafter. But the scheme worked only because of specific economic factors combined with the usual persuasion and coercion techniques used in other campaigns. The food campaigns failed to mobilize widespread support for the war, instead widening the gulf separating people and government.

The government had a simple message for American farmers: Produce more food! Woodrow Wilson appealed to farmers as the people who decided the issue of all great wars, claiming they would be crucial in this one by breaking "the domination of Prussian Plunder and Hunnish Hate." An assistant agriculture secretary put it rather less gracefully, insisting that any farmer who did not increase production was a slacker. Governor Gardner, in outlining "new truths in new forms," told farmers that they competed in a world market whether or not they chose to admit it, and Germanism threatened to destroy that market.[3] As an agricultural state, third in corn production in the nation and seventh in wheat, Missouri's primary task would be to feed the fighters.

Frederick B. Mumford needed no urging. As United States food administrator for Missouri and chairman of the Missouri Council of Defense, with the federal government behind him and the war crisis driving him on, Mumford and his followers could finally modernize Missouri agriculture. Missouri farmers now must increase production through expanding acreage and using improved techniques because it was "as much a patriotic duty as carrying a gun." "Conquer the Hun by Corn," proclaimed Mumford's office, and "Breed Every Female on the Farm." "Even a rusty rake is proof of

1. *Food and Fuel Administration Reports, 1917*; Robert D. Cuff, "Herbert Hoover: The Ideology of Voluntarism and War Organization During the Great War"; Mumford to Saunders, 22 September 1917, Papers of the Missouri Council of Defense *(Papers)*, WHMC, Collection no. 2797, folder 79; Saunders to Harvey J. Hill, 17 October 1917, *Papers*, folder 26.

2. Quoted in Christopher C. Gibbs, "Missouri Farmers and the World War: Resistance to Mobilization," p. 22.

3. Missouri State Board of Agriculture, *Monthly Bulletin* 16 (January 1918): 2–5; ibid. (July 1918): 6; also Danbom, *Resisted Revolution*, esp. pp. 97–119.

Why is it necessary to eat less Meat and less Wheat Bread?

THE UNITED STATES FOOD ADMINISTRATION asks you to get behind our soldiers, sailors and Allies by sending them now the most food possible in the least shipping space. Every man, woman and child in America can help by eating less wheat, beef, pork, fats and sugar, more of other plentiful foods which can not be shipped, and by avoiding waste.

What the food situation is

THE men of England, Scotland, Ireland, France, Italy and Belgium are fighting; they are not on the farms. The food production of these countries, our Allies, has therefore been greatly reduced. Even before the war it was much less than the amount consumed. The difference was supplied by the United States, Canada and other countries, including Russia, Roumania, South America, India, and Australia.

This difference is now greater than ever, and, at the same time, food can no longer be obtained from most of the outside countries.

Therefore our Allies depend on North America for food as they have never depended before, and they ask us for it with a right which they have never had before. For today they are our companions in a great war against a common enemy. For the present it is *they* who are doing the fighting, the suffering, the dying—in *our* war.

One million of the finest young men in the United States will soon be fighting side by side with the millions of brave soldiers of France, Great Britain, Belgium, Italy and Russia.

Millions of the men, women, and children of the United States can not go abroad and fight the enemy face to face. But they can fight by helping the fighters fight.

WHY IT IS NECESSARY TO EAT LESS WHEAT BREAD

France, Great Britain, Italy and Belgium must now import sixty per cent of their breadstuffs instead of the forty per cent they imported before the war.

America must supply the greater part of this need. To send them the least that they can live on we must increase our export of wheat from 88,000,000 bushels to 220,000,000 bushels.

We can not send them corn because they have not enough mills to grind it. We can not send them corn meal because it spoils in shipping. The oats, rye, barley, etc. that we send will not support them unless mixed with wheat. WE MUST SEND THEM MORE WHEAT, and to do this WE MUST EAT LESS WHEAT BREAD.

WHY IT IS NECESSARY TO EAT LESS MEAT

Because of the lack of fodder and the increased need of meat to feed the soldiers and war workers, France, Great Britain, Italy and Belgium have on hand today 33,000,000 less head of stock than they had before the war. Their herds are still decreasing in spite of the fact that we are now sending them three times as much meat as we did before the war. We must send them more meat this year than ever before.

WHY IT IS NECESSARY TO EAT LESS FATS

The chief source of fats for eating is in dairy products. We are able to produce no more of these now than before the war. Yet last year we sent our Allies three times as much butter and ten times as much condensed milk as we used to send them. Because their milk cows are still decreasing we must send even more butter and condensed milk this year. Because their Hogs are decreasing we must send them more lard.

WHY IT IS NECESSARY TO EAT LESS SUGAR

Before the war France, Italy and Belgium raised all their own sugar. Great Britain bought sugar from Germany.

Now France, Italy and Belgium can not raise much sugar because their men are fighting and Great Britain can not buy sugar where she used to buy it.

All must now get sugar where we get it, and there is not enough to go around unless we save.

How you can help

EAT LESS WHEAT BREAD

Have at least one meal a day without wheat bread. Use instead corn, oat, rye, barley, or mixed cereal breads.

Eat less cake and pastry.

Order wheat bread from your baker at least 24 hours in advance so that he will not bake too much. Cut the loaf of wheat bread on the table. Use all stale wheat bread for toast or cooking.

If every person in America consumes four pounds of wheat flour a week instead of five, we can ship the 220,000,000 bushels which our soldiers and our Allies must have.

EAT LESS MEAT

Eat fish and other sea food, poultry and rabbits, instead of beef, mutton and pork. Fish, chicken, etc. can not be shipped in compact form like meat, and are more perishable.

Do not use either beef, mutton, or pork more than once a day, and then serve smaller portions. Use all left-over meat cold or in made dishes. Use more soups. Use beans; they have nearly the same food value as meat.

Remember that no grain or other human food was used to feed the fish that gives you nourishment. Save the products of the land.

EAT LESS FATS

Use no butter in cooking except left-overs that would otherwise go to waste. Cook with olive or cottonseed oil instead. Save lard by eating less fried foods.

Try to use up all left-over fats in cooking, but if there is some you can not use save it carefully, make scrubbing soap out of it, or sell it to the soap maker.

If every person in America saves one-third of an ounce of animal fat a day we can ship enough for our soldiers, sailors and Allies.

EAT LESS SUGAR

Cut down on candy and sweet drinks. Eat half as much sweets as before and you are still eating more than the Englishman or Frenchman gets.

Use honey, maple sirup and corn sirup on the breakfast table instead of sugar.

Serve cake without frosting or icing. Eat plenty of fruit.

If every person in America saves an ounce of sugar a day our soldiers, sailors and Allies will be provided for

BURN LESS COAL

The railroads can not carry coal to you and also handle military supplies in the quickest way. Help by burning less coal.

Coal supplies power for electric light and steam heat. Turn off both when you don't need them.

If you can get wood, use it instead of coal.

Eat plenty, wisely, without waste, and help win the war

UNITED STATES FOOD ADMINISTRATION
No. 7.   Washington, D. C.

This U.S. Food Administration poster called for voluntary restraint to aid the war effort. Courtesy Western Historical Manuscripts Collection, Columbia, Missouri.

lack of patriotism," and any farmer who used inferior, or "slacker," seed was to that extent himself a slacker. The Missouri Food Administration urged farmers to experiment with purebred stock, to use fertilizers, to plow more land more carefully. Mumford sought cooperation with the state's bankers in providing easy loans for farmers who undertook modernization.[4] Most important of all in increasing production, the government urged farmers to organize.

Farmers interested in modern farm organizations had two alternatives, the new Missouri Farmer's Association and the growing farm bureau movement. The two had roughly similar goals but divergent methods. Each had its journal: *Missouri Farmer* for the MFA; *Missouri Ruralist* for the farm bureau movement, the agriculture college, and the extension system. Both organizations backed the war, though with varying degrees of enthusiasm. Both achieved about equal measures of success during the war in their efforts to organize Missouri farmers.

William A. Hirth, a newspaper man and ex-populist, founded the Missouri Farmer's Association a few years before America entered the war.[5] Hirth wanted to improve farm life in general and to improve the economic position of the farmer in particular. He hoped to see once again the farm as the "citadel of the Republic," where life was simple and families read the Bible in the evening. In more mundane terms, Hirth complained that farmers had no control over the prices they received for their goods, nor the prices they paid for necessities. In order for farmers to achieve control over their economic lives, which would in turn enable them to return to their former exalted state, they had to organize, diversify, and seize control of the marketing of agricultural goods. While Hirth's aims ran counter to the government's preference for specialization, he hoped to realize his Jeffersonian vision through modern pluralistic tactics.

Hirth knew exactly what he did not want. He resisted the initiatives of local bankers, merchants, and commercial clubs in organizing farmers, retaining the populist notion of the businessman as the farmer's enemy. Nor did Hirth favor self-styled experts from the College of Agriculture imposing themselves on farmers. He thought expert advice should be available when farmers sought it voluntarily, and he urged farmers to maintain friendly relations with local merchants, but his farmer's association would be made up of and run by farmers. Hirth sought the creation of a pure interest group motivated by sound business principles, by which he meant the profit motive. He was for farmers first, last, and always and was quick to point out advantages to them: "We cannot permit humanitarian sentiment," he said

4. *Missouri on Guard* 1 (July 1917): 2; Missouri Council of Defense Letterbook, 22 May, 5 August 1918; *Missouri Farmer*, 15 July 1917; *Slater Rustler*, 28 February 1918; *Springfield Republican*, 27 April 1917.

5. *Missouri Farmer*, 15 January, 15 February, 15 July 1917; 1 January 1918.

regarding the war, "to blind us to the new obligations and opportunities which the European calamity thrusts upon the United States."[6] By organizing along simple interest-group lines, Hirth believed farmers could achieve a position of power comparable with, but separate from, similar groups of organized workers and capitalists.

Hirth spoke in terms of traditional goals. More than anything else, he believed that farmers could succeed only by joining "the hands of the producer and consumer in the elimination of the food speculator and grafter." He constantly cautioned his followers to attend to the needs of consumers, for only through a union of producers and consumers could farmers strike out at "the industrial parasites who preyed on both." At the same time, Hirth sought to minimize the farmer's own position as a consumer. While he supported marketing cooperatives to cut out middlemen, he strongly opposed farmers' consumerist activity. Such "farmers' stores" had, he felt, been the death of the populist movement, for they had alienated local merchants. Therefore, while Hirth did support cooperative purchasing of such trust-dominated items as binder's twine, he urged his followers to do as much business as possible with local merchants. Through organization and cooperation among themselves, farmers could end harmful competition and restore a sense of community in rural Missouri while solving natural problems by using purebred stock, controlling disease and parasites, and planting tested seed. They could correct human error by using better farming techniques. All of this would regain for the farmer the power in American society he deserved and had once held.[7]

But if Hirth and the MFA spoke in traditional terms about employing modern techniques, Mumford and the farm bureau supporters offered a somewhat different approach. In the first place, the farm bureau movement in Missouri was started and supported by bankers, merchants, commercial clubs, and farm experts from the College of Agriculture. These men and women urged farmers to improve their position by adopting the techniques of modernization employed by large corporations, which would help them improve production and establish a better place in the market network. All over the state, local businessmen's groups set out to persuade farmers to organize under this banner. In the southwest the Springfield Young Men's Business Club sent carloads of representatives to meet with farmers and urge them to acquire a county agent and to impress upon them the value of scientific farming and of close cooperation with businessmen. In Houston, Missouri, in the south-central region, the commercial club organized, with the aid of the College of Agriculture, local extension meetings to teach farmers to "raise the level of their farming." In the north, the Milan press reported that the Milan Commercial Club wished to establish a local farm

6. *St. Louis Republic,* 6 August 1914, p. 2.
7. *Missouri Farmer,* 1 February, 1 June, 1 August, 1 September 1917.

bureau. The Northeast Missouri Agricultural and Industrial Association called a meeting in Hannibal to hear a talk by a local county farm advisor. No farmers attended, so the agent gave his talk to the assembled businessmen.[8]

The farm bureau movement in Missouri sought, like the MFA, to improve the market power of farmers and farm life for all rural people. But their different approaches revealed the differences between the two groups. Hirth sought to restore unity of production and consumption insofar as it was possible in modern America, and to that end the improved market power of farmers along interest group lines was a means; the farmer's enemies, the corporations, were the consumer's enemies as well, so unity would benefit both. The farm bureau movement sought to turn farmers away from such anticorporate attitudes: "Get acquainted with your railroad, you might like it," they suggested.[9] In the triumvirate of farmers, farm experts, and businessmen, farmers were clearly the weakest, and farm bureau and College of Agriculture propaganda consistently portrayed them as backward and recalcitrant. Where Hirth found farmers to be hesitant about joining, Mumford and his followers found them to be stubborn, ignorant people who obviously had to be modernized for the benefit of society and themselves.

While both organizations saw the war as an opportunity, it clearly helped one rather than the other. Hirth was so ambivalent about the war as to cast doubt on the sincerity of his claims of patriotism. He admitted that farmers had not wanted the war, that it would hurt them by drawing young men away from the farms and by increasing the power of the corporations. He continually criticized Hoover, the Food Administration, and the farm bureau, which he believed was intent on swallowing MFA. While he urged farmers to try to profit from the war, he cautioned them to keep their heads and warned that the war could not last forever, that boom times could quickly go bust. Further, the war led Hirth to seek a third party in the producer-consumer war against the corporations. Although he did not like it at first, Hirth finally admitted that the sudden growth of the federal government could benefit the people, for the government could use its war powers to regulate middlemen right out of existence. Ultimately, however, Hirth admitted that the average farmer "refuses to get his feet wet" in the matter of joining the Missouri Farmer's Association, and by the end of the war he could claim only thirty to forty thousand members.[10]

The farm bureau movement was also just barely getting off the ground when the war began. Only a scattering of Missouri counties had farm advisors, and some that did were trying to get rid of them as a waste of tax

---

8. *Springfield Republican,* 30 March 1917; *Houston Herald,* 8 March 1917; *Milan Republican,* 15 March 1917; *Missouri Ruralist,* 20 June 1917.

9. *Missouri Ruralist,* 5 December 1917.

10. *Missouri Farmer,* 15 February, 15 April, 15 June 1917.

dollars.[11] But the war put Mumford in control. The Federation of Missouri Commercial Clubs claimed that "every farmer . . . will be organized in the food . . . campaign." Farmers who sought federal loans were required to organize into groups of no fewer than ten and to apply for not less than $20,000. Tenants could not apply.[12] The College of Agriculture sent out experts to urge improved farming techniques and to organize farmer groups with county advisors. The college maintained that only through extension service and county agents could farmers meet the demands for increased production. The *Missouri Ruralist* admitted that county farm bureaus were designed "primarily for national service in increased production" and pointed out that since the farm bureau was a war measure, anyone who resisted it was as much a traitor as one who opposed enlistment in the military. Congress appropriated $155,000 for the college to spend on county agents, insisting that "it is imperative that the state and nation have a representative in each county." Finally, in May 1918, the Council of National Defense made it official, instructing state councils to consider local farm bureaus as being in charge of increased production for the war.[13]

Yet, with all this help, the farm bureau in Missouri did little better than the MFA. True, to the extent that county councils of defense were county farm bureaus, every county in the state had a farm bureau. But many lacked county agents, and the movement's historian notes that in "some of [the counties] the local organization existed rather in theory than in fact."[14] Mumford admitted, "If farm folk would only believe that we have no selfish motive and that we are only trying to help them there would be no trouble." This tone, similar to that of a missionary speaking of savages, pervaded the farm bureau system and did not help to organize farmers. Mumford began to sound anxious by 1918: "Criticisms of the government leading to more or less open and direct attacks on war activities border closely upon disloyalty." He added, "There can be no compromising now. Every American citizen is either for or against the government. Those who are against the government are clearly disloyal. Every action public and private of every individual during the present war emergency must be judged from the standpoint of the effect of such action upon the purpose of the nation to destroy the ruthless, cruel, and unrighteous power of the imperial government of Germany." But after a considerable organizing campaign, Mumford counted only thirty to forty thousand members for his movement. Unfortunately, there is no way of knowing whether it was the same group that Hirth claimed, but some overlapping may well have occurred. In any case, when the county councils of defense disappeared at the end of the war, so did most of the county farm

11. *Springfield Republican*, 5 January, 24 January 1917.

12. Ibid., 27 April 1917; *Slater News*, 12 April 1917.

13. *Ellington Press*, 19 April 1917; *Slater Rustler*, 24 May 1917; *Missouri Ruralist*, 5 June, 5 August 1917; Council of Defense Letterbook, 23 August 1917, 18 May 1918.

14. Vera B. Schuttler, *A History of the Missouri Farm Bureau Federation*, p. 19.

bureaus. Only about thirty existed in 1919, and fewer than 10 percent of Missouri farmers reported participating in cooperative activities that year.[15] It would take the crisis of the 1930s to get the farm bureau movement in Missouri off the ground.

Missouri farmers were a conservative lot, but in a much deeper sense than is suggested by that overused term. Farming is a hard way to make a living today, and it was harder still in 1918, closer to the forces of nature, lonelier, not as cash oriented, and a long way from a Jeffersonian utopia. No air-conditioned tractor cabs insulated farmers from the weather; indeed, few had tractors. Farm wives cooked over wood stoves and pumped water from wells or cisterns or drew it from springs. The telephone diminished the loneliness for many, but farm people lived isolated lives. The average farmer made about $1.35 a day, supplemented by the egg money of the women and winter trapping by the boys. Farmers handled little cash, however, running up tabs in stores in town and paying off once or twice a year. The new Internal Revenue Service complained that Missouri farmers kept no account books and seldom knew where they stood in terms of money, which made them difficult to tax. But farmers could describe their lives in detail in terms of nature and usually did. The weather was good or bad, the crops were good or bad, the animals did well or poorly. Farmers always had to deal with natural forces beyond their control; increasingly they had to deal with market forces beyond their control also. They resented the towns and cities that attracted their best young people and that seemed bent on profiting from the vulnerability of rural folk. As one Franklin County farmer put it, "There is no money in the country . . . no entertainments, no schools, no roads, no loveliness, only ceaseless toil and chores . . . . Why blame the boys and girls for leaving home?"[16]

And yet farmers did not jump at the chance to get out from under, whether by joining a farm organization or by appealing for government aid. They suspected the motives of the leaders of farm organizations, and they worried more about what their government would do *to* them than about what it might do *for* them. Nor were they happy about a war whose spokesmen in government and business were not to be trusted. The impact of the war, depriving the farm of young men and scarce money, confirmed their worst fears.[17]

Actually, neither Hirth nor Mumford expected Missouri farmers to go along with the demands for increased production without some inducement. Both the *Ruralist* and the *Farmer* called on the government to regulate the middlemen. They also demanded money. In July 1917 Hirth sent a tele-

15. *Missouri Ruralist*, 5 June 1917, 5 May 1918, 5 July 1917; *Missouri on Guard* 2 (July 1917): 1; *Fourteenth Census: Agriculture*, 6:48–49.

16. *Missouri Farmer*, 1 May, 15 May 1918; *Slater News*, 1 February 1917; *Missouri Ruralist*, 5 July, 20 November 1917; *Springfield Republican*, 19 January 1918; *Papers*, folder 198.

17. Danbom, *Resisted Revolution*, pp. 3–22, 98–117.

gram to Sen. Thomas P. Gore, chairman of the agriculture committee: "Time has come when farmers should know what Congress intends to do about fixing wheat and oat prices because threshing season is about to begin . . . If price of less than two dollars per bushel is fixed on wheat few farmers will sow wheat this fall . . . ."[18] In August, Mumford telegraphed Herbert Hoover, "Does government guarantee farmers two dollars bushel for wheat? Very important definite statement regarding this matter be made immediately otherwise wheat acreage will not be increased."[19] The government responded, and before planting time it had guaranteed prices for winter wheat at over $2.25 per bushel, or about a dollar over the prewar price. It fixed prices on no other crop, however, and only fixed hog prices the following October, a few days before the war ended.[20]

Of course not all farmers would respond to such an inducement. Some had the cash flow and the inclination to respond positively to modernization and the benefits of a war economy, plus the land and machinery to devote to specialization in staple crops. These were the men who joined farm organizations and did increase their production through expanded acreage and improved methods. Over time, they grew in power as their less flexible and less efficient neighbors were driven out. Even the labor crisis benefited a few farmers by accelerating modernization as the Missouri Council of Defense, the farm press, and implement dealers urged the importance of the gasoline engine in meeting the demands of the war. With so many farm boys, as well as mules and horses, off to war, there was a real possibility that the vital 1917 crop might rot in the fields. Agricultural experts scorned the notion of enforced levies of townsmen to work the harvest, claiming that their lack of experience would only hamper the war effort. Tractors, however, were the wave of the future, and manufacturers spread the word, holding tractor shows to demonstrate their wares and conducting schools to teach farmers the new technology. They suggested that buying a tractor might be a patriotic act. And some farmers responded, but not so many that purchase of a tractor ceased to be a big story for the local press; and by the end of the war only about 3 percent of the state's farmers had actually bought tractors.[21]

Those farmers who did modernize their operations did so for a variety of reasons. No doubt support for the war was one. And the prospect of making a killing in wheat must have been attractive. Many farmers in Missouri agreed with the agricultural experts in Columbia that adaptation to modernization was easier, and more profitable, than resistance. And unquestion-

18. *Missouri Farmer*, July 1917.

19. Copy in Council of Defense Letterbook, 18 August 1917.

20. *St. Louis Post-Dispatch*, 27 October 1918, p. 5B.

21. *Missouri Ruralist*, 20 April 1917; 4 January, 20 July 1918; *Slater Rustler*, 5 May 1917; *Springfield Republican*, 9 June, 3 August 1917, 21 March 1918; Council of Defense Letterbook, 22 May 1918; Ira Reed to Saunders, 28 May 1918, *Papers*, folder 67.

ably many benefited, at least financially, although the collapse of the rural economy in the 1920s must have come as a cruel blow. But for a time they reaped the harvest. They also helped feed a world at war.

Missouri saw significant changes in agricultural production during the war years. Corn, the state's leading crop, declined, while wheat, the war crop, increased. The percentage of farms growing corn dropped off slightly, from 87 to 86 percent during the decade 1909–1919.[22] Farms growing wheat rose from 28 percent to 54 percent during the same period. Acreage changed more radically: corn fell 21.7 percent while wheat rose 126 percent. The actual amount of acreage indicates the nature of the change. Corn acreage dropped from approximately 7.1 million in 1909 to 5.6 million in 1919; wheat jumped from 2.0 million acres to 4.6 million. Obviously farmers shifted from corn to wheat, probably during the war years, when it paid them to do so. Wheat increased in value by 368 percent during the decade, thanks mainly to high demand, and corn rose only 104 percent. Yet by the end only slightly more than half Missouri's farmers were growing wheat, while well over three-fourths still grew corn. Furthermore, at the end of the war, when only 14 percent of farm land was in wheat, 17 percent was still in corn, while 47 percent was in pasture. The shift to wheat, therefore, was dramatic, but perhaps not quite so dramatic as increased prices and the urgings of war boosters might have predicted.

A close look at three counties of roughly the same size serves to illustrate. Knox County, in the northeast corner of Missouri, had 302,841 acres in farm land and saw an increase in wheat acreage from 660 in 1917 to 22,220 in 1919. (The 1917 wheat crop was in the ground long before America entered the war, and the 1919 crop had been planted before the Armistice and its price was guaranteed by the government.) The jump in acreage in Knox County was over 3,000 percent. Lincoln County, just north of St. Louis, had 343,700 acres in farm land and experienced only an 80 percent rise in wheat acreage. But Lincoln was already producing 52,642 acres of wheat in 1917 and increased its output to 95,130 in 1919. Ste. Genevieve County, south of St. Louis, experienced an increase in wheat acreage of only 18 percent, one of the lowest in the state. The county had 229,762 acres in farm land, and wheat went from 17,793 acres in 1917 to 21,110 in 1919.

Corn acreage in these three counties changed as well. In Knox, where wheat production grew so remarkably, corn remained paramount, going from 67,005 acres in 1917 to 79,640 in 1918 before dropping to 39,670 in 1919, still almost twice the acreage in wheat. In Lincoln and Ste. Genevieve, wheat overtook corn. In Lincoln County corn went from 53,882 acres to 72,130 by 1919. In Ste. Genevieve County corn dropped from 23,813 acres to 14,840 acres in 1919. Thus Knox County had such a dramatic increase in wheat because it had grown almost none in 1917; it was chiefly a corn county and

22. *Fourteenth Census: Agriculture*, 6:567–615, for crop data.

remained so throughout the war, though the increase in wheat acres planted could be accounted for by the drop in corn acreage. In the other two counties corn and wheat had been fairly evenly balanced before the war, but wheat had taken the lead by 1919. And it appears that farmers interested in growing a war crop of wheat did so by turning corn fields into wheat fields rather than by plowing up pasture land, which takes more time and money to accomplish.

Other significant changes occurred. The number of farms, which had grown between 1860 and 1900, declined 2.7 percent between 1900 and 1910 and dropped another 5.1 percent during the next decade. Improved land in farms grew by over 15 percent each decade from 1880 to 1900, grew 7.3 percent between 1900 and 1910, but rose only 1 percent by 1920. Since so much Missouri farm land was unimproved during the war years, this cannot suggest that farmers ran out of land to improve. At the same time, the number of small and average-size farms (average being about 130 acres) declined while the number of large farms grew. Farms under 20 acres dropped 15.8 percent between 1909 and 1919; farms 20 to 49 acres dropped 13.3 percent; farms 50 to 99 acres declined 9.1 percent; those between 100 and 174 fell off less than 1 percent. Farms between 500 and 999 acres and those over 1,000 acres, which had declined during the previous decade, reversed the trend, growing 7.5 percent and 19.3 percent respectively during the 1909–1919 period.

Other data shed more light. The number of farms reporting expenditure for fertilizer rose 157 percent, but only 6.6 percent of farmers reported using fertilizer in 1909 and 18 percent reported using it in 1919. The amount of money spent on fertilizer rose sharply, from $671,073 in 1909 to $3,941,488 in 1919. Thus a fairly small number of farmers accounted for a fairly large increase in the amount of money spent on fertilizer. The change in mortgage indebtedness suggests who may have accounted for the increases in farm size and improved farming techniques (as indicated by the use of fertilizer). Between 1909 and 1919, only 7.4 percent of all farms reported an increase in the amount of mortgage indebtedness, but the amount of increase reported was 92 percent. Thus a handful of farmers accounted for a large increase in indebtedness. Perhaps they used the money to buy up smaller farms, or to improve farming techniques. Certainly a farmer with enough money, or who was willing to go into debt, could put in a couple of quick wheat crops on already prepared land more easily than he could open new acreage on his own. Thus, given government wheat prices, buying another farm might be a safe gamble.

Mumford and his allies urged farmers to increase output, especially of wheat, for the war and offered price supports as inducement. Wheat output did increase, but farmers did not abandon corn in favor of wheat. Further, after the war ended, and price supports with it, acreage data for 1920 indicates that those Missouri farmers who had put acreage to wheat returned to planting corn. Almost half of Missouri farm acreage was still in pasture in 1919, which means that Missouri farmers did not rush to increase acreage under cultivation as a war measure. They just cut back on corn, or bought a small neighboring farm, and turned the land to wheat for a few years. Obviously some people must have made money this way, but they probably kept it for themselves, since most were not buying war bonds. So few farmers went into debt, and so few bought fertilizer or invested in a tractor, that it is clear that there was no rush to modernize by the vast majority. In the meantime, the war had precisely the impact predicted by many opponents. The total number of farms, especially of small and medium-sized farms, declined, while the number of large farms grew. Perhaps, as in the case of war bonds, it was the big operators who supported the war, made the change from corn to wheat, expanded acreage and improved techniques, and made money in the process.

But if some farmers expanded to take advantage of government price supports, it took time for that expansion to take effect. When America entered the war, the 1917 wheat crop was just beginning to sprout, and it would be more than a year before the 1918 crop could be harvested. A similar time lag prevented any sudden increase in livestock production, since animals bred for the war would not bear for some months. Nature has its own seasons and does not mobilize well. The American people would have to tighten their belts and feed themselves and their allies from existing supplies for months to come. The federal government recognized the problem and hurriedly began a nationwide program of food conservation. While asking producers to grow more, the government pressured consumers to eat less.

Specifically, the fighting men needed fats (mainly beef and pork), wheat, and sugar. To secure the needed supplies Congress created the United States Food Administration. Relying on a philosophy of voluntarism and eschewing bureaucratization, food administrator Herbert Hoover hoped to bring together dedicated professionals like himself to run the agency, men who, despite their particular areas of expertise, understood large organizations and the economy, men who were problem solvers, who could make executive decisions. He sought a flexible, decentralized agency that worked with existing local institutions and leaders. Primarily, he intended to rely on "the unselfish patriotic spirit engendered by the war . . . the intense longing for participation in war service on the part of [a] thoroughly aroused citizenship." Like McAdoo, Hoover also hoped to teach thrift, economy, simple living, and efficiency.[23]

Thus Hoover and his followers saw themselves as a living embodiment of that "unselfish patriotic spirit" that longed for a role in some great national enterprise, and they assumed people shared this sentiment. They did not

23. Hoover to R. A. Green, 15 October 1917, *Papers*, folder 47; William C. Mullendore, *History of the United States Food Administration, 1917–1919*, pp. 80–81.

Courtesy Western Historical Manuscripts Collection, Columbia, Missouri.

recognize that while they, as a new class of professionals, sought to justify their rise to power through participation in the war, most farmers, workers, and housewives did not.

The Missouri Food Administration worked to implement various conservation programs under the direction of Hoover's office. It encouraged gardening and canning, warned against hoarding, and asked people to pledge to follow certain guidelines in eating less. It tried to restrict consumption by asking people to observe meatless and wheatless days, whether at home or dining out. It tried to teach housewives greater efficiency. It engaged in a massive advertising campaign for conservation. Yet voluntarism failed to yield enough food, or enough war supporters, and so the government began a program of quasi-rationing, controlling processing and distribution through licensing powers and federal supervision, through government purchases, and in some cases by simply ordering reduced consumption of certain needed foods. There were no ration cards, nothing like the system that prevailed in the next generation's war, but the combination of scarcity and high prices, plus a strong measure of chaos, achieved the same ends. Consumption decreased and America fed herself and her allies.

One approach was organized gardening. Missourians had been gardening and canning for years. With wartime inflation after 1914 it became more popular, especially in urban areas. After April 1917 the Food Administration tried to turn this activity into a war measure. Libraries listed books on gardening. Local newspapers published instructions on the best methods of growing, the best crops to grow, and the best ways to preserve the produce. Large corporations did their part by offering their vacant land to "responsible" people at as little as a dollar a year for gardening; mining companies donated land to the wives and children of employees.

The Missouri Food Administration sought to achieve control of preservation of garden produce. It tried to arrange to have all information on, and supplies of, canning materials channeled through its offices. Working with the College of Agriculture, the administration disseminated information on growing and preserving foods and sent home demonstration agents around the state. These agents, young ladies from the college's new "home economics" department or middle-class housewives from the suburbs, were to teach proper methods of homemaking to rural and urban women in much the same way that college experts and businessmen would teach Missouri farmers how to farm better. The home demonstration agents would not only show women how to conserve food for the war, but also how to manage a modern home in a clean, healthy manner, making it a joy to live in and a service to the state for years to come.[24]

24. St. Louis Post-Dispatch, 4 March 1917, p. 8; 16 March 1917, p. 1; 18 June 1917, p. 16; 6 January 1918, p. 4B; Milan Republican, 19 April 1917; Springfield Republican, 1, 3, 4 May, 24 June, 10 July, 18 December 1917; 23 February, 24 March 1918; Missouri on Guard 1 (July 1917): 1.

The gardening and canning movement was largely a failure. In the first place, garden produce could not overnight replace meat, wheat, and sugar in the average diet; and fresh vegetables could not be sent overseas. Also, successful gardening takes time and skill. Ground must be prepared and plants tended. Farm wives had experience with gardening and canning, but urban gardeners often lacked the time, the land, and the skill to grow enough to make a difference in either their food bills or the war effort. Housewives, furthermore, proved just as resistant to Mumford's ideas of efficiency as they had before the war. By 1918 fear of the federal government was so widespread that the Council of Defense felt compelled to remind people that rumors that the government intended to confiscate their preserved food were "false, and come originally from the enemy or from friends of the enemy."[25]

The Food Administration hoped to win public approval by controlling food middlemen. Hoover's opponents in the Senate, Missourian James Reed among them, harped constantly on this theme, claiming that the new war agency would benefit the big packers and millers and hurt consumers and farmers. The Missouri farm press and editorials in urban dailies kept up a constant harassing fire against food processors.[26] Hoover promised that he would work to control speculators and profiteers, that the great power he sought would be used for the public good.[27]

And, indeed, the Food Administration began with the best intentions. In order to prevent a food crisis, and to quiet criticism, it sought to prevent speculation in needed foodstuffs, to keep food moving to consumers both at home and in the trenches, and to prevent the kind of uncertainty that led to hoarding.[28] Agencies such as a federal wheat corporation would regulate supply, distribution, and consumption, including all purchasing and exporting for military purposes. Thus the Food Administration could regulate prices and perhaps avoid the kinds of "embalmed beef" scandals that had occurred during the previous war. Food processors had to acquire licenses if they did over a specified amount of business. Smaller middlemen could be dealt with by regulating their suppliers. Profits were to be restricted to prewar levels, 2.5 percent in the case of meatpackers, for instance. Violators were subject to fine and imprisonment.[29]

Food retailers also came under Food Administration guidelines. Grocers were told to display administration posters ordering people to conserve. This the Food Administration took as a sign of voluntary support for its

25. *Missouri on Guard* 1 (April 1918): 1.

26. *St. Louis Post-Dispatch*, 17 March 1917, p. 14; 18 June 1917, p. 12; 6 August 1917, p. 4; *Springfield Republican*, 1 July 1917.

27. *Springfield Republican*, 11 July 1917.

28. *Missouri on Guard* 1 (December 1917): 2.

29. *Springfield Republican*, 4 November, 25 November 1917; Missouri Food Administration Letterbook, 10 December 1917, 5 January 1918.

programs by retailers. The administration instructed its agents at the local level that it was "the purpose of the poster pledge campaign . . . to put every retailer on record, either for or against the government." And it added, "It is entirely optional with the retailer whether he signs . . . or not." But the administration ordered its workers to keep an eye on their local dealers. "If the poster is not exhibited, we should know the reason why."[30]

Thus the new voluntarism.

One of Hoover's professionals, a leading hotel man, organized a section on public eating places within the Food Administration. Clubs, dining cars, hotels, and restaurants were to demonstrate their patriotism by reducing food portions and taking sugar bowls off tables. They also were to observe wheatless and meatless days and to display Food Administration posters. It quickly became apparent, however, that only about half the eating establishments in Missouri would participate voluntarily, so public eating houses fell under federal licensing regulations, and by late 1918 certain conservation measures were compulsory. Customers complained about this state of affairs because, while the quantity and quality of the food fell, prices remained the same.[31]

Hoover's efforts to regulate food middlemen also amounted to little. Just as many restaurants refused to lower prices to accompany smaller portions, other middlemen profiteered as well. Hoover's assertions that his administration constantly had its finger on the food production and distribution pulse of the world were challenged by Senator Reed, who claimed that Hoover wielded dictatorial power and that his agency protected the packing and milling trusts. The press seconded Reed's charges. In his *Missouri Farmer* column, William Hirth insisted that "centralized wealth starves the people" and that food speculators were "camp followers . . . ghouls who do not hesitate to coin human misery into personal gain." And Federal Trade Commission reports that large packing firms had doubled their profits while millers had tripled theirs lent support to these and other attacks.[32]

Hoover's voluntarism campaign reached a peak in the food pledge drives. During the summer of 1917 the government tried to get housewives to sign a pledge promising to try to conserve food for the war effort. Mrs. Walter McNab Miller led the campaign in Missouri. Mrs. Miller accepted the Council of Defense's characterization of food conservation as "women's work" and sought to demonstrate that women could make a significant contribution to the war effort as organizers and workers. Mrs. Miller and her fol-

30. Food Administration Letterbook, 29 January 1918; *Missouri on Guard* 1 (February 1918): 1.

31. Mullendore, *History*, pp. 96–97; Saunders to Mumford, 17 December 1917, *Papers*, folder 89.

32. *Springfield Republican*, 29 January, 12 April, 9 July 1918; Food Administration Letterbook, 29 January 1918; *St. Louis Post-Dispatch*, 18 August 1918, p. 2; 29 June 1918, p. 3; *Missouri Farmer*, 15 April, 15 May 1917; *Savannah Reporter*, 25 May 1917.

Do you know the crooked people
Who have a crooked smile
And give a crooked reason
To cover up their guile?
They eat their white bread
          every meal,
Make syrup of their tea:
They eat their meat
And do their bit
For Bill and   Germany.
                    -George Nardin-
                    -Copyright-

This offbeat piece of propaganda, which appeared in the *Columbia Missourian* on 15 April 1918, is an example of the more heavy-handed approach to encouraging cooperation that often occurred at the local level. The poem is credited to George Nardin, the artwork to "G. M. Wheat." Courtesy State Historical Society of Missouri, Columbia.

lowers enthusiastically sought to enroll as many of the women in Missouri as possible, instructing teachers to enroll all female students over the age of sixteen. She told one worker to get signatures from all the patients at the local "feeble minded sanitarium." Women set up registration booths in rural towns on market day and went out into the countryside in search of signatures.[33] In urban areas, middle-class women accompanied by policemen ventured into ethnic and racial neighborhoods trying to sign up Italian, Polish, and black women. One worker positively bubbled at her success: "We met not one who refused to take the pledge that made them privates in Hoover's Army."[34] In addition, women who claimed that they were already saving as much as possible simply to live on were enrolled as having taken the pledge.

Actually, this campaign failed to get the desired number of signatures. Mrs. Miller admitted the failure, as did Food Administration historian William Mullendore years later. Both put it down to lack of time to organize, lack of money for publicity, and lack of organizing experience on the part of women workers.[35] But, while Mrs. Miller and her followers won the respect of the council's leaders, few Missouri women went along. They had not favored entry into the war any more than men had. Even those who wanted to help often lacked experience in the kind of mobilization required, and Miller complained that the time allowed was too brief to let new ideas of total participation sink in.[36] Despite these excuses, Missouri housewives often responded with a vehemence that indicates not mere inefficiency, but actual opposition. Some set dogs on the food campaign workers who called, or angrily slammed doors in their faces. And under these circumstances, some workers were reluctant to push their neighbors too far. "I'm sorry that you did not feel that it was worth while to make an extra effort to get signatures," chided Miller in a letter to a colleague.[37]

The food pledge drive could not have come at a worse time. Many farm women were busy with harvest and could not be bothered. Many urban women were afraid to sign up. The campaign unfortunately coincided with conscription, and some women worried that the government would draft them as well, confiscating their preserved food and pressing them into service once it had their names and addresses. "People have come to me in tears," Miller wrote Hoover, "saying that the government was going to take them out of their homes and send them to France and various other places,

33. Mullendore, *History*, p. 86; Miller to Mrs. E. M. Shepard, 6 July 1917, *Papers*, folder 888; Miller to R. W. Wilbur, 3 September 1917, folder 409.

34. *St. Louis Post-Dispatch*, 15 July 1917, editorial section, p. 1.

35. Mullendore, *History*, p. 86; Miller to Wilbur, 10 September 1917, *Papers*, folder 410.

36. ? to Mumford, 13 September 1917, *Papers*, folder 78; Saunders to Hill, 17 October 1917, folder 26.

37. Miller to Wilbur, 10 September 1917, *Papers*, folder 410; Miller to Mrs. C. S. Bohn, 5 September 1917, folder 1126.

as soon as they could get their names . . . ." Food campaigners insisted that the pledge was voluntary and simply gave women a chance to promise to do what they could to aid the war effort. They would certainly not be drafted, nor would their food be taken. But conscription provided women with a working model of mobilization, and no appeals could overcome their fears, especially if there was a policeman standing by.[38]

A revised Hoover Food Pledge got underway in the fall. Donald Farnsworth, a federal official stationed in Kansas City, supervised the campaign for Missouri, Kansas, and Oklahoma. Farnsworth immediately antagonized the chief war boosters in Missouri. As a result, though in theory the council was not supposed to get involved, Mumford and the county councils, especially the women's committees, did the organizing and legwork involved.[39] This time, however, the government sought the participation, not just of housewives, but of virtually the entire population. "Under no circumstances," directed the council, "should the campaign cease until EVERY MAN, WOMAN, AND CHILD [over age ten] in every Missouri county has had a chance to sign a pledge list."[40] In this way the council sought a minimum of two million signatures, or about 70 percent of the population.[41]

The war boosters had various goals in the food pledge campaign. For Hoover it doubtless appeared to be a perfect test of voluntarism. William F. Saunders, secretary of the Missouri Council of Defense, hoped the pledge drive would educate people on the importance of food conservation and the Food Administration's role in winning the war. To Mumford the pledge drive served as a measure of war support that would enable every Missourian to show exactly where he stood.[42]

The pledge was also designed to persuade people to conserve food. The Food Administration disseminated guidelines on how to do this. Of twenty-one possible meals during the week, Americans were to go without wheat at eleven of them and without meat another eleven: no wheat at all on Wednesdays, no meat on Thursdays, no pork on Saturdays. No meat at breakfast and no wheat at supper, seven days a week. Even Mumford admitted, "The practical housekeepers tell me that it's almost impossible to serve a single meal without some wheat," and avoiding meat so extensively was almost as difficult.[43]

38. *Springfield Republican*, 15 July 1917; Bohn to Miller, July 1918, *Papers*, folder 1126; Miller to Hoover, 10 July 1917, folder 164; Breen, *Uncle Sam at Home*, p. 124.

39. Mumford to Saunders, 22 September 1917, *Papers*, folder 79; Saunders to Hill, 17 October 1917, folder 26.

40. See "Apportionment Lists—Cities and Counties," n.d., *Papers*, folder 62.

41. A. J. Meyer to Saunders, 17 October 1917, *Papers*, folder 63; Ferrell, *Woodrow Wilson and World War I*, p. 94, for results nationwide.

42. Hoover to Robert Green, 15 October 1917, *Papers*, folder 47; Saunders to Hill, 17 October 1917, folder 26; Mumford to "Bankers of Missouri," n.d., folder 70.

43. *Slater Rustler*, 14 February 1918; Food Administration Letterbook, 18 February 1918; Mumford to Saunders, 18 October 1917, *Papers*, folder 82.

In practice, the people running the food pledge campaign regarded it more as a means of mobilizing mass participation in the war effort than as a practical method of conservation. The Food Administration launched a massive public relations campaign designed to confront people at every turn with propaganda. Food pledge workers distributed films, cartoons, and slides and saw to it that posters appeared "on all available outdoor premises." They sent out hundreds of speakers and home demonstration agents.[44] With the help of education groups and of Uel Lamkin, Missouri school superintendent, the Food Administration bombarded thousands of schoolchildren with "lessons on Community and national life" and told them how to save food by signing the pledge and helping Mom at home. Some twenty-five hundred clergymen received prepackaged sermon outlines to present on the Sunday before the campaign began, and some, at least, complied.[45] The campaign sought to appeal to deeply entrenched beliefs and community values, such as neighborliness in a crisis. However, it also attempted to redefine the community by enlarging it to include the entire nation, by focusing goals outward, against the Hun or for worldwide democracy, rather than inward, on improving life within the community.

Some Food Administration propaganda sought to exploit anticorporate sentiment. One film included a "strong melodramatic attack on the food speculator through a romantic story of which the farm girl is the heroine," in an effort to reach both producer and consumer. One of the administration's cartoons showed the "food speculator, a loaf of bread in one hand, and squeezing some of the common people in the other, smoke forming a dollar mark coming from the cigar in his mouth."[46]

The campaigners also tried scare tactics. Signatures on the food pledge would be regarded by "everyone" as the "yardstick of patriotism" by which Missourians would be measured. In addition, if people did not sign the pledge in great numbers, Americans would appear weak and irresolute, which would cause despair among the Allies and rejoicing among the enemy, with unforeseen consequences. Most important, failure to sign would fatally weaken America's war effort. It would "sign the death warrant for a large part of the half million American boys who will soon be at the fighting front."[47]

The war workers in Missouri took precautions to prevent anyone from slipping past them. They saw to it that "children will be registered at the schools, the men at their places of business, the women in their homes." Preachers took names after services. Nine thousand teachers, under orders from Lamkin, enrolled their students during classes, and their county su-

44. Saunders to Hill, 2 November 1917, *Papers,* folder 46; Mullendore, *History,* pp. 89–93.

45. Mumford to County Chairmen, n.d., *Papers,* folder 70; Saunders to Mumford, 22 October 1917, folder 82; Saunders to Fleming, 7 June 1918, folder 29.

46. Saunders to Hill, 25 October 1917, *Papers,* folder 46.

47. *St. Louis Post-Dispatch,* 5 November 1917, p. 2; *Missouri on Guard* 1 (November 1917): 1.

perintendents followed up to make sure they did their jobs well. Workers went door to door. Government officials at all levels were enrolled. The Food Administration called upon bankers to enroll influential business-men. War workers even gave pledge cards to city policemen, who stopped people on the streets and asked them to sign.[48]

In spite of all this effort on the part of so many, the food pledge campaign to enlist support for the war failed: war workers obtained fewer than half the number of signatures they sought.[49] Enrollment of students was considered "a stroke of genius" since children enrolled at a much higher rate than adults in some areas, often running as high as 98 percent participation.[50] At least they were recorded as having enrolled. Teachers under pressure from supe-riors'might simply have enrolled entire classes without consulting the indi-viduals in them. The rate of enrollment of workers in some factories ran as high as that of students, but, given the evidence of the bond drives, it is at least possible that coercion was at work here as well.[51] Preachers often wielded considerable influence locally, and it was no doubt difficult to avoid the parson with a pledge list while leaving the church after the sermon. Putting enrollment blanks in the hands of policemen was equally inspired, for it resulted in thousands of additional signatures.[52]

As in the case of the bond drives, everywhere people turned they were confronted with someone asking them to sign up to support the war. And the issue was put in precisely those terms, with various threats, implied or stated, often lying behind them. The Missouri Food Administration wanted very much to succeed in this campaign, and it continued to accept names long after the enrollment period had officially ended. Finally, however, Mumford could claim only slightly more than a million names, or about half the target figure.[53]

The campaign did poorly in part because of economic forces beyond any-one's control. With prices high, food scarce, and the newspapers full of sto-ries about food profiteers, Missourians complained bitterly about being asked to conserve food. They resented being told to starve themselves by "fat, pampered advocates of economy," whether they were millionaire min-ing engineers in Washington or well-to-do women in their hometowns. One war worker complained that it was a "nasty, thankless job trying to get poor

48. *St. Louis Post-Dispatch*, 2 November 1917, p. 16; Saunders to Hill, 24 October 1917, *Papers*, folder 46; Saunders to Mumford, 22 October 1917, folder 82; Mumford to County Chairmen, n.d., folder 70.

49. Saunders to T. J. Talbert, 20 December 1917, *Papers*, folder 178; Breen, *Uncle Sam at Home*, p. 123.

50. Saunders to Hill, 2 November 1917, *Papers*, folder 46; *St. Louis Post-Dispatch*, 18 November 1917, p. 16.

51. See *Papers*, folder 1000.

52. Saunders to Farnsworth, 11 November 1917, *Papers*, folder 17.

53. Saunders to Mumford, 3 January 1918, *Papers*, folder 70; Talbert to Saunders, 27 May 1918, folder 180.

people to save with teaspoons." A farm wife, confronted by pledge workers while working in her field, "said if we would give [a pledge card] to her she would wipe her butt with it, [she] wasn't going to feed rich people."[54]

The council feared that "alien influences," which they insisted had worked against the bond drives, were also hampering the food pledge. The council admitted that German influence was very strong in some areas of the state and in many cases was "hindering enrollment by cautious discouragement." In rural Missouri, whole settlements of German-Americans refused to sign. In other areas, where German-Americans were not concentrated, "almost all [canvassers] have tales of encounters with vicious women who are not in sympathy with" the food drive. Thus, while Missourians could not easily avoid the draft, they could refuse to sign a pledge promising to support the war. And even if the pledge workers worked hard to get signatures, people could, and did, retreat into their communities and their homes, reasonably secure in the knowledge that neighbors and family members would not ostracize them for resisting the war in one of the few ways open to them.[55]

Whether other ethnic communities had the same insulating effect as did the German-American is impossible to confirm. The fact that pledge workers took policemen with them when visiting certain neighborhoods suggests that they expected to find a situation that might require a blue uniform to overcome. But other ethnic communities in Missouri were much smaller and were often less entrenched, less cohesive, so that particular tactic may have succeeded. In any case, ethnicity alone cannot account for the failure of the pledge workers to reach their goal.

The Food Administration demonstrated with its pledge drive that the war lacked support in Missouri. Mumford had intended it to be a measure of support for the war, and by his own yardstick, Missourians had failed to measure up, especially considering the considerable pressure applied. Too many people resented Wilson's promising to keep America out of war while running for office in 1916, then leading the nation into war when in office. As a woman in Savannah, Missouri, put it, "The president has not treated us right . . . when he was running for President he promised to keep us out of WAR." Mrs. Wirt Ball, also of Savannah, refused to sign the food pledge because "she don't think this is a free country any more."[56]

Some refused because they felt the government made unfair demands on consumers. A man in Marion County became very aggressive when approached, claiming that the government "couldn't touch him, couldn't dic-

54. *Missouri Ruralist*, 5 July 1917, p. 1; C. E. Fields to Council of Defense, 30 November 1917, *Papers*, folder 1128; see also lists of names in folder 887. Such lists often appear in county folders, listed alphabetically in the Council of Defense Papers.

55. Saunders to Hill, 2 November 1917, *Papers*, folder 46; *Missouri on Guard* 1 (November 1917): 3; *Springfield Republican*, 11 November 1917.

56. See Andrews County folder in *Papers*.

tate to him about his family." When a Marion County schoolgirl told her family she had registered for the food drive in class, they "gave her corn bread for supper that night and when she didn't like it they told [her she] had to eat it." The girl's eldest brother was "in the draft army," and the family thought they had done enough for the war. Many people claimed that they could not economize any further, and some insisted they would eat all that they could afford regardless of the federal government.[57]

The Missouri Food Administration's efforts failed when people withdrew into their homes, their families, their communities. People locked their doors and would not answer the pledge worker's knock. They withstood propaganda from the pulpit, from teachers, from community leaders; they withstood pressure from the police and from government agents. The people in charge of the food drive insisted that resistance was more than mere refusal to sign a pledge card: it was slacking, opposition to the war, treason, it was killing American soldiers. But Missourians still refused to sign.

By January 1918 the failure of voluntarism combined with a severe wheat shortage caused a crisis in the Allied camp. The Food Administration announced that Americans would be required to cut wheat consumption by forty-two million bushels per month. Hoover decided that, since there would always be slackers, "some repressive regulation must be used," even in Missouri, which made a better showing than almost every other state in the nation. Obviously there were more slackers than first suspected.[58]

The Food Administration began in early 1918 to issue instructions to food processors, manufacturers, and consumers on how much food to save and how to save it. With wheat in short supply, bread attracted most of the attention, but the government also needed sugar. Producers of candy, soft drinks, and chewing gum had to cut the amount of sugar used by 20 percent. Sugar regulations restricted consumers to two pounds per person per month, although three pounds was closer to the average consumption rate.[59] Bakers were ordered to use only 75 percent wheat flour; the rest was to be such wheat substitutes as oat flour or corn meal. Bakers were to devote one business day a week to the sale of products made with wheat substitutes. The habit of selling day-old bread back to wholesalers, who then sold it for hog feed, was stopped, and hog growers turned to garbage as a substitute.[60]

The government also tried to impose controls on wheat middlemen. The Food Administration told flour millers to inventory everything they had, to get more flour out of their wheat, and to cut waste and raise efficiency. Mil-

57. Marion County folder, ibid.

58. Cuff, "Herbert Hoover," p. 370; *Missouri on Guard* 1 (February 1918): 4.

59. Mullendore, *History*, pp. 112–14; Food Administration Bulletin, 3 August 1918; *Missouri on Guard* 2 (August 1918): 3; Food Administration Letterbook, 18 May 1918.

60. Mullendore, *History*, pp. 104–7; *Springfield Republican*, 26 January 1918; *Missouri on Guard* 2 (July 1918): 4.

lers were also to cut shipments of flour to private dealers by 30 percent, which was in turn to be sent to the government.[61] Most important, the government sought to restrict sales to consumers. From mid-February 1918 to near the end of the war, consumers had to purchase substitutes with their wheat flour on a one-for-one basis. Farmers exchanging wheat for flour at mills did not have to take substitutes, but farmers buying flour in stores did. Purchases were restricted to six pounds per person per month, although ten pounds per adult was average. Nor could consumers keep more than one month's supply on hand, to prevent even the appearance of hoarding. In this way the United States saved some eighty-five million bushels of wheat, which, along with an additional twenty-one million imported from Argentina and Australia, enabled America and its allies to survive until the harvest was in.[62]

There were problems with compliance. The job of enforcing federal restrictions fell upon retailers, who had to keep track of who bought how much and to report unusually large purchases, or unfamiliar purchasers, to their local food administrator. At the same time, retailers had to deal with customers angry about scarcities, about restrictions, about high prices. Consumers blamed retailers for price gouging, and retailers blamed consumers for hoarding and getting them into trouble with the Council of Defense. Both blamed millers of substitutes for profiteering. Some retailers, however, violated regulations in favor of their customers, selling them wheat flour without substitutes in violation of regulations.[63]

Regulations meant considerable impositions on consumers. Department of Agriculture encouragement to grow more food, combined with Food Administration seed allocations to producers, caused a surplus of potatoes. They began to clog the system, and soon eating them became a war measure: "Eat Another Potato and Help Win the War." The government especially urged consumption of potato chips.[64] Also, because of other miscalculations, there was a large surplus of certain wheat products that the military did not need, and which had formerly occupied only a marginal place in the average diet. Consequently the increased consumption of pasta and breakfast cereal also became patriotic acts.[65]

In effect the government attempted temporary changes in diet for the

61. *Springfield Republican*, 10 January 1918; Food Administration Letterbook, 10 December 1917.

62. Food Administration Letterbook, 29 January, 19 February, 22 March 1918; Mullendore, *History,* pp. 104–6.

63. Food Administration Letterbook, 17 May, 29 June, 13 July 1918; *Missouri on Guard* 2 (June 1918): 4; *Springfield Republican*, 12 April, 18 April 1918.

64. Food Administration Letterbook, 20 April 1918; *St. Louis Post-Dispatch*, 6 May 1918, p. 3; Robbins to Mumford, 28 October 1918, *Papers*, folder 111.

65. *St. Louis Post-Dispatch*, 4 June 1918, p. 19; Food Administration Letterbook, 4 April 1918; Food Administration Bulletin, 27 July 1918.

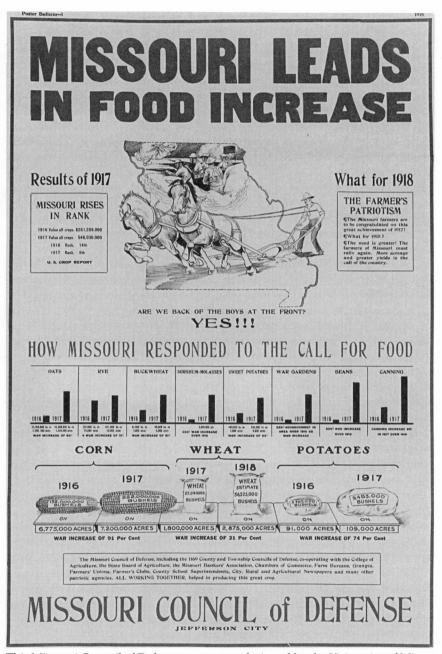

This Missouri Council of Defense poster was designed by the University of Missouri School of Journalism. Posters like this one masked a deeper reality regarding the attitudes and activities of Missouri farmers. Courtesy Western Historical Manuscripts Collection, Columbia, Missouri.

purpose of winning the war. Consumers responded poorly. At the least they complained; many hoarded food; others persuaded retailers to help them evade regulations; and a surplus of oat flour and corn meal quickly became a problem. But there was little else to do. People today who remember the war remember "Victory Bread" as coarse and unappetizing. Indeed, a popular joke at the time had a young mother asking her son, "What on earth are you doing smashing up those strawberry boxes?" He responds, "Aw, we're grindin' 'em up inta flour. Then we're goin' ta make some war bread like yours mamma."[66]

In dealing with the wheat shortage, the Food Administration disrupted local conditions without solving the problems of profiteering and hoarding. When local people complained about high prices, the administration suggested that local middlemen combine to regulate each other and bring down prices. At the same time it instructed local groups, women's committees, or local food administrators to investigate and report violations.[67] But at the national level, despite FTC reports and congressional concern, the packers and the millers continued to profiteer. As a result, the onus of regulation fell on local people, as it had in the draft and bond drives, creating a climate of suspicion and hostility among consumers, retailers, producers, and local war workers. While the local community fragmented, corporations grew in power, and local leaders took much of the heat off national administrators, receiving, in return, political legitimacy that derived not from local loyalties, but from the central government. At the same time, the community, and traditional institutions and relationships within it, often failed to provide protection for those who relied on them.

The government's efforts to increase food supplies during the war produced the necessary food but failed to mobilize support for the war. The government set people against each other by rewarding big producers at the expense of consumers and small producers, by setting retailers against their customers, by encouraging people to spy on each other, by threatening, bribing, coercing people to work for the war. These efforts worked toward a reorganization of society to create a mass loyalty to the central authority, a loyalty that was to transcend, even erase, local ties. The intent was to break down horizontal bonds among people at the local level, replacing them with vertical bonds to Washington. And if this process was not entirely accomplished, it was greatly advanced as people, hoping to avoid the bond salesman, the draft board, the official name-taker, retreated into their homes and into silence, or, in search of workable forms of communication and organization, relied on class as a measure of resistance.

66. *St. Louis Post-Dispatch*, 21 June 1918, "Women's Page." The author followed the recipe for "Victory Bread," and the result was something like cattle feed.

67. Food Administration Letterbook, 21 February, 29 July, 13 July 1918; *St. Louis Post-Dispatch*, 5 April 1918, p. 5; *Springfield Republican*, 10 July 1918; *Missouri on Guard* 2 (June 1918): 4.

Chapter 7

Workers

As it had with agriculture, so the war disrupted American industry. Despite the best efforts of preparedness advocates, the economy proved unable to provide the most basic goods and services necessary for modern warfare. Men and supplies sailed to Europe in the confiscated ships of foreign nations, and the federal government finally had to commandeer the snarled and tottering railway system. Despite glowing promises from inventors and corporate executives, Americans flew British and French planes throughout the war and blasted the Hun with foreign-made tanks and guns. At the same time, taxes and prices rose dramatically, and waste, inefficiency, corruption, and profiteering severely hampered the war effort.[1] To compound matters, the war intensified the struggle between employers and employees.[2]

During the war the government desperately needed and anxiously sought the cooperation of the nation's workers. The specter of antiwar syndicalism haunted war leaders, and even the prospect that conservative trade unions might seek to strengthen their position during the crisis threatened to slow production. Events justified these fears. Just as American participation in the war began, Socialists met at St. Louis in a hastily called convention and overwhelmingly condemned the war. A few months later John H. Hammond of the National Civic Federation told businessmen that, based on a recently completed tour of the nation, workers had failed to respond to the government's efforts to generate enthusiasm for the war. Indeed, American workers, regardless of political orientation, participated only reluctantly in the war effort, and in some cases they resisted vigorously.[3]

The war caused considerable labor unrest in Missouri. A brief glance at

1. Alexander M. Bing, *War-Time Strikes and Their Adjustment*, pp. 1–10, 117–19, 225–35; Russell F. Weigley, *History of the United States Army*, pp. 356, 360–69; Daniel R. Beaver, *Newton D. Baker and the American War Effort, 1917–1919*, pp. 54–59; Edward M. Coffman, *The War to End All Wars*, pp. 20–54 passim.

2. Richard L. Watson, Jr., *The Development of National Power: The United States, 1900–1919*, p. 297; James Weinstein, *The Corporate Ideal in the Liberal State, 1900–1918*, pp. 233–47.

3. Weinstein, *Corporate Ideal*, pp. 136, 233–34; Herbert Peterson and Gilbert Fite, *Opponents of War*, pp. 3–8, 17–19; Bing, *War-Time Strikes*, pp. 1–10, 117–19; Maurine W. Greenwald, *Women, War, and Work: The Impact of World War I on Women Workers in the United States*, pp. 32–35; William Preston, Jr., *Aliens and Dissenters: Federal Suppression of Radicals, 1903–1933*.

the urban press during late 1917 and most of 1918 suggests that Missouri workers had exploded in an endless series of strikes. Workers and bosses fought violent battles over such traditional issues as union recognition, the closed shop, and wages and hours, while the government demanded that they all quit squabbling and return to war production. Both groups took advantage of the crisis: management tried to grasp windfall profits and crush unions, and workers sought to expand organization and capture some of the windfall for themselves; and both sought government intervention to tip the balance in their favor. The result was class conflict throughout Missouri that solidified both groups into contending camps, confirmed the government's role as mediator, and seriously crippled war production in the state.

The federal government had hoped to avoid trouble by granting labor representation in the high councils of war. President Wilson appointed Samuel Gompers of the American Federation of Labor as the workers' representative on the Council of National Defense. After the declaration of war, Gompers helped develop the American Alliance for Labor and Democracy, a Committee of Public Information front group that was to provide a haven for the few prowar socialists and labor radicals that existed.[4] The government also tried to stabilize employer-employee relations. It opposed competitive bidding for workers by employers, since this led to excessive mobility among the labor force and threatened to leave crucial industries without enough workers at a crucial stage of production. Thus the government established a federal employment service to serve as a clearing house for the needs of employers and an agency for allocating workers. Unfortunately, this program did not get fully underway until the war was almost over.[5]

The government also established numerous agencies to deal with potential labor problems, especially wage and hour disputes, within specific industries. Agencies like the Emergency Construction Wage Commission, which oversaw the wages of men building the army's new training camps, and others often went so far as to write into government contracts specific clauses favorable to workers. Other agencies sought to serve as mediators between employers and workers in particular industries, such as the Marine and Dock Industrial Relations Commission or the Shipbuilding Labor Adjustment Board.[6]

The government made some major concessions in its attempts to gain labor's support for the war. In April 1917 the secretary of labor acknowledged labor's right to organize and bargain collectively. In 1918, pressed by continued labor unrest, the government created the War Labor Board in April and the War Labor Policies Board in May. These would serve as mediation,

4. Weinstein, *Corporate Ideal*, pp. 245–47.
5. Missouri Council of Defense Papers, folders 418–22, 424.
6. Bing, *War-Time Strikes*, pp. 318–19.

"The world must be made safe for Democracy!"
— WOODROW WILSON —

"To the men who run the railways of the country, whether they be managers or operative employees, let me say that the railways are the arteries of the nation's life and that upon them rests the immense responsibility of seeing to it that those arteries suffer no obstruction of any kind, no inefficiency or slackened power."

Courtesy Special Collections, Ellis Library, University of Missouri–Columbia.

fact-finding, and policymaking agencies for the government in the area of labor relations. In exchange for a promise from Gompers that labor would avoid strikes for the duration of the war, the government promised to allow workers to protect themselves by joining unions, and it furthermore promised all workers the right to a living wage.[7]

The government failed to secure the widespread, enthusiastic cooperation of American workers, despite its efforts. Many unions, both within and outside the AFL, came to support the government's war policies. But neither the government nor the unions could alleviate the main sources of labor's complaints: rising prices, paternalistic or blatantly oppressive employers, the endless war drives and mobilization campaigns. Nor could labor agencies move fast enough to solve specific problems. Sometimes it took them months to raise wages in accordance with inflation that had already risen past the point at which the request had been made. The labor agencies had a difficult time controlling employers as well. While industrial organizations, trade associations, and businessmen's groups promised to support federal labor policies, they complained about the government coddling workers while they circumvented regulations wherever it was possible and profitable. Many an employer resolved not to knuckle under just because there was a war on and his trade association had sworn loyalty. The war provided

7. Ibid., pp. 165–66, 191–93.

too many chances, not just to make fantastic profits, but to resolve the union problem once and for all. The federal government and various state legislatures seemed to offer some help by suspending certain worker-protection laws for the duration; and Washington supplied secret service agents to corporations to help uncover spies and saboteurs. Employers often used these agents to report on union activity or worker discontent, claiming that such behavior constituted espionage and sabotage. As corporate earnings rose along with prices, wage increases came in grudging driblets, and employers could and did characterize as pro-German slackers and traitors any workers who sought to improve their condition. Employers consistently refused to accept worker bargaining committees, ignored government requests for arbitration of labor disputes, and tried to break up existing unions by firing members and withholding recognition.[8]

The government tried to establish a tripartite pact among business, organized labor, and itself for the duration of the war. It sought to foster interest-group development in labor as it did in agriculture because interest groups could be defined more clearly and dealt with more efficiently than such inchoate groups as "consumers" or "citizens," which lacked formal structure. But interest groups did not prove especially effective in mobilizing the country for war, partly because relatively few Americans saw themselves strictly in interest-group terms. The vast majority of workers, for instance, did not belong to unions, either before or after the war. Workers functioned and thought of themselves as consumers and citizens, as family members, as parishioners, lodgefellows and neighbors, as well as workers. If the government promised to benefit people as producers, it seemed to threaten them in their other roles through high taxes, conscription, and the kind of coercion that often accompanied the food and bond drives. As a result, the war generated a complex set of responses among workers. Obviously workers were among the people in Missouri who sought to avoid buying bonds or signing the food pledge, and relying on family and friends no doubt helped. But they also sought to protect themselves on the shop floor, where class served as a valuable resource upon which they could draw during the crisis. It also offered them an alternative form of community. If much of the government's mobilization efforts tended to fragment the community, identification with class could bring people together. If workers had a difficult time protecting their families from war taxes and the draft and from high prices, perhaps they could find recourse in the traditions of worker solidarity and the strike, which might serve as more effective means of resisting the impact of the war. The union hall or the shop floor or the picket line could be arenas for localism, democracy, and anticorporate sentiment as well as

8. Ibid., pp. 156–59, 225–33; David Montgomery, "The 'New Unionism' and the Transformation of Workers' Consciousness in America, 1909–1922"; Greenwald, *Women, War, and Work*, pp. 35–39.

the neighborhood or the village. Consequently, as the traditional resistance to modernization by Missouri farmers frustrated war mobilizers, so too were they frustrated by the class action of Missouri workers, action that brought the state's major cities to a halt, hampered war production, and won new victories for organized labor as well.

When America went to war approximately 1.5 million Missouri men, women, and children were gainfully employed. Agriculture employed about 480,000, more than any other field. Manufacturing employed 285,000 people; trade, commerce, and finance, 114,000; transportation, 100,000; mining, 32,000. There were about 155,000 clerical workers, domestics, professionals, and public service and government employees. Leading manufacturing activities in terms of workers employed were railroad car repair (21,000); boot and shoe making (19,000); printing, binding, typesetting (15,000); lumber (13,000); foundry and machine workers (10,000); electronics (10,000); men's clothing (8,000); baking (8,000); brewing (7,000); and meat packing (6,000). There were about 6,900 manufacturing establishments in the state, over 4,000 owned by individuals, 2,500 by corporations. Corporations were considerably more important to the economy, however, employing over 87 percent of the wage earners in manufacturing and producing 90 percent of the value of all goods manufactured. These figures rose during the war.

Only a handful of Missouri's nonagricultural workers, fewer than 15 percent, belonged to a labor union. About half the state's railroad workers and miners were organized, and brewery workers, boot and shoe makers, and construction workers were well organized. Half the workers in St. Louis were organized and about 16 percent in Kansas City, with lower percentages in other towns and cities. Most members belonged to craft unions, but about 20 percent belonged to industrial unions.[9] At the same time, Missouri had a tradition of labor radicalism of the deepest sort, reaching back to the Great Strike of 1877, when workers of all types, led by railroad employees, seemed to be on the verge of seizing control of the entire state for several days.[10]

Organized labor in Missouri was led by the Missouri Federation of Labor (MFL), which was founded in 1891. Although by 1917 the MFL, as well as the vast majority of organized labor in the state, was at least formally associated with the American Federation of Labor, Missouri unionism had a strong socialist tradition. The St. Louis Central Trades and Labor Union (CTLU) had helped found the MFL and as late as 1905 accounted for up to two-thirds of the delegates to the state convention. The CTLU was socialist, calling for

9. John C. Crighton, *Missouri and the World War*, pp. 17–18; *Missouri Red Book, 1916–1917*, pp. 388–95, 1157–58; also *Fourteenth Census, Missouri Compendium*.

10. See David Thelen, *Paths of Resistance: Tradition and Dignity in Industrializing America*, pp. 77–85, especially on the democratic base of the uprising.

the collective ownership of the means of production and demanding that Samuel Gompers quit the employer-oriented Nation Civic Federation; but, like most Missouri socialists, it was gradualist rather than revolutionary in its approach. Despite this, the CTLU received frequent threats of expulsion from the AFL.

Kansas City labor lacked a socialist tradition, but the antiunion bias of the city's employers nevertheless generated a high level of militancy among workers and led to bitter confrontations. Outstate labor tended to be less centralized and less narrowly class conscious than urban workers, but many small-town unions called for a broad spectrum of local reforms, including such popular causes as municipal ownership of utilities.

According to the leading historian of organized labor in Missouri, the MFL worked hard to implement a coherent political program at the state and local levels by lobbying legislators and by voting for candidates sympathetic to their causes. For the first two decades of the century, labor's program consisted mainly of promoting more direct democracy. The MFL supported initiative and referendum, direct primaries, direct election of senators, and women's suffrage, and it fought hard to prevent emasculation of the state's direct democracy laws once they were on the books. The federation's economic program called for certain specific reforms, such as equal pay for women, child labor and compulsory education laws, the eight-hour day, and the abolition of the convict leasing system. They also demanded that workers be paid in "lawful money" rather than in company scrip. On a broader scale, the MFL sought redistribution of wealth and power through such measures as the extension of the public domain to mines and quarries, as well as to timber, oil, and water resources. They advocated the abolition of the wage and profit system and the takeover of the means of production and distribution by workers.[11]

When America entered the war, Reuben Wood, a socialist from Springfield, led the MFL. In 1915 the MFL had issued a plea to world leaders, including President Wilson, to try to end the "horrible war conflagration" in Europe.[12] At the 1916 convention President Wood expressed shock that the war still raged. He pointed to the human cost and spoke of the "capitalist business war between the ruling classes." Turning to America, he criticized the preparedness movement, calling it American militarism under the "cloak of Republicanism and Democracy."[13] Local labor organizations also came out against the war. The socialist *St. Louis Labor* editorialized constantly against "the boss's war," and the St. Louis CTLU and labor groups in Kansas City voted overwhelmingly against preparedness. Unions in Sedalia,

11. Gary Fink, *Labor's Search for Order,* pp. 2–5, 13, 25, 34–39.
12. Missouri Federation of Labor, *Proceedings of the Twenty-third Annual Convention, 1914,* p. 40.
13. Missouri Federation of Labor, *Proceedings of the Twenty-fifth Annual Convention, 1916,* pp. 42–43.

Missouri, supported Senator Stone's stand against the armed-ship bill, and the St. Joseph Central Labor Council called for a referendum on the war.[14]

After April 1917, however, the MFL leadership came out in favor of the war. Wood pledged the federation's "undivided support . . . in this tremendous world struggle against militarism and autocracy and for the establishment of a world democracy." The MFL then aligned itself with "that sterling, loyal, and purely American" American Federation of Labor, thereby cutting ties with more radical labor groups and turning its back on its own past. Wood called for the conscription of wealth and attacked the "Kaisers of Industry" who paraded their "alleged loyalty and patriotism," but that was almost pro forma for opponents of war who changed their minds that spring.[15] All of which was in line with Gompers's position in his Labor Day speech that year, in which he outlined a plan for the nation's workers. The war, Gompers said, had caused the shifting of the economic center of the nation to Washington. This in turn required a close understanding between labor and the federal government. In return for labor's loyalty the government would guarantee "justice to labor" and the removal of "industrial anarchy" and inhuman living and working conditions.[16]

To some extent Gompers, and especially Wood, were simply being practical. After the declaration of war there was no turning back, and resistance would only bring federal retaliation of the kind organized labor knew only too well. Besides, the government had begun to admit, however grudgingly, the justice of some of labor's demands. Thus Wood and the MFL were willing to trade an ideological position that was no longer tenable for organizational legitimacy. At the 1918 convention Wood pointed to the great progress made by the unionization movement. Whereas the number of union members had actually fallen between 1914 and 1917, it had grown since the declaration of war. There were now more new unions and more affiliations with the MFL. The number of union members grew from 108,000 in 1917 to 160,000 in January 1919, and the percentage of members associated with the federation had gone from 80 percent to 87 percent. Wood himself devoted much time during the war to the organization movement, dashing about the state unionizing domestics in Lexington, teamsters in Deepwater, and firemen in Joplin, all with at least the implied approval of the government. Further, organized labor won representation on the Missouri Advisory Board of the Fuel Administration and on district draft exemption boards.[17]

14. Fink, "The Evolution of Social and Political Attitudes in the Missouri Labor Movement, 1900–1940" (Ph.D. diss., University of Missouri–Columbia, 1968), pp. 128–29; *Springfield Laborer,* 9 March 1917.

15. Missouri Federation of Labor, *Proceedings of the Twenty-seventh Annual Convention, 1918,* pp. 41, 42; *Missouri Red Book, 1916–1917,* p. 200.

16. *Missouri Red Book, 1916–1917,* p. 230.

17. *Missouri Red Book, 1918–1920,* pp. 651–53, 876–77; Fink, "Social and Political Attitudes," pp. 136–37.

Wood himself served as labor's representative on the Missouri Council of Defense. Despite his brave words about the benefits the war would bestow on labor, however, he soon grew tired of struggling against the overwhelming business domination on the council. He tried on several occasions to get the council to deal with antilabor employers. He accused Swift & Company of treating its workers unfairly and called for an investigation. After much delay the council finally appointed as investigator the manager of the St. Joseph stockyard owned by Swift. The investigation halted. Wood continued to pester the council, though, asking them to look into the matter of employers with government contracts replacing male workers with lower-paid women. The council refused to get involved. Wood tried to resign in early 1918, but the federation, perhaps afraid of what would happen to it without at least token representation, persuaded him to stay on until the end of the war.[18]

If Wood grew frustrated dealing with employers, so did Missouri's workers. According to the State Bureau of Labor Statistics, the war years saw a sharp increase in labor unrest.[19] Indeed, Springfield transit workers were on strike when the war began, and America's entry into the conflict hardly caused them to break stride in their march against the traction company. When other newspapers in town turned their attention to the declaration of war, the *Springfield Laborer*, begun by strikers because they believed the regular press would not tell their side of the story, barely mentioned it, devoting most of its columns and editorials to labor's struggle against capital.

The strike began in October 1916, when the Springfield Traction Company began firing members of a newly formed transit workers' union. The workers struck and called on citizens to assist them by boycotting the company, a traditional approach to labor problems in Missouri.[20] Soon hundreds of commuters and shoppers were walking or riding the jitneys provided by the strikers.

The company found that it confronted not only angry workers, but angry citizens as well, plus a city government determined to see that the company did not trample on anyone's rights. The company imported strikebreakers, and violence broke out when mobs attacked them. Mayor (formerly Councilman) Gideon and the city government refused to allow the police to be used as strikebreakers and insisted that the company discharge the scabs, who it said were the real cause of the trouble. Local businessmen sided with the traction company, claiming the city government was prolabor. In January 1917 the Jobber's and Manufacturer's Association tried to form a vigilante band of armed businessmen to be called the "Law and Order League." They promised to offer one thousand armed men to city officials, but the first

18. Fink, "Social and Political Attitudes," p. 135.
19. *Missouri Red Book, 1916–1917*, p. viii; *Springfield Republican*, 1 March 1918.
20. Thelen, *Paths of Resistance*, pp. 194–95, 222, 228–29.

meeting was attended by one thousand workers and their allies, who condemned the company for lawlessness and praised the police for maintaining order. The "Law and Order League" never recovered.

The efforts of the company and its allies continued to meet resistance from the community. A grand jury called to investigate labor violence was dismissed after failing to indict anyone. The business community forced a recall election, but Gideon was retained in office. In June, after more than two hundred fifty days, the company surrendered, agreeing to recognize the union, to rehire men fired during the strike, and to grant a small wage increase.

Neal W. Moore, president of the Ozark Labor History Society and an expert on the strike, maintains that the strike must be seen in the context of the region's radical tradition of anticorporate sentiment reaching back to the end of the nineteenth century. That tradition led the city government to insist that the transit company, owned by a New York utility holding company, had to obey local laws. Gideon's role was central. He enjoyed wide popularity in part because of his stand against the corporations in the 1912 electric rate controversy. Local businessmen, however, supported the corporation in this case and threatened to boycott the *Springfield Laborer* by refusing to buy advertising space. A threatened counterboycott by the Women's Trade Union League raised the possibility of reduced trade, and the merchants, fearing consumer revolt, backed down. Later, during the recall campaign, labor supporters engaged in a massive voter-registration drive, concentrating on the working-class neighborhoods. This drive, and the later vote, helped convince the company that it could not win. Thwarted at every turn by workers and citizens, finally defeated at the polls, the company quit.[21]

The strike may also be understood within the context of the war. In 1912 local businessmen, who were hurt by high utility rates, had sided with Gideon and other consumers against the company. By 1916, however, some of these men had war orders and hoped for more after America entered the conflict. As employers they sided with the traction company against organizing workers. The MFL agreed that it was a class issue. They had resolved to organize the notoriously antiunion traction industry throughout the state and had chosen Springfield to fight it out, in part because it was Reuben Wood's hometown, thereby simplifying links between local and state organizations, and partly because the city and the region had a reputation for anticorporate attitudes, thereby guaranteeing the union the base of popular support it would need to survive. The same radical traditions that made slackers of Springfield residents in the bond drives and the food pledge also made them allies of labor against capital, though as streetcar riders they

21. See *Springfield Laborer* for the first week of April 1917; *Springfield Republican*, 4 January, 4, 5, 7 May, 16, 23 June 1917; Fink, "Social and Political Attitudes," pp. 142–45.

probably did not view matters in the same terms as the workers.[22] In any case, workers, too, opposed the war. The *Laborer*, when it took time away from the class struggle in Springfield, argued regarding the sinking by Germany of the *Algonquin*, "When Mr. Morgan ships ammunition or loans money to the allies it seems to be called 'business.' When Germans loan money or ship arms to Mexico . . . it is a plot." While not closely reasoned, the paper made similar arguments occasionally until late April, when it pointed out that those who were too vocal in their opposition to the war tended to "disappear," snapped up, no doubt, by the "secret service." After that the paper became tepidly, and safely, loyal.[23]

St. Louis also experienced a wave of strikes, but, while the community generally supported the workers, the city government was not as helpful as in Springfield. During the first quarter of 1918, St. Louis was second only to New York City in the number of strikes.[24] Transit workers were the first. In late January there were rumors that workers were unhappy about the employment of a few women conductors. By 1 February organizers from the Amalgamated Association of Street and Electric Railway Employees had come to town to organize Local 788, and the issue quickly became one of wages and hours, the right to organize, and the closed shop. (The company's Mutual Benevolent Society had been the only union since the 1900 strike.) The question of women conductors faded when workers asked the new employees to join the union and two did.

The transit strike took place amid lingering hostility against United Railways (UR), a subsidiary of North American Company, another New York utilities holding company. United Railways sought a new operating franchise. The public opposed the franchise bill then before the Board of Aldermen because it granted a franchise for thirty-one years, because the claimed sixty million dollars in capitalization contained too much water, and because the bill exempted UR from most city taxes. At the same time the company had cut many stops and instituted procedures requiring passengers to change cars more frequently. Passengers rebelled, refusing to change cars, or suing the company for returning them to the shed when they refused to get off as ordered. Citizens threatened a referendum if the unpopular franchise bill passed.

The traction company encountered mass opposition immediately. The union appealed to the public for a boycott, and commuters complied. Passengers cheered when motormen announced the strike and insisted on getting off at once rather than be carried to their destination despite offers of

22. Telephone interview with Neal W. Moore, 16 June 1980; Fink, "Social and Political Attitudes," pp. 144–45; *Springfield Laborer*, 14, 29 March, 19, 21 April 1917.

23. See *Springfield Laborer* through the end of April 1917; Fink, "Social and Political Attitudes," p. 155.

24. For details, see *St. Louis Post-Dispatch* and *St. Louis Globe-Democrat* from late January through mid March 1918, when strikes were a constant source of news.

rides from workers. Throughout that first week in February, people were piling into jitneys, braving winter winds rather than riding streetcars. Joseph Woracek, president of the CTLU, appealed to Newton Baker and Samuel Gompers to intervene, claiming that the company had discharged men for joining the union, something they were supposed to be able to do under the wartime compromises. Further, the union came out against the franchise bill, linking their cause to that of consumers and taxpayers. Violence broke out as scabs tried to run the cars and mobs tried to stop them. The city ordered police to guard company property, and Home Guards went on alert. City police shot two innocent bystanders.

The company made its position clear. UR was "one big family." President Richard McCulloch told how UR had paid for an operation for one worker's wife and provided free legal advice for a worker seeking to buy a home. The men were loyal to the company, he insisted, but had been "pulled from their cars" by outside agitators. He said that these agitators were "willing to inflict injury on this community and help the country's enemies by tying up St. Louis' numerous war supply industries." Large advertisements claimed that UR was a St. Louis firm, for St. Louisans, and asked the people to help oppose the outsiders. To prove UR was a local company, the president of the North American Company even came in from New York, protesting all the while that, since it was not an operating concern but a holding company, North American was not involved in the matter at all.

The workers denied the company's charges. It was obvious that UR was owned by New Yorkers and was bringing in strikebreakers from the outside. The workers insisted that they were loyal to America, but argued that the company was unfair to its employees, forcing them to work long hours for low pay and denying them the right to organize. They promised to cooperate should the government take over and run the system. Backed by the CTLU, the workers acknowledged the seriousness of their actions, but insisted that the company was being disloyal by refusing to adhere to federal labor guidelines. Finally, on 8 February, only a few days after the strike had begun, the company agreed to recognize the union and to discuss wages and hours later.

The company may have yielded so quickly because of pressure from traditional allies. In 1900 it had taken on the workers and the people and had won. In 1918, however, other corporations, with the aid of the government, may have tipped the balance the other way. The strike tied up transportation for four working days, and thousands of workers stayed home. Several munitions plants had to close. War plant output during the first day of the strike was only 10 percent of normal. By the end, even with companies providing transportation, production was still only half of normal at the nearly two hundred firms with war contracts. Jackson Johnson, president of the St. Louis Chamber of Commerce, wired Washington to ask about the possibility of a government takeover if the matter were not settled. "Output our factories supplying Quartermaster already reduced 80 percent," he said. Valuable time was being lost, and war contracts were too lucrative to be jeopardized by a transit strike.

In any case, almost as soon as the transit strike ended, others began. Women at the Liggett and Myers tobacco plant sought to unionize and struck when the company opposed them. "Our purpose," said a worker, "is not to strike, it is to get better organized." The CTLU acknowledged that the success of the transit strike should encourage others. The "present time is especially favorable" for unionization, said Woracek, and he agreed to support the women at L&M as well as the men and women who worked as retail clerks in downtown department stores, who had just decided that they wanted a union for themselves as well. When employers rejected them entirely, the clerks walked out. By 8 March, hundreds of grocery store and hardware clerks had joined them. In the following weeks more workers began organizing and demanding recognition, higher pay, shorter hours, and better conditions. Workers in war plants as well as bakery employees, elevator operators, and janitors struck despite pleas not to hamper war production and despite threats that they might lose whatever deferred draft status they held by virtue of working in important industries. Workers struck for the right to organize at Wagner Electric, St. Louis's largest munitions manufacturer. The St. Louis (railway) Car Company had war contracts and was nonunion. Workers struck there when efforts to organize were rejected by the company. Workers at the city's two largest chemical plants, Monsanto and Mallinckrodt, virtually shut down war work due to strikes. Approximately 90 percent of the employees of ten garment factories went on strike, causing a severe slowdown in the manufacture of uniforms. Workers at Plumb Tool, temporarily making bayonets, went on strike. By mid-February as many as ten thousand workers were on strike, and industry throughout the city had virtually ceased.

The government tried to end industrial unrest in St. Louis first by sending individuals to mediate. An army officer, Maj. William Rogers, was sent as a representative of the secretary of war to try to end the strikes. Rogers failed. He openly sided with the employers and was relieved of his duties after Reuben Wood and other labor leaders traveled to Washington to complain to federal officials about his lack of fairness. Rogers was not long out of work, however, for he was immediately hired by the Employers' Association, which had been formed to deal with the strike.

The government also sent a labor representative, James H. Hahn, former president of a New York typographers' local. Hahn had no better luck than Rogers. He tried preaching loyalty. He warned against Germans, IWWs, Bolsheviki, pacifists, and conscientious objectors, any or all of whom might try to corrupt St. Louis workers. He asked labor leaders to pause and consider before calling another strike. St. Louis labor leaders responded that they intended to secure justice for workers and hinted that folks in Washington either help them or leave them alone. A few days later another thousand workers went on strike. By early April, St. Louis marked the anniversary of the declaration of war by having had between thirty and fifty thousand workers on strike at different times since January.

The Chamber of Commerce appealed for an end to the strikes, begging both workers and employers to do nothing that might weaken America's warmaking capability. Jackson Johnson asked workers to adhere to federal requests not to take advantage of the war crisis by trying to change labor's status; and he appealed to employers to raise wages to meet inflation. The president of Simmons Hardware, whose workers were also out, responded that the strikers were pro-German and deserved no concessions. The *Post-Dispatch*, while accusing employers of causing some of the unrest, asserted that strikes during the war took on "almost the dismaying quality of mutiny in the army." Wilson denied that workers had the right to halt production until all avenues of conciliation had been explored. As the *Post-Dispatch* continued, "We cannot have industrial unrest at home and win our war with autocracy in the field."

Striking workers refused to budge, but they were clearly stung by the accusations of lack of patriotism. A telegram signed by Woracek, Wood, and others to the Chamber of Commerce claimed that the strikers "are all loyal citizens," but that the strikes had been precipitated "by the cruel and unjust methods used by some employers in dealing with their unprotected and unorganized employees." These employers, in their "avarice and greed," drove up prices and tried to crush unions. The CTLU pointed to a story in the papers about 30 men whose combined income equaled that of 350,000 workers. It was not the workers but the bosses, insisted the CTLU, who were disloyal and unpatriotic, who reaped huge profits while forcing their employees to work in poor conditions and to go hungry at home. No nation could wage a war for democracy if it allowed a class of profiteers to crush the efforts of workers to exercise their "God-given right of organization." To permit such oppression meant the end of freedom and the rise of "an imitation of industrial Kaiserism and Czarism if our free American workmen and women are deprived of the right to organize . . . ." The CTLU went on, "Gentlemen, it is a question of bread and butter with us. We must help our country . . . but we can only do so by protecting our families . . . ."

Finally the government sent federal mediators from the War Labor Board to deal with matters. They offered concrete proposals rather than exhortations, and one by one St. Louis employers agreed to allow workers to organize and bargain collectively. Employers also agreed to wage increases, though many wanted to raise their prices to compensate; and they promised to look into the matter of poor working conditions. Workers drifted back to work, but many remained unsatisfied, claiming that the bosses would not live up to their promises. For the remaining months of the war, St. Louis was the fourth-ranking city in the nation in the number of strikes.[25]

25. Fink, "Social and Political Attitudes," pp. 160–61.

In the summer of 1917, shortly after the Springfield strike ended, a transit strike began in Kansas City. It followed, up to a point, the pattern of similar strikes. The company tried to break a new union. The public sided with labor against the company. But the city government supported management and ordered policemen to protect strikebreakers. When forty-three cops refused to perform such duty, they were fired. The transit strike succeeded eventually, however, in that transit workers won the right to organize; but the city government would promise only to rehire policemen as vacancies occurred.[26]

The transit strike was in any case only a prelude to a conflict that peaked with a general strike in the spring of 1918 that brought Kansas City to a complete halt for six days.[27] It began with a strike by the city's laundry workers. The Laundry Owner's Association, quickly formed to oppose cooperation among employees, allied with the antilabor Kansas City Employer's Association. The laundry workers had gone out in February. The employers hired strikebreakers to replace them and, with the approval of the city government, special police to protect the new workers. Skirmishing began between strikers and scabs, and employers stood firm against any hint of compromise with the women on strike.

An investigation of the laundries by the Women's Committee of the Jackson County Council of Defense revealed low pay and terrible working conditions. The employers tried to undermine the strike by offering a wage increase, but the strikers refused to return to work without union recognition and improvement of conditions. In mid March, Kansas City labor leaders called for a general strike in support, to begin on 25 March unless the owners agreed to a compromise. The labor leaders later extended the deadline in the hope of arbitration, but still companies refused, and on 27 March the general strike began. Construction and brewing halted. Cooks, bakers, motion-picture operators and stage hands, barbers and transit workers all went out on strike. Soon factories with war contracts were shutting down as the number of strikers reached twenty-five thousand.

The city government, fearing civil disorder, called out the Home Guards. Saloons were closed. Patrick Gill, a federal mediator who was also trying to deal with the St. Louis strikes, arrived and tried to persuade the Employer's Association and the laundry owners to compromise with the strikers. W. D. Mahon, of the transit workers, came to town to urge labor to take a more conciliatory stand. Finally, with the help of these men and the mayor of Kansas City, labor and management reached an agreement, despite the fact that the employers constantly refused to meet with labor leaders. Under the

26. *Springfield Republican,* 9, 12, 17 August 1917.

27. See the *Kansas City Journal* for March and April 1918; also Fink, "Social and Political Attitudes," pp. 147–52; Bing, *War-Time Strikes,* p. 30; *St. Louis Post-Dispatch,* 15 March 1918, p. 8; 27 March 1918, p. 4; 28 March 1918, p. 4; 29 March 1918, pp. 3–4; 31 March 1918, p. 4.

terms of the compromise, striking workers could return to work under their old contracts. The owners agreed to reinstate striking women with a pay increase but refused union recognition. Some Kansas City workers wanted to continue the strike until the women won recognition, but Mahon threatened to sign a separate agreement with the Employer's Association that would put transit workers back on the job. Threatened with the defection of so important an element in the alliance, organized labor agreed to end the strike.

The unorganized laundry workers, abandoned by their allies, gained little from the strike. The unions had demonstrated their power, but nonunion women ended up getting little help either from unions or from government. And within a few weeks it became clear that the laundry owners were not about to honor their commitments. The women complained that their wages had not been raised and that former strikers were not being rehired. Organized labor ignored them. The general strike had amply demonstrated union militancy and employer obstinacy, as well as the willingness of Washington to deal with the two groups, but in the end the unorganized were left with no protection.

The Kansas City strike thus revealed variations in the pattern of class conflict during the war. The Kansas City labor movement was relatively new, lacking the long socialist tradition of the movement in St. Louis as well as the deep-seated anticorporate attitudes and close community ties of the Springfield workers. Kansas City unions had demonstrated their ability to organize transit workers and had brought the city to a halt in defiance of business and government leaders, as close adherence to the new trend toward interest-group politics indicated they should. But they were not willing to fight to the end for female laundry workers. This may have been the result of attitudes toward women, although other unions in the state indicated a willingness to include women in their ranks, if only to maintain wages for men. It also may have resulted from craft unions' attitudes toward industrial unions. At the same time, the unions faced unified employers, which apparently workers in St. Louis had not, and they confronted a hostile city government, unlike workers in Springfield. Consequently, once they had flexed their muscles, Kansas City unions may not have felt it worthwhile to fight such determined opponents over so small an issue. It is also possible, furthermore, that the federal government felt that in encouraging union organization in exchange for labor peace it had unbottled a genie, for, while many workers rushed to take advantage of the opportunity to organize, many employers proved unwilling to grant workers a right they insisted upon for themselves.

Elsewhere in Missouri, responses to America's entry into the war involved not just efforts to organize unions, but outright violence. In May 1917 the St. Louis and San Francisco Railroad office in Springfield asked its employees to be patriotic and cautioned them against hampering the war effort by interfering with rail traffic. A few months later there were several attempts to dynamite Frisco bridges in the area, in one case just before a troop train was to pass over. Harry Durst, a Springfield attorney, took the possibility of such action for granted. In July he had written Governor Gardner, "We are bound to have some internal disturbances, and . . . the greatest caution should be taken to preserve law and order" while the country mobilized for war. Other local attempts at sabotage occurred. Shortly after the 1918 harvest, arsonists destroyed much valuable wheat in Barry and Livingston counties. And in December 1917 a bomb went off in the Aurora Iron Works in Springfield.[28]

The violence in southwestern Missouri may have been inspired by the antiwar "Green Corn Rebellion" in Oklahoma, but labor unrest in other parts of the state lent broader significance to Harry Durst's concern. In May 1917 the mayor of Moberly, in the north-central part of the state, asked Governor Gardner for state troops to deal with rioting Brown Shoe Company workers. Over a dozen had already been arrested, and the mayor claimed the police were overwhelmed. Violence had erupted in the strikes in Springfield, St. Louis, and Kansas City. Employers and elected officials saw disloyalty behind the unrest and pointed to radical influences in the labor movement. One particular incident of labor violence, in the lead-mining region of St. Francois County, suggests yet another variation in the pattern of the war's impact on Missouri workers.[29]

By July 1917 four or five large national companies owned most of the mines in Missouri's "Lead Belt." They also owned land they leased to farmers and homeowners, stores through which they sold goods to their employees, and even whole neighborhoods they had built to house newly imported immigrant workers. As a St. Louis newspaper noted, the Lead Belt was "a Feudal Domain of the lead mining companies."

The mining companies aroused great discontent in local communities. Local merchants complained that they could not compete with company stores. Company property was assessed at much lower rates than privately owned property. The mining and smelting processes were destroying the environment. Acres of land were covered with huge "chat piles," and "the streams," according to one observer, "are so polluted with slime from the lead mills that they are unfit to be used for laundry purposes to say nothing of being used for human consumption." But the companies used their influence in the legislature to prevent the two principal towns in the area, Bonne Terre and Flat River, from incorporating. These towns were not wholly controlled by the companies, and incorporation meant that citizens would be able, among other things, to pass local laws regulating corporate activity. The companies could not allow this.

28. *Springfield Republican*, 5 May, 5 August, 10 August, 27 December 1917, 9 July 1918; *Missouri Ruralist*, 5 June 1917; Durst to Gardner, 14 July 1917, Council of Defense Papers, folder 888.

29. See Christopher C. Gibbs, "The Lead Belt Riot and World War One."

In the meantime, the war caused a lead boom in the United States. At first, during the last months of 1914, prices fluctuated wildly, then soared as war in Europe and revolution in lead-rich Mexico caused increasing demand and declining supply. Production in the United States increased 22 percent in the first year of the war, and prices jumped from 3.5 cents a pound to 12.2 cents by 1917. With America's entry into the war, lead company managers went to Washington to serve on the various new boards and agencies, there to ensure that the price of lead remained as high as possible. By 1917 the United States was producing 45 percent of the world's lead and had become for the first time the world leader in lead production. Missouri led the nation in lead production, and the Lead Belt was the chief lead-producing region in the state. In 1907, for instance, St. Francois County produced slightly less than 100,000 tons of lead; in 1917 it produced well over 200,000 tons, or 34 percent of all the lead smelted in the United States.

All of this bore heavily on the man at the rock face, the miner with a pick and a drill. Technological advances had included the introduction of the diamond-bitted drill for prospecting, and underground rail systems and power lifts to facilitate the movement of ore to the surface. But the sort of work done by the average miner had not changed significantly. It was "brutal, man-killing" work, done with hand tools wielded by men working far underground, stooped over, standing in water to their ankles.

Most of the native-born miners had been reared on farms in the area and had been first attracted to mining by the boom times of the 1890s and the promise of good wages. A St. Louis reporter described them as " 'hill-billy' types" who were good enough workers, "but of a shiftless type, not easily managed . . . likely to rebel against orders [and] new efficiency methods and those new wrinkles that are supposed to get the best results out of any industry" (*St. Louis Star*, 17 July 1917). The miners probably felt there were already enough wrinkles, and the nature of the work and the background of the workers combined to make for casual work patterns. Miners received a daily wage based on the amount of ore they dug. A man had only to work long enough to make a satisfactory amount of money, to "make his score," and he could quit early for the day, or for the week. Many of the native-born miners in any case sought work only through the winter months, when the weather made farming impossible.

The lead companies permitted this situation to prevail as long as the lead market remained fairly stable. But then came the war and with it the chance for fantastic profits. The companies were developing an underground power shovel to do much of the actual digging, but in the meantime they tried to get more work out of their men. They tightened up on regulations against drinking and absenteeism, both fairly common practices that had not seemed so important before the war. They tried to replace the casual work habits of their men by instituting an hourly wage system. And when the native-born miners proved intractable, the owners imported immigrants through labor agents in St. Louis. The immigrants, from Hungary, Italy, and Britain, were eager to work hard at high American wages in order to make enough money to allow them to return home as wealthy men or to establish themselves in this country. They were more willing to compromise, in any case, than were the native-born men. Certainly the owners assumed that they could exploit the immigrants fully for the short time they needed them, that is until technology or peace rendered them expendable, and they hoped they would prove more manageable than the "hillbillies" they were to replace. Finally, as an added bonus, the owners believed that the immigrants would not be subject to conscription.

At 6:30 p.m. on 13 July 1917, the native-born miners employed by the St. Joe Lead Company sought to spoil the company's plan. These men were about to be replaced by immigrant workers who bragged that they would have all the jobs and the women when the others went off to war. By nightfall a mob of nearly one thousand rampaged through Flat River, throwing rocks at the homes of immigrants, stopping immigrant miners on the street, and beating several. The rioters also stopped cars and searched them for company officials on whom to vent their anger. The next morning the native-born miners met, elected leaders, listened to speeches, and then formed up behind an American flag and headed for the offices of the mining company. They demanded that all foreign-born miners be discharged and advised to leave the district. They also threatened company officers, several of whom left town. Those who remained claimed that they could not act without word from headquarters in New York. The miners refused to wait, however, and, accompanied by women and children, went cheering and shouting toward the immigrant neighborhoods. One witness described it as a "Saturday holiday atmosphere" (*St. Louis Post-Dispatch*, 15 July 1917, p. 1).

The rioters rounded up the foreign born, whether at home or at work. They lined them up and marched them to the company pay windows where reluctant clerks, encouraged by flourished pistols, gave the departing immigrants their last paychecks. The procession moved on to a bank in Flat River, where the immigrants cashed their checks. From there they went to the railroad depot. The rioters saw to it that the immigrants all had tickets, even purchasing tickets in some cases, then gave them a loud send-off, cheering and firing their weapons as the train pulled out. After that most of the mob went home; a few looted the recently abandoned houses of the immigrants. Some looted company stores.

In the meantime the company had asked for military protection. County Sheriff Charles Adams refused to get involved, but did agree to ask the governor for state troops. At the same time, the lead companies located in the district appealed directly to Washington. Irwin B. Cornell, president of the St. Joe Lead Company and adviser on lead to the Council of National Defense, pleaded with Newton D. Baker for federal assistance. Baker referred the matter to Governor Gardner, and by late on the evening of 14 July, state troops began arriving in the Lead Belt.

The presence of the troops sparked new unrest. The companies, apparently satisfied that the troops would keep order, refused to meet with a grievance committee of workers who wanted to discuss working conditions in the mines. The companies refused requests by State Labor Commissioner William Lewis to submit to arbitration, insisting that the grievance committee represented no recognized body of miners. The miners, who had no union, could come to management individually, however, and management would supposedly listen to whatever that miner had to say. In this way the companies hid behind procedural minutia while the troops began arresting miners and anyone else who had participated in the riot. Throughout the remainder of 1917 the troops continued to arrest people, thus enforcing strict control in the area. They arrested so many people that they filled the county jail to overflowing and had to send prisoners to neighboring counties for confinement. They shot at people in the streets, wounding several, and then threatened to destroy the shop of an editor who protested their unruly behavior. When the Missourians were federalized and sent to train for encounters with an armed enemy, the federal government sent in federal troops to keep order. Under this umbrella the companies reimported the immigrant miners and resumed the profitable and vital wartime production of lead.

The people of the Lead Belt sided with the rioters throughout. No one would serve as sheriff's deputy during the violence. Adams himself came under severe criticism from the military commander in the area, who complained that Adams dragged his feet during the investigation and released suspected rioters as fast as the soldiers put them into jail. Circuit Judge Peter H. Huck hesitated to invoke the full weight of the law against the rioters, but the companies insisted. A grand jury, which Huck had initially opposed calling, brought 113 indictments. And despite the objections of the county prosecutor, two company attorneys appeared in court to help prosecute.

It did the companies little good, for community opposition continued to restrict proceedings. The military commander complained that his investigations were complicated by prospective witnesses who demonstrated an "astonishing lack of memory" about what had happened during the riot (*St. Louis Republic*, 16 July 1917). No one seemed able to recall, for instance, any damage to company property. The company lawyers complained that there were almost no witnesses for the prosecution but more than enough for the defense. Indeed, as the trials dragged on, Huck simply dismissed many cases, while the jury found many other accused rioters innocent. A few were found guilty, but the jury waived the maximum penalty in favor of a small fine and no jail time.

The people of the Lead Belt were the fertile soil from which the rioters sprung. As the editor of the *Lead Belt News* claimed on 20 July 1917, the riot was due to "long pent up prejudices against both the companies and the foreigners." The Lead Belt Ministerial Alliance criticized the miners for depriving the immigrants of their rights, and the companies for poor treatment of native-born workers. The actions of the rioters support the claim that they were as angry at company officials as they were at the immigrants, and they surely would have handled roughly any company officer they found in their searches that first evening. Expulsion of the immigrants came only after failure to get satisfaction from company officials. Finally, the stores and houses they looted were company property, and, with a few exceptions, the mob was careful not to damage any property belonging to individuals, immigrant or native.

None of which is to suggest that the native-born miners liked their foreign-born counterparts, or that their actions were somehow pardonable because they were under a lot of pressure. The Lead Belt Riot seems to have been a case of one group of victims punishing another rather than the common enemy of both. At the same time, it is important not to mistake the riot for some ill-defined prowar nativist uprising against anyone not 100 percent American. The riot took place in the context of the war, but not in support of it. The timing of the riot was directly due to the war. There were immigrants in the Lead Belt before 1917; and during the riot, selected immigrants, especially those with some tenure in the area, were protected by rioters. But not until after April 1917 did the lead companies crow about their patriotic contributions and lick their lips publicly over prospective profits. Only with the war did the companies attempt to modernize the workplace with new work patterns, machinery, and imported labor. Finally, the riot occurred just after draft registration ended and just before the first call-ups began.

Just as people in the Lead Belt disliked the companies that made the region economically viable, so they opposed the war that seemed to be showing them a future they did not want to see. During February and March of 1917 they were content to let Senator Stone and Congressman Hensley speak for them. And only one local newspaper favored American entry into the war.

Most contemporaries saw the riot as an expression of local antiwar sentiment. Governor Gardner used the Lead Belt Riot as an example of the kind of antiwar radicalism that threatened mobilization in Missouri. The lead companies agreed, claiming that the rioters were trying to damage the war effort. After the riot, the council of defense chairman from neighboring Madison County began to agitate for Home Guards to prevent similar disturbances (see above, Chapter 3, note 22).

The issue in the Lead Belt Riot was not union recognition or wages and hours; the miners acted in opposition to war-related modernization by their employers. For years the miners and their neighbors had resented the companies' influence over them. They were willing to let representatives in

Congress and the press take the lead in opposing the war. By July 1917, however, these sources had fallen silent; the companies were replacing native-born miners with immigrants; and conscription was about to begin, with its uncertainty and potential dangers. Out of work in an inflationary economy, on the verge of being forced to fight in a war they opposed while aliens took their jobs, abandoned by traditional spokesmen, the native-born miners of the Lead Belt exploded in violence, expressing their frustration at the war and those in charge of it in the only way that appeared useful to them.

Thus class was one of the resources Missourians drew upon in their responses to the war, and class could be expressed in several ways. In sanctioning organization among workers, the government sought a particular kind of class consciousness, one that was narrowly interest-group oriented, willing to compromise within a system inhabited by other contending interest groups, willing to cooperate to keep the war going. This is what Gompers had promised, what Reuben Wood and others tried to achieve. But something different occurred. Not only did workers resist buying bonds, refuse to sign food pledge cards, and try to avoid conscription by claiming exemptions, but they also turned class into a war issue, behaving as slackers on the production line as they did at home, often bringing war production to a complete stop. They ignored their leaders' promises of peace and sought, not simply a share of power within a pluralist framework, but control over their lives for themselves all the time, and they proved willing to use violence to achieve their goals. Some relied on class action to strengthen their class position as represented by union recognition; others sought simply to improve conditions in the workplace; still others seem simply to have struck out at their oppressors. Like so many other Missourians during the war, the workers seem often to have acted incoherently, inefficiently, against their own best interests. Certainly the position of workers in general was not improved by the war, as the few limited gains achieved were wiped out after the Armistice, either by direct employer action or by general economic conditions. But their actions do help expand understanding of the war's impact.

Class conflict between workers and their employers ultimately made slackers of workers, bosses, and often the rest of the community as well. Employers were willing to fight unions at the expense of production. Workers were willing to fight back. And the public, more often than not, was willing to support the workers, whether union members in Kansas City, prospective union members in St. Louis and Springfield, or the unorganized in the Lead Belt. As a consequence, labor unrest in various locations kept Missouri on the boil through the end of the war and beyond.

Chapter 8

Afterword

The guns in Europe fell silent on 11 November 1918, but the echoes could be heard, and felt, in Missouri for months, years afterward. Wartime conditions prevailed nationwide well into 1919 as crisis followed crisis, as various war agencies sought continued existence, and as local leaders called upon their neighbors for continued sacrifices. Missourians responded to these calls as they had before the Armistice, by slacking when possible, resisting where necessary, and going along when no other course of action was available. But, as the war had affected different people in different ways while it was being fought, so its influence had varied effects after it was over.

Some of the immediate aftershocks of war could neither be resisted nor avoided, and their effect was indeed wide ranging. In part this arose from the fact that neither Woodrow Wilson nor Congress offered any kind of plan for postwar domestic reconstruction.[1] This absence of national leadership, especially after almost two years of vigorous attempts to run the war from Washington, effectively jerked the rug from under local war boosters, who had relied on links to the capital to underwrite their legitimacy. The result was chaos since many problems caused by the war were inevitably beyond local control.

Inflation continued to plague consumers for months following the war, and food prices were especially high. Prices did not drop until 1921, and when they did thousands of farmers, in Missouri and elsewhere, began the Great Depression ten years early. The farmer's costs of doing business rose, and prices failed to keep up. Modernization continued to have only a limited impact on most farmers. For instance, the number of tractors in use more than tripled in the decade following the war, but that meant that only about 10 percent of Missouri farmers were using them. In 1924, one-fourth of all farmers in Missouri did business with either the Farm Bureau or the MFA, and this dropped to 22 percent by 1929. And as Missouri's farms lagged, so did rural communities and the local firms that did business with those farmers. Indeed, the entire state seemed to slow down. Missouri's ranking by population dropped to tenth during the postwar decade.[2]

1. Burl Noggle, *Into the Twenties: The United States from Armistice to Normalcy,* pp. 8–9.
2. Richard S. Kirkendall, *A History of Missouri, Volume V: 1919 to 1953* (Columbia: University of Missouri Press, 1986), pp. 41–43, 55–61.

More short-lived was the influenza epidemic that swept through military camps and the civilian population during the fall of 1918. Schools were closed and public meetings were outlawed by frightened local governments, thereby muting celebration over the Armistice without slowing the epidemic. The asafetida bags and gauze masks people wore were no more effective. Between October and December some three thousand Missourians died.[3] In response to popular demand, and in the absence of policy, the government did bring the troops home quickly, where approximately four million were welcomed by over four hundred fifty parades. At the same time, however, the government effectively discharged between three and four million workers as it canceled wartime contracts. The result was an explosion in unemployment that the U.S. Employment Service struggled valiantly to deal with until the business lobby killed it off shortly after the Armistice.[4]

At the local level, war boosters must have seemed as tenacious as unemployment, disease, and high prices. Despite the fact that "the people were sick of wheatless days and meatless meals [and] hated this constant prodding to exercise thrift, give money, buy bonds," the prodding went on. "Life in America is just one 'drive' after another," complained an observer, and "the end of the war has not stopped it."[5] Both the Salvation Army and the Boy Scouts conducted fund drives in Missouri in 1919, and a new emergency arose with fund drives to aid the starving Armenians in Turkey. Local chamber of commerce organizers warned prospective participants in this cause not to "wait to be visited by a committee" before joining. The Red Cross, after several wartime drives to enroll every family in the state (and after claiming total success in each one), in 1919 conducted yet another drive to enroll everyone in the state. The charitable organization was still promising to root out slackers, threatening vaguely that "reports will be made," though with the war over the final destination of such reports was unclear.[6]

People who resisted these drives during the war only increased their resistance when the war was over. Volunteers for the United War Work Fund planned late in the war to enroll every citizen as a subscriber, and their work had barely gotten off the ground when peace intervened. Undeterred, they continued their drive; equally undeterred, Missourians in large numbers refused to participate. Many who refused pointed to the advent of peace as their excuse for not contributing to a war fund. So too did Missourians who

3. For food prices, see Department of Commerce, Bureau of the Census, *Historical Statistics of the United States, Colonial Times to the Present*, 2d printing (Washington: Government Printing Office, 1961), pp. 124–27; for the flu epidemic, see *St. Louis Post-Dispatch* for the last three months of 1918; C. Kevin McShane, "The 1918 Kansas City Influenza Epidemic," *Missouri Historical Review* 63 (October 1968): 55.

4. Noggle, *Into the Twenties*, pp. 68–75.

5. *Springfield Republican*, 7 February, 18 June 1919.

6. Ibid., 11 December, 21 December 1918; 6 February, 12 February, 11 June, 3 August 1919.

Courtesy Western Historical Manuscripts Collection, Columbia, Missouri.

sought to avoid buying war bonds. The final Liberty Bond drive, its name hastily changed to Victory Drive, had been planned for the spring of 1919, and it met a wall of apathy from the small subscriber. The participation rate was only about half what it had been in the Liberty Bond drive of the previous fall.[7]

Part of the problem lay in the fact that in the midst of these drives the organizational network that had supported them ceased to operate. As has been noted, many local councils of defense in Missouri were all but dormant before the Armistice. The rest quit as soon as the state headquarters closed its doors in early 1919. Local boosters tried to maintain local agencies, however. Fund drives were held around the state to provide local support for the now-marooned county farm bureaus, for example, but they usually failed. Nevertheless, these local drives adhered to wartime patterns, with exhortations to participate and widespread slacking, and with wealthy individuals and organizations finally meeting the quotas.[8]

The Red Scare, with labor unrest, lynchings, and official cries of alarm, also reverberated in Missouri. During the war, authorities had seen such outbreaks as the Lead Belt Riot and the Kansas City general strike as examples of the same kind of German-sponsored radicalism that had overthrown Russia. Thus for many in Missouri the Red Scare began in the spring of 1917, and the helmeted Hun was replaced on cartoon pages by the bearded bomb thrower long before the Armistice. The unrest of 1919 should therefore be seen as a continuation of wartime unrest rather than a sudden postwar surge of dissent. Springfield's doughty Colonel Dickerson perceived Bolshevik influence in the strikes around Missouri in 1919 and asked Congress for help. He wanted war-surplus machine guns and grenades to be sent to local law enforcement officers, who, reinforced by bands of veterans, would suppress revolution in the state. Once again Dickerson was disappointed, but only in his specific solution to a situation that many others in Missouri perceived as well.[9] Indeed, the problem went deeper than Dickerson and others supposed. Some thirty-two IWW leaders were tried in Kansas City for resisting the draft and for violating food and fuel regulations during the war.[10] If this was subversive activity, as the government suggested in court, then hundreds of thousands of Missourians reading about the trial in the newspapers must have felt a chill, for they had committed similar offenses, and the only thing that saved them was that they did not belong to notorious organizations. Missouri was, by the government's measure, full of dangerous revolutionaries, and the message to these people was clear. The prominent war resisters were tried, convicted, jailed, deported; what would

7. Ibid., 29 June 1919.
8. Ibid., 18 December 1918; 12 October, 9 November 1919.
9. Ibid., 2 February 1918, 23 November 1919.
10. Ibid., 5 December 1919.

be the fate of the plain citizen who had secured a draft exemption for her son? Would a casual remark to a neighbor about hoarding flour lead to court? Could refusal to buy a bond mean jail?

Questions like these were profoundly serious to people in 1919 and indicate one important aspect of the war's impact. It is clear that the mobilization process brought the federal government into the daily lives of Americans in new and often wrenching ways. It is also clear that, whatever the actions of the president and Congress, many wartime leaders saw this as an opportunity to change radically the relationship between people and government by securing Washington's role as the focus of loyalty, thereby overleaping previously important state and local institutions. Under this new arrangement the federal government would lead and the people would follow, all of them, 100 percent, and the government's local allies would achieve great prestige and power. But in 1919 the government suddenly backed out, and most people had refused to go along anyway, and by the end of the war the leaders at all levels found themselves out in the open with mostly each other for company. In turn they accused the people, with justification, of slacking. But it is important to emphasize that they equated slacking with radicalism, subversion, and treason, and they sought to bring the full force of their power to bear on the slackers, both prominent and obscure. Missourians responded, during the war and after, with still more slacking. They could not be led where they did not want to go, and they were hard to intimidate. Of course, as Randolph Bourne noted, the government did not really need them and so got on with its war, but the gulf between the self-appointed leaders and their putative followers was wide and growing wider.

For years World War I has served as a kind of fault line for understanding twentieth-century America. That assessment is not entirely unfair. If the period before the war was characterized by reform movements, political unrest, and widespread popular involvement in the major issues of wealth and power in an increasingly urban-industrial society, then the years following the war seem to have been dominated by political apathy accompanied by growing interest in the trivial: booze, baseball, new cars, flappers, and quick financial success. In the twenties, and even into the thirties, Americans were evidently willing to leave important matters to people who claimed to be in charge, and this tendency increased until it was all but impossible for people working from below to force their attentions on their leaders. It was as if the fires of reform had exhausted themselves in the muddy trenches and labyrinthine diplomacy of Europe. The more government tended to impose its versions of change on citizens, with new deals and fair deals and new frontiers, the more the numbers of those willing to engage in the bitter struggles for real change dwindled. Barring major disasters, Americans turned in growing numbers away from reform in search of something, anything, to take their minds off their troubles. They wearied, perhaps, of fighting a system that seemed to have all the money and all the votes and all the guns. Meanwhile, the alternatives beckoned brightly. It was much more pleasant to improve the "inner man," to make money instead of trouble. The insurgents of 1910 gave way to the Babbitts, the "me generation" of 1921. New York and Hollywood glittered like Berlin and London and Paris before the fall. The war was the point of change.

This is a widely accepted view, one with a great deal of evidence to justify it. And yet. If one of the lessons of the war was that America had to accept the responsibilities of world power, America seemed to reject that lesson. And if the ways in which the government organized for war offered a model for running the new industrial state, it would take many years and another world crisis before that model would again be tried. While the war was a four-year ordeal that blighted an entire generation of Europeans, there were a scant nineteen months between America's declaration of war and the Armistice, and the vast majority of American troops who fought were engaged for less than a third of that time. These few months were certainly enough to kill and maim tens of thousands, but from the vantage point of someone in the middle of the United States, the whole thing might have seemed a brief adventure, a remote irritant, or a barely noticeable rumbling from afar.

Reaction to the war was not a carefully considered program, but a product of the cultural resources and social and natural environments of the people involved. Intellectuals, whether for or against, may be able to deal with war in abstract terms; ordinary people have to live with it. Within a few months of electing a president who had kept America out of the conflict in Europe, Missourians discovered that the president had severed relations with Germany and was openly talking war. A few welcomed this joyously, some accepted it reluctantly, most hoped to avoid the thing altogether. In avoiding it they relied on traditional measures. They held local meetings, as though they were dealing with their local utility company. They conducted straw polls. They petitioned their representatives because they believed it would have an impact on the course of events. They called for a national referendum on the war, a national straw poll, because they believed that a nation that preached democracy should, and would, practice democracy, and because straw polls were something they understood well from direct experience. Events demonstrated that such measures possessed limited utility, and almost at once Missourians were dealing with mobilization for war. Few had any experience with this kind of thing, and the circumstances made resistance difficult. The federal government functioned, in part intentionally, as a hydra with several heads in each community, and opponents did not know, or know how, to go to the center. Threatening phone calls to the local draft board, attacks on the local grocer, only served to turn neighbors against each other; such actions touched Crowder, Hoover, or Wilson not at all. At the same time, the cop on the beat could arrest an indiscreet drunk or demand a bond subscription in lieu of a summons despite Wilson's orders against infringing on anybody's rights. Both sorts of action were strictly local in nature, but one sort was much more effective than the other.

The responses to mobilization, efficient or not, arose from the people involved. Traditional political resources were severely strained in the attempt to prevent entry into the war. Resistance to mobilization relied therefore on a narrower base in many instances, the neighborhood, the family, sometimes just the individual alone refusing to answer the door, refusing to sign up. In well-defined communities with strong ethnic ties, such as the German villages along the Missouri River, collective action worked. In much the same way, class solidarity also helped organized workers resist certain aspects of the war's influence. The same may have been true in remote Ozark counties. But in many cases, individual criminal behavior had to suffice: fraud when dealing with the draft board, for example; theft of certain food items; attacks on war workers. Some relied on other forms of pathological behavior, from self-mutilation or even suicide to evade the draft to the kind of social self-mutilation evident in the attacks on immigrant miners in the Lead Belt during the war and in Klan attacks on blacks and others in Missouri during the twenties.[11]

Others sought to turn the system to personal advantage. Bankers could profit from bond sales. Local leaders could enhance their power through council of defense work, whatever their opinion on the war itself. Some scaled the heights, like Irwin B. Cornell of the St. Joe Lead Company and Robert Brookings of Washington University in St. Louis, both of whom went to Washington to serve.

But according to the complaints of the mobilizers—and the available numerical data support them—the most common response was slacking, a response rooted in tradition. Faced with a war they had been unable to prevent, and with a government they could not effectively resist, Missourians simply boycotted the war every chance they got. Where geographical isolation, strong ethno-cultural ties, or strong class consciousness existed, this boycotting—slacking—may not have required much effort: few war workers ventured into German-American enclaves, or "Kerry Patch" in St. Louis, or into the rough Ozark hill country. But sometimes slacking required overt defiance. To refuse to buy a bond, or to refuse to sign the Food Pledge, despite direct, personal, face-to-face exhortation to do so, was active resistance with vague, possibly dangerous, consequences.

The more people refused to go along, the more the war boosters had the field to themselves. They sought to impose new definitions on old words. Democracy ceased to mean popular contention over issues, with the eventual outcome determined by majority rule; during the war, and increasingly in the years that followed, democracy came to mean total support of the

11. For Klan activities in Missouri after the war, see Kirkendall, *History of Missouri, Volume V*, pp. 67–70, 92–94, 99.

president, the government, and their programs, instant loyalty with no questions asked. Patriotism had meant love of country; during and after the war, patriotism meant agreeing with whoever was in the White House, and parroting the government's interpretation of events. Thrift no longer meant living within one's means; the war hurled the government deeply into debt, and McAdoo urged the American people to follow suit. During the war thrift was defined as "giving until it hurt," going into debt if necessary to pay for the war. Thrift meant not only submitting to government conscription of money through high prices, high taxes, and tax breaks for the privileged, but it also meant a kind of frantic consumption of Liberty Bonds, Red Cross flags, YMCA banners, Salvation Army stars, and Boy Scout pins. And if charity had traditionally been demonstrated locally through churches and benevolent orders working within the community, during and after the war charity came to mean lining up and signing up to give money to an agency that sent it to national headquarters, where it was distributed by professional experts. Thus people began to lose control of language, and the war workers began to forge certain words into weapons for use against slackers and other troublemakers.

The war and those who supported it also worked to corrode the bonds that held communities together. In some cases, the German-Americans for example, the war might actually have forced them to draw together more closely. But any community is cemented by webs of relationships that are comprised of, but transcend, class, ethnicity, and family. Already under attack in industrializing America, these bonds came under increased strain during the war. Food growers and food consumers, for instance, began railing at each other, whereas ten years before they had allied against food middlemen. Commuters of all classes could unite against the streetcar company, but there could be no unity when the burdens of war were perceived to fall unequally depending on wealth. Leaders lost the respect of followers to the extent that the leaders supported the war and the followers did not. And, with the government designating some groups and individuals as official enemies, local war leaders spied on people, lied to them, and armed themselves against their neighbors; and they urged others to do likewise. The bonds of community often broke down under this kind of assault, sometimes with devastating consequences for the less powerful, including the poor, the unorganized, and racial and ethnic minorities. In the years before the war, many of these, blacks especially, had enjoyed marginal community status at best; the tumult of 1917 and after frequently meant a plunge into the abyss.

If most people did not go along with this, some did. Under the circumstances, that was enough. It became unsafe, virtually impossible, to talk openly about the war. Even a careless word to a gossipy friend might bring the "committee" knocking on the door. Few topics were safe for discussion while words were losing their accustomed meanings, when a political argument, or a complaint about high prices, could be interpreted as treasonous and might mean a night in jail, or worse. No wonder, as the chairman of the Cape Girardeau County Council of Defense pointed out, all *signs* of opposition to the war eventually disappeared. Official canvassers reported time after time on whole neighborhoods in which people known to be at home refused to answer a knock on the door. As the war and the war boosters thus cut people off from each other even as united action was being praised as one of the war's great achievements, people fell silent or turned to safe topics of conversation. A person could go pretty far with subjects like baseball and cars, even to the point of open conflict, without running the risk of being called a traitor. Consequently, if people in the twentieth century seem increasingly to have immersed themselves in the trivial, perhaps in part it is because the experience of World War I taught that the trivial was also safe; and leaders who point to the "silent majority" as their basis of support build on sand.

The family also suffered. On the one hand, families, like communities, often turned in upon themselves as a reliable institution untainted by mobilization. But the war affected the family directly. Food regulations disrupted the usual diet while home economics experts with their new authority invaded the domain of the housewife to turn every family function to the service of the state. Taxation, high prices, and bond drives undermined the economic stability of the family. The draft removed husbands, fathers, and brothers from their homes, killing some and maiming others, returning still others shattered in spirit, their health ruined by the gas, nursing dark memories that isolated them from friends and relatives, from anyone who had not been *there*, who had not shared those indescribable, inexplicable experiences.

Even the individual suffered. Most people try to get along and live their lives with as much security, comfort, and pleasure as is consistent with their talents and their notions of right and wrong. Mostly they try to do right, playing by the rules as they understand them most of the time. But what happens when, literally overnight, the rules change? What happens to a person who is called a traitor if he does not buy a war bond, if she hoards food to feed her family, if he avoids the draft because he does not want to die in someone else's war? What happens to a person constantly bombarded by propaganda, constantly pressured by war workers, constantly harangued, threatened, exhorted? What happens when an agent of the federal government, in the name of patriotism, deprives a person of political influence, denies him or her the right to speak on certain subjects, attacks an individual's economic position? What are the feelings of a person who reads about prominent individuals arrested and tried for offenses he or she has also committed? So many bowed to the pressure, but many more did not, and often they paid the price, growing fearful of each other and of federal institutions, frustrated by their lack of power, apathetic or embittered in the face of overwhelming odds. And so, like their leaders before them, they too fell silent.

But in their silence, how deeply had they been changed? Some had been shaken to their roots: the wounded soldier; the farmer who grasped modernization as though it were salvation; the suffragist who demanded her quid pro quo; men like Mumford who had seen the future and believed it worked; the black veteran who insisted he be treated like a man; the housewife, bent on acquiring the latest conveniences, developing her domestic skills to perfection to make better citizens. People for whom slacking, dropping out, keeping silent becomes a way of life have been affected deeply; so have those who keep talking, but only about acceptable subjects.

And yet. Many may have been changed hardly at all. Nor was the silence total; consider the following. Much debate arose in 1919 over what to do with the railroads, which were still under federal control. Shippers lobbied Congress for a secretary of transportation to oversee matters, ICC regulation, cooperation among lines to ensure efficiency, and the return to private control of all lines taken over by the government during the war. Security holders opposed a secretary of transportation and any federal incorporation of the railroads, favoring instead immediate return to private control. State transportation commissioners agreed, preferring to retain their own authority. But for many, federal control of the railroads meant the fulfillment of a dream at least as old as the People's party platform of 1892, and they opposed any return to private control. And in Missouri, four hundred members of Ozark Lodge 233 of the International Association of Machinists, who opposed returning control to "promoters, grafting schemers, Wall Street buccaneers, etc.," offered a solution common to the prewar period: Congress should submit to the people a referendum on the question. Thus the issue could be decided democratically. Obviously the experiences of the war had not changed their minds regarding the best way to solve large national problems.[12]

Another incident, several years later, may further our understanding of the war's impact on Missouri. Artist Thomas Hart Benton had avoided the trenches by volunteering for the navy. In 1924 he visited his dying father at his home in southwest Missouri. Benton found, as Homer Croy had years earlier, a strong sense of community that seemed unshaken by wider events. Missouri, Benton noted,

> is a rural-minded country. The flavor of a premachine-age past hangs in its drawling speech. In the skepticism of its people there is a good deal of the old doubting backwoods farmer who isn't going to be dragged into new-fangled situations without long consideration. Missouri is a state which

12. *St. Louis Post-Dispatch*, 6 December 1918, p. 3; *Springfield Republican*, 13 December 1918.

does not rush wildly to decision. . . . [T]here are no gag laws on the Missouri statutes and its people as a whole are pretty genuinely democratic. Missouri has come out of the great exploitative rages of yesterday, not with an unscarred soil and soul but with one less scarred than you find in most other places.[13]

In other words, the war had not extinguished all fires of democracy. And while the "rages" of yesterday had their impact, they had not worked fundamental changes everywhere. All of which only indicates what we have already seen, that the war workers were just not as effective as they claimed. In some cases their hearts were not in the work; in others their seed fell on barren ground, for there was no traditional basis for the kind of work they were doing; and many people were sheltered by circumstances. People in Missouri and in Washington were consolidating their positions, reviewing the lessons they had learned during the war, and they would continue to advocate their solutions to problems, but the war had given one set of solutions greater viability. In the meantime people on farms, in villages, in neighborhoods began to rebuild their families and their communities, to shore up traditions, to try to return, in fact, to some kind of normalcy. Missouri after the war continued to be a state in transition, though the course of change was clearer than it had been in 1914. Value systems would continue to clash, but after the war, advocates of one set of values now enjoyed an edge. The world was unfortunately less safe for democracy than it had been, as events in Europe, Japan, and the United States were soon to prove. But for many Missourians, the corporation was still the greatest threat. Democracy was still the myth that explained reality; and at the local level it could still be the reality itself: for some the last, best appeal in all great human cases.

13. *An Artist in America,* pp. 75–76.

Selected Bibliography

Books

Beaver, Daniel R. *Newton D. Baker and the American War Effort, 1917–1919.* Lincoln: University of Nebraska Press, 1966.

Benedict, Murray. *The Farm Policies of the United States, 1790–1950.* New York: The Twentieth Century Fund, 1953.

Benton, Thomas Hart. *An Artist in America.* 4th rev. ed. Columbia: University of Missouri Press, 1983.

Bing, Alexander M. *War-Time Strikes and Their Adjustment.* New York: E. P. Dutton & Co., 1921.

Bourne, Randolph S. *War and the Intellectuals: Essays by Randolph S. Bourne, 1915–1919.* Ed. Carl Resek. New York: Harper & Row, 1964.

Breen, William J. *Uncle Sam at Home: Civilian Mobilization, Wartime Federalism, and the Council of National Defense, 1917–1919.* Westport: Greenwood Press, 1984.

Coffman, Edward M. *The War to End All Wars: The American Military Experience in World War I.* Madison: University of Wisconsin Press, 1986.

Crighton, John C. *Missouri and the World War, 1914–1917: A Study in Public Opinion.* Columbia: University of Missouri, 1947.

Croy, Homer. *Country Cured.* New York: Harper & Bros., 1943.

Cuff, Robert D. *The War Industries Board.* Baltimore: Johns Hopkins University Press, 1973.

Danbom, David. *The Resisted Revolution: Urban America and the Industrialization of Agriculture, 1900–1930.* Ames: University of Iowa Press, 1979.

Detjen, David W. *The Germans in Missouri, 1900–1918: Prohibition, Neutrality, and Assimilation.* Columbia: University of Missouri Press, 1985.

Faculty of the St. Louis School of Social Economics. *Studies in Social Economics.* St. Louis: Washington University, 1914. Vol. 1, no. 2, *The Immigrant in St. Louis,* by Ruth Crawford.

————. Vol. 1, no. 1, *Industrial Conditions Among Negroes in St. Louis,* by William Crossland.

Ferrell, Robert H. *Woodrow Wilson and World War I, 1917–1921.* New York: Harper & Row, 1985.

Fink, Gary. *Labor's Search for Order.* Columbia: University of Missouri Press, 1972.

Gerlach, Russel L. *Settlement Patterns in Missouri: A Study of Population Origins.* Columbia: University of Missouri Press, 1986.

Gilbert, Charles. *American Financing of World War One.* Westport: Greenwood Publishing Co., 1970.

Greenwald, Maurine Weiner. *Women, War, and Work: The Impact of World War I on Women Workers in the United States.* Westport: Greenwood Press, 1980.

Handlin, Oscar. *The Uprooted.* 2d ed. Boston: Little, Brown, 1973.

Hawley, Ellis W. *The Great War and the Search for a Modern Order: A History of the American People and Their Institutions, 1917–1933.* New York: St. Martin's Press, 1979.

Jensen, Joan M. *The Price of Vigilance.* Chicago: Rand McNally & Co., 1968.

Jenson, Richard J., Steven L. Piott, and Christopher C. Gibbs, eds. *Grassroots*

167

Politics: Parties, Issues, and Voters, 1854–1983. Westport, Conn.: Greenwood Press, 1983.

Karp, Walter. *The Politics of War, 1890–1920.* New York: Harper & Row, 1979.

Kennedy, David M. *Over Here: The First World War and American Society.* New York: Oxford University Press, 1980.

Kolko, Gabriel. *The Triumph of Conservatism.* New York: The Macmillan Company, 1963.

Lane, Franklin K. *The Letters of Franklin K. Lane, Personal and Political,* ed. Anne W. Lane and Louise H. Wall. Boston: Houghton Mifflin, 1922.

Lawson, V. L. *The Lead Belt Riot of 1917.* Privately printed, 1976.

Leuchtenberg, William E. *The Perils of Prosperity, 1914–1932.* Chicago: University of Chicago Press, 1958.

Link, Arthur S. *Woodrow Wilson and the Progressive Era, 1910–1917.* New York: Harper & Row, 1954.

Livermore, Seward. *Woodrow Wilson and the War Congress, 1916–1918.* Seattle: University of Washington Press, 1968.

Luebke, Frederick C. *Bonds of Loyalty: German-Americans and World War One.* DeKalb: Northern Illinois University Press, 1974.

May, Ernest R. *The World War and American Isolation.* Chicago: Quadrangle Books, 1966.

McConnell, Grant. *The Decline of Agrarian Democracy.* New York: Atheneum, 1969.

Mullendore, William C. *History of the United States Food Administration, 1917–1919.* Palo Alto, Cal.: Stanford University Press, 1941.

Noggle, Burl. *Into the Twenties: The United States from Armistice to Normalcy.* Urbana: University of Illinois Press, 1974.

Peterson, Herbert, and Gilbert Fite. *Opponents of War.* Madison: University of Wisconsin Press, 1957.

Piott, Steven L. *The Anti-Monopoly Persuasion: Popular Resistance to the Rise of Big Business in the Midwest.* Westport: Greenwood Press, 1985.

Preston, William, Jr. *Aliens and Dissenters: Federal Suppression of Radicals, 1903–1933.* New York: Harper & Row, 1963.

Rayburn, Otto E. *Forty Years in the Ozarks: An Autobiography.* Eureka Springs, Ark.: Ozark Guide Press, 1957.

Reid, Loren. *Hurry Home Wednesday: Growing Up in a Small Missouri Town, 1905–1921.* Columbia: University of Missouri Press, 1978.

Rodgers, Daniel T. *The Work Ethic in Industrial America, 1850–1920.* Chicago: University of Chicago Press, 1974.

Rosenblum, Gerald. *Immigrant Workers: Their Impact on American Labor Radicalism.* New York: Basic Books, 1973.

Ryley, Thomas W. *A Little Group of Willful Men.* New York: Kennikatt Press, 1975.

Salutous, Theodore. *The Greeks in the United States.* Cambridge: Harvard University Press, 1964.

Schuttler, Vera B. *A History of the Missouri Farm Bureau Federation.* Springfield: Missouri Farm Bureau Federation, 1948.

Shannon, David A. *Between the Wars: America, 1919–1941.* Boston: Houghton Mifflin, 1965.

Slosson, Preston W. *The Great Crusade and After, 1914–1928.* New York: The Macmillan Co., 1930.

Snow, Thad. *From Missouri.* Boston: Houghton Mifflin, 1952.

Stokesbury, James L. *A Short History of World War I.* New York: William Morrow & Co., 1981.

Thelen, David. *Paths of Resistance: Tradition and Dignity in Industrializing Missouri.* New York: Oxford University Press, 1986.

————. *Robert M. La Follette and the Insurgent Spirit.* Boston: Little, Brown & Co., 1976.

Trask, David F., ed. *World War I at Home: Readings on American Life, 1914–1920.* New York: John Wiley & Sons, 1970.

Vaughn, Stephen. *Holding Fast the Inner Lines: Democracy, Nationalism, and the Committee on Public Information.* Chapel Hill: University of North Carolina Press, 1980.

Watson, Richard L., Jr. *The Development of National Power: The United States, 1900–1919.* Boston: Houghton Mifflin, 1976.

Weigley, Russell F. *History of the United States Army.* New York: The Macmillan Company, 1967.

Weinstein, James. *The Corporate Ideal in the Liberal State, 1900–1918.* Boston: Beacon Press, 1968.

Wiebe, Robert H. *The Search for Order, 1877–1920.* New York: Hill and Wang, 1967.

Articles

Billington, Ray A. "The Origins of Midwest Isolationism." *Political Science Quarterly* 40 (March 1945): 44–64.

Bourne, Randolph S. "A War Diary." *The Seven Arts* 2 (Sept. 1917): 535–47. Rpt. in *War and the Intellectuals: Essays by Randolph S. Bourne, 1915–1919*, ed. Carl Resek. New York: Harper & Row, 1964.

Corzine, Jay, and Irene Dabrowski. "The Ethnic Factor and Neighborhood Stability: The Czechs in Soulard and South St. Louis." *Bulletin of the Missouri Historical Society* 33 (January 1977): 88–93.

Cuff, Robert D. "Herbert Hoover, The Ideology of Voluntarism and War Organization During the Great War." *Journal of American History* 64 (September 1977): 358–72.

Cushing, Charles P. "Floating Through the Ozarks." *Outing*, August 1911, pp. 435–42.

————. "The Ozarks." *The Mentor*, July 1927, pp. 23–31.

Flad, E. "St. Louis' New Charter." *American City* 14 (April 1916): 150–51.

Gibbs, Christopher C. "Missouri Farmers and World War One: Resistance to Mobilization." *Bulletin of the Missouri Historical Society* 35 (October 1978): 17–25.

————. "The Lead Belt Riot and World War One." *Missouri Historical Review* 71 (July 1977): 396–418.

Gutman, Herbert. "Work, Culture, and Society in Industrializing America, 1815–1919." *American Historical Review* 73 (June 1973): 531–88.

Hilton, O. A. "Public Opinion and Civil Liberties in War Time, 1917–1919." *Southwestern Social Science Quarterly* 28 (December 1947): 202–8.

Johnston, Clifton. "Life in the Ozarks." *Outing*, January 1906, pp. 435–42.

McLean, Norman. "Working Together in St. Louis." *Survey*, 10 August 1912.

Miller, William T. "The Progressive Movement in Missouri." *Missouri Historical Review* 22 (July 1928): 456–561.

Montgomery, David. "Workers' Control of Machine Production in the Nineteenth Century." *Labor History* 17 (Fall 1976): 485–509.

———. "The 'New Unionism' and the Transformation of Workers' Consciousness in America, 1909–1922." *Journal of Social History* 7 (Summer 1974): 509–29.

Mormino, Gary R. "Over Here: St. Louis Italo-Americans and the First World War." *Bulletin of the Missouri Historical Society* 30 (October 1973): 44–53.

Mumford, Frederick B. "A History of the Missouri College of Agriculture." *Agriculture Experiment Station Bulletin*, no. 483 (1944).

Nelson, W. L. "A Rural Survey of Morgan County, Missouri." *Monthly Bulletin of the State Board of Agriculture*, no. 14 (February 1916).

Owens, Elizabeth W. "The Year Was 1908: A Personal Reminiscence." *Bulletin of the Missouri Historical Society* 33 (October 1976): 27–39.

Polsby, Nelson W. "The Institutionalization of the U.S. House of Representatives." In *American Political Behavior: Historical Essays and Readings*, ed. Lee Benson et al. New York: Harper & Row, 1967.

Senn, Gerald. "Molders of Thought, Directors of Action: The Arkansas Council of Defense, 1917–1918." *Arkansas Historical Quarterly* 36 (Autumn 1977): 280–90.

Syrett, Harold C. "The Business Press and American Neutrality." *Missouri Valley Historical Review* 32 (September 1945): 215–30.

Venable, Austin. "The Arkansas Council of Defense in the First World War." *Arkansas Historical Quarterly* 2 (Spring 1943): 116–26.

Public Documents

Department of Commerce, Bureau of the Census. *Fourteenth Census of the United States, State Compendium, Missouri*. Washington: Government Printing Office, 1924.

Kansas City Board of Public Health. *Fourth Annual Report, April 15, 1912–22 April 1913*. N.p., n.d.

Missouri Bureau of Labor Statistics. *State Sociology of Missouri, 1913*. Jefferson City: Missouri Bureau of Labor Statistics, 1913.

Missouri State Board of Agriculture. *Monthly Bulletins*.

———. *Annual Reports*.

Office of Secretary of State. *1910 Census of Missouri . . . Collated From the Thirteenth Decennial Census Statistics of the United States*. Jefferson City: n.p., n.d.

Unpublished Studies

Donohue, Steven. "No Small Potatoes: Consumer Consciousness in the American Food Crisis, 1914–1917." Master's thesis, University of Missouri–Columbia, 1976.

Muraskin, Jack D. "Missouri Politics During the Progressive Period, 1896–1916." Ph.D. diss., University of California–Berkeley, 1969.

Pfabe, Jerrald K. "Missouri Congressmen and Neutrality, 1914–1917." Ph.D. diss., St. Louis University, 1962.

Sullivan, Margaret L. "Hyphenism in St. Louis, 1900–1921." Ph.D. diss., St. Louis University, 1962.

Towne, Ruth. "The Public Career of William J. Stone." Ph.D. diss., University of Missouri–Columbia, 1953.

Manuscript Collections

Library of Congress, Manuscripts Division, Washington, D.C.
    William Jennings Bryan Papers
    Robert M. La Follette Papers
    Woodrow Wilson Papers
Missouri Historical Society, St. Louis, Missouri.
    Third Liberty Loan, County Sales Plan
Western Historical Manuscripts Collection (WHMC), Columbia, Missouri.
    Herbert S. Hadley Papers
    Frederick B. Mumford Papers
    Papers of the Missouri Council of Defense
    William J. Stone Papers

Missouri Newspapers and Periodicals

American Zinc and Lead Journal
Atlanta Post
Bethany Democrat
Bonne Terre Register
Bonne Terre Star
Desloge Sun
Ellington Press
Farmington News
Farmington Times
Hannibal Morning Journal
Hopkins Journal
Kansas City Journal
Kirksville Daily Express
Lead Belt News
Linneus Bulletin
Milan Republican
Missouri Farmer
Missouri On Guard
Missouri Ruralist

National Ripsaw
New Hampton Herald
Princeton Post
Ridgeway Journal
St. Francois County Record
St. Joseph News-Press
St. Louis Labor
St. Louis Post-Dispatch
St. Louis Republic
Savannah Democrat
Savannah Reporter
Slater News
Slater Rustler
Springfield Laborer
Springfield Republican
Warrensburg Star-Journal
Wayne County Journal
Weekly Saline Citizen

Index